THE FUTURE OF ATHEISM

Alister McGrath *&* Daniel Dennett *in Dialogue*

Edited by Robert B. Stewart

Fortress Press
Minneapolis

THE FUTURE OF ATHEISM
Alister McGrath and Daniel Dennett in Dialogue

Cover photo © iStockphoto / song mi
Cover design: Kevin van der Leek
Book design: Christy J. P. Barker and Douglas Schmitz

Library of Congress Cataloging-in-Publication Data is available.
ISBN 978-0-8006-6314-8

The paper used in this publication meets the minimum requirements of American National Standard for Information Sciences—Permanence of Paper for Printed Library Materials, ANSI Z329.48-1984.

Manufactured in the U.S.A.

12   11   10   09   08   1   2   3   4   5   6   7   8   9   10

For
James Leo Garrett Jr.

Teacher, Mentor, Friend

Contents

Contributors

Paul Copan (Ph.D. in philosophy, Marquette University) is the Pledger Family Chair of Philosophy and Ethics at Palm Beach Atlantic University in West Palm Beach, Florida. He is the author of several books, including *Loving Wisdom: Christian Philosophy of Religion* (Chalice, 2007) and *True for You, But Not for Me* (Bethany House, 1998), and he is coauthor of *Creation Out of Nothing: A Biblical, Philosophical, and Scientific Exploration* (Baker Academic, 2004). He has coedited a number of books such as *The Rationality of Theism* (Routledge, 2003), *The Routledge Companion to the Philosophy of Religion* (Routledge, 2007), and *Philosophy of Religion: Classic and Contemporary Issues* (Blackwell, 2007). In addition, he has written many articles in professional philosophical and theological journals. He is the current president of the Evangelical Philosophical Society, and he lives with his wife Jacqueline and their five children in West Palm Beach.

William Lane Craig is Research Professor of Philosophy at Talbot School of Theology in La Mirada, California. He earned a doctorate in philosophy at the University of Birmingham, England, before taking a doctorate in theology from the Ludwig-Maximilians-Universität München, Germany, where he was for two years a Fellow of the Alexander von Humboldt-Stiftung. Prior to his appointment at Talbot he spent seven years at the Higher Institute of Philosophy of the Katholike Universiteit Leuven, Belgium. He has authored or edited over thirty books, including *The* Kalam *Cosmological*

Argument; Divine Foreknowledge and Human Freedom; Theism, Atheism, and Big Bang Cosmology; and *God, Time, and Eternity,* as well as over a hundred articles in professional journals of philosophy and theology, including *The Journal of Philosophy, American Philosophical Quarterly, Philosophical Studies, Philosophy,* and *British Journal for Philosophy of Science.*

Daniel C. Dennett is University Professor and Austin B. Fletcher Professor of Philosophy, and Co-Director of the Center for Cognitive Studies at Tufts University. He is the author of *Breaking the Spell* (Viking, 2006), *Freedom Evolves* (Viking, 2003) and *Darwin's Dangerous Idea* (Simon & Schuster, 1995). He was born in Boston in 1942, the son of a historian by the same name, and received his B.A. in philosophy from Harvard in 1963. He then went to Oxford to work with Gilbert Ryle, under whose supervision he completed a Ph.D. in philosophy in 1965. He taught at U.C. Irvine from 1965 to 1971, when he moved to Tufts, where he has taught ever since, aside from periods visiting at Harvard, Pittsburgh, Oxford, and the École Normale Supérieure in Paris. His first book, *Content and Consciousness,* appeared in 1969, followed by *Brainstorms* (1978), *Elbow Room* (1984), *The Intentional Stance* (1987), *Consciousness Explained* (1991), *Kinds of Minds* (1996), *Brainchildren* (1998), and *Sweet Dreams* (2005). He coedited *The Mind's I* with Douglas Hofstadter in 1981. He is the author of over three hundred scholarly articles on various aspects on the mind, published in journals ranging from *Artificial Intelligence* and *Behavioral and Brain Sciences* to *Poetics Today* and the *Journal of Aesthetics and Art Criticism.*

Evan Fales obtained his Ph.D. in philosophy from Temple University and is presently an associate professor in the philosophy department at the University of Iowa. His primary interests are in metaphysics, epistemology, and philosophy of religion. He has published two books, *Causation and Universals* and *A Defense of the Given,* and published articles on the nature of God, the problem of evil, the interpretation of Scriptures, and various other topics within the philosophy of religion.

Hugh J. McCann is Professor of Philosophy at Texas A&M University. He received his B.A. from Villanova University, and his M.A. and Ph.D. from the University of Chicago. He has taught at Northern Illinois University, the University of Virginia, and the University of Notre Dame. He is the author of *The Works of Agency: On Human Action, Will, and Freedom* (Cornell University Press, 1998) and is presently completing a book on the subject of creation. He has published numerous articles in the philosophy of religion, philosophy of action, and related areas in metaphysics, philosophy of mind, and value theory.

Alister McGrath, after twenty-five years at Oxford University, was recently appointed to the Chair of Theology, Ministry, and Education at King's College, London. He holds Oxford doctorates in both molecular biophysics and Christian theology. His research focuses on the relation of science and Christianity, especially in relation to the biological sciences. Among the many books that he has authored are the three-volume *A Scientific Theology*; *The Twilight of Atheism: The Rise and Fall of Disbelief in the Modern World*; and *Dawkins' God: Genes, Memes and the Meaning of Life*, the first book-length assessment of the religious ideas of the Oxford atheist writer Richard Dawkins. His most recent book is *The Dawkins Delusion? Atheist Fundamentalism and the Denial of the Divine.*

J. P. Moreland is Distinguished Professor of Philosophy at Talbot School of Theology, Biola University. With degrees in chemistry, theology, and philosophy (Ph.D., University of Southern California), he has authored, edited, or contributed to thirty-five books, including *Does God Exist?* (Prometheus, 1993); *Philosophy of Religion* (Oxford, 1996); *Naturalism: A Critical Analysis* (Routledge, 2000); *Universals* (McGill-Queens, 2001); *Philosophy of Religion: A Reader and Guide* (Edinburgh University Press, 2002); *Consciousness and the Existence of God* (Routledge, 2008); and *Blackwell Companion to Natural Theology* (forthcoming). He has also published over sixty articles in professional journals, including *American Philosophical Quarterly, Australasian Journal of Philosophy, MetaPhilosophy, Philosophy and Phenomenological Research, Religious Studies,* and *Faith and Philosophy.*

Keith M. Parsons is Professor of Philosophy at the University of Houston, Clear Lake. He has a doctorate in the history and philosophy of science from the University of Pittsburgh (1996), a Ph.D. in philosophy from Queen's University, Canada (1986), and a Master of Theological Studies from Emory University (1981). He has published broadly in the fields of the history of science, the philosophy of science, and the philosophy of religion. His books include *God and the Burden of Proof* (Prometheus, 1989), *Drawing Out Leviathan: Dinosaurs and the Science Wars* (Indiana University Press, 2001), *The Great Dinosaur Controversy* (ABC-Clio, 2003), *The Science Wars: Debating Scientific Knowledge and Technology* (Prometheus, 2003), and *Copernican Questions: A Concise Invitation to the Philosophy of Science* (McGraw-Hill, 2005). Professor Parsons was the founding editor of the philosophical journal *Philo* and has served in numerous venues as a lecturer, debater, and workshop leader.

Ted Peters is Professor of Systematic Theology at Pacific Lutheran Theological Seminary and the Graduate Theological Union in Berkeley, California. He serves as coeditor of *Theology and Science,* published at the Center for Theology and the Natural Sciences. He is author of *GOD—The World's Future* (Fortress Press, 2000); *Science, Theology, and Ethics* (Ashgate, 2003); *The Stem Cell Debate* (Fortress Press, 2007); and *Anticipating Omega* (Vandenhoeck & Ruprecht, 2007). He is coauthor with Martinez Hewlett of *Evolution from Creation to New Creation* (Abingdon, 2003) and *Can You Believe in God and Evolution?* (Abingdon, 2006). He is coeditor of *Bridging Science and Religion* (Fortress Press, 2003) and *The Evolution of Evil* (Vandenhoeck & Ruprecht, 2008).

Robert B. Stewart (M.Div.BL, Ph.D., Southwestern Baptist Theological Seminary) is Associate Professor of Philosophy and Theology at New Orleans Baptist Theological Seminary, where he is Greer-Heard Professor of Faith and Culture. He is editor of *The Resurrection of Jesus: John Dominic Crossan and N. T. Wright in Dialogue* (Fortress Press, 2006); and *Intelligent Design: William A. Dembski and Michael Ruse in Dialogue* (Fortress Press, 2007). He is author of *The Quest of the Hermeneutical Jesus: The Impact of Hermeneutics on the Jesus Research of John Dominic Crossan and N. T. Wright* (University Press of America, 2008). A contributor to the *Cambridge Dictionary of Christianity* and the *Revised Holman Bible Dictionary,* he has published articles or book reviews in numerous journals.

Preface

The purpose of the Greer-Heard Point-Counterpoint Forum in Faith and Culture is to provide a venue for fair-minded dialogue to take place on subjects of importance in religion or culture. The intention is to have an evangelical Christian dialogue with a non-evangelical or non-Christian. The forum is intended to be a dialogue rather than a debate. As such, it is a bit more freewheeling than a traditional debate, and it is not scored. The goal is a respectful exchange of ideas, without compromise. So often in our culture the sorts of issues that the forum addresses stoke the emotions, and consequently the rhetoric is of such a nature as to ensure that communication does not take place. There may be a place and time for such preaching to the choir, but minds are rarely changed as a result of such activity—nor are better arguments forthcoming as a result of gaining a better understanding of positions with which one disagrees. The result often is that what passes for argument is really nothing more than a prolonged example of the Straw Man fallacy.

The subject of the 2007 Greer-Heard Point-Counterpoint Forum in Faith and Culture was "The Future of Atheism." The dialogue partners were Alister McGrath, then of Oxford University, and Daniel Dennett of Tufts University. One can hardly imagine a question more fundamental than the existence or nonexistence of God, or two protagonists more distinguished than Dennett and McGrath. Given the recent spate of publications promoting atheism that have climbed the best-seller lists in America, the topic was certainly a timely one.

The dialogue took place February 23–24, 2007, in the Leavell Chapel on the campus of the host institution, New Orleans Baptist Theological Seminary. The chapel was filled with an enthusiastic and appreciative crowd. The atmosphere was pleasant and the exchanges between Dennett and McGrath respectful and serious, with dashes of humor added at timely moments. I think it is safe to say that never before had the seminary played host to so many atheists. By all accounts the event was a model for how this sort of public discourse can take place and how groups with different viewpoints on crucial issues can conduct themselves in a way that is refreshing and honest. One of the consistent fruits of the forum has been the realization that disagreement does not have to be shrill or heated in nature, and that one does not have to check one's convictions at the door in order for respectful dialogue to take place.

Along with my introductory chapter, this book includes a transcript of the February 23, 2007, dialogue between McGrath and Dennett as well as the papers presented the following day by William Lane Craig, Evan Fales, Hugh McCann, and Keith Parsons. Craig offers a vigorous defense of certain types of cosmological arguments for God's existence—based largely upon the findings of contemporary science. Fales puts forward an existential moral critique of the Judeo-Christian God based upon problematic passages in the Old and New Testaments. Keith Parsons offers a thorough critique of McGrath's book *The Twilight of Atheism*.[1] Hugh McCann takes up the task of critiquing the extent to which the knowledge claims made by religious believers are subject to appraisal by standards that, in one way or another, may be considered scientific—and what follows if at least some of those claims are.

In addition to these essays, which were presented at the Greer-Heard Forum, three other essays are included. The authors J. P. Moreland, Paul Copan, and Ted Peters were invited to contribute because they each brought different skills to the task and addressed different questions. J. P. Moreland updates a recurring theistic critique of naturalism—that naturalism undermines, or at least offers no clear support for, human reason—by addressing a contemporary atheistic response to this charge. Paul Copan's chapter addresses the question of the (necessary) relationship or lack thereof between the existence of God and objective moral values. Finally, Ted Peters offers the perspective of a mainline theologian on some theological issues related to the question of God's existence.

While one could easily note issues that are still not addressed in this volume, or think of significant thinkers who are not included in this book, we believe these chapters make for a fuller treatment of the issue. No doubt readers will have to judge for themselves if this is in fact the case.

I am grateful that Fortress Press has seen fit to allow us to present the fruit of the 2007 Greer-Heard Forum to you. I trust that you will read it with an open mind and consider carefully what each author has to say. If you will, I have no doubt that you will be the richer for having done so.

Robert Stewart
New Orleans Baptist Theological Seminary

Acknowledgments

Thanking others in print always causes me a bit of anxiety because I fear that I will fail to recognize someone who truly deserves a word of appreciation. But many deserve to be publicly thanked, and even praised, so I must go on. First of all, I must thank Bill and Carolyn Heard for their passion to have a forum where leading scholars can dialogue about important issues in faith and culture in a collegial manner and on a balanced playing field—and their willingness to fund such a project. Without them the Greer-Heard Point-Counterpoint Forum in Faith and Culture would be a dream rather than a reality. As always I thank Dr. Chuck Kelley, president of New Orleans Baptist Theological Seminary (NOBTS), for his support and encouragement.

My right-hand man throughout this entire process was Rhyne Putman. He did everything he was asked to do and more—and all of it with a cheerful attitude. He produced the index in addition to making numerous forays to various libraries to find resources that I needed, as well as doing anything that didn't fall under somebody else's job description. The event would never have come off successfully without the efforts of Linda Jackson and her staff. She endured countless meetings and thousands of questions while showing great flexibility throughout.

I also am grateful to Vanee Daure and her staff for the work they did in media support. Additionally, Bob Waldrep, Allan McConnell, and Rick Sutton of Watchman Fellowship must be thanked for audio CD reproduction, order fulfillment, and website management related to making the forum available to others via audio CDs and MP3 files. Sheila Taylor and the NOBTS cafeteria staff must be applauded for serving numerous meals of all varieties to large numbers. Lisa Joyner of Johnson Ferry Baptist Church in Marietta, Georgia, deserves a word of recognition for her work in producing the programs and CD covers. Without the high-quality graphic art and public relations work of Jeff Audirsch, Boyd Guy, and Gary Myers, the task would have proven too great.

Jeremy Evans must be thanked for organizing the Evangelical Philosophical Society special event program that took place in conjunction with the Greer-Heard Forum, as must the EPS executive committee for supporting the idea. I also thank Scott Smith for his efforts in publicizing the event, and Joe Gorra for providing EPS support materials.

Our conference speakers, Alister McGrath, Daniel Dennett, William Lane Craig, Hugh McCann, Keith Parsons, and Evan Fales, must all be thanked. In addition, the contributions of our other authors, Paul Copan, J. P. Moreland, and Ted Peters, are much appreciated. All are outstanding scholars and true gentlemen.

I am grateful to NOBTS provost Steve Lemke for making it possible for Baptist college groups to attend the event. His efforts, along with those of Archie England and Rick Morton and their respective staffs, were much appreciated.

Brantley Scott and the staff at Lifeway Books deserve a word of thanks for working so hard at the book signing and for going the extra mile to ensure that all the books ordered actually arrived on time. This was a massive undertaking but they never complained.

Michael West, editor-in-chief of Fortress Press, must be thanked for his enthusiasm for fair-minded respectful dialogue on important issues and for choosing to publish the fruit of the Greer-Heard Forum. Michael's knowledge of contemporary theology, coupled with his judicious recommendations, significantly strengthened this book. Susan Johnson of Fortress Press also deserves a word of thanks. Her cheerful attitude and eagerness to help in any way possible are much appreciated. I am especially grateful for the expert editing of Carolyn Banks, the Senior Project Director for this publication. Her patience and skill were vital to the success of this project.

As always, my wife and family must be thanked. I suspect that they enjoy the rush that accompanies an event like the forum, but they still make numerous sacrifices in order to make sure things comes off without a hitch.

Finally, I am grateful to all those through the years who have contributed to my growth as a Christian and a scholar. Perhaps nobody has done more to mentor me as a Christian scholar than James Leo Garrett Jr., professor emeritus of theology at Southwestern Baptist Theological Seminary in Fort Worth, Texas. Years ago he asked me to serve as a grader for him. I was thrilled to have the opportunity. At every point he has modeled for me what it means to be a Christian gentleman and scholar. I know I don't always measure up to that ideal, but when I fall short it is not for lack of desire. It is to him that I gratefully dedicate this book.

Introduction

The Future of Atheism

An Introductory Appraisal

Robert B. Stewart

Predicting the future of any belief system is difficult. Predicting the future of atheism is an even more difficult task than is the case with most belief systems. This is so for several reasons. First, atheism is a difficult term to define. Simply put, people don't always mean the same thing when they say "atheist." In this sense atheism is a fairly imprecise term. Unbelievers have several terms with which to describe themselves; among their options are agnostic, humanist, secularist, skeptic, naturalist, or freethinker, as well as various types of atheist (positive or negative; friendly, unfriendly, or indifferent; broad or narrow, and so on). But the problem runs deeper than a multiplicity of terms.

The second difficulty is that many who don't believe in God or gods, who deny, either explicitly or implicitly, the existence of supernatural beings, nevertheless also avoid the label of atheist. Some do this out of indifference. They understand atheism to be a religious position, albeit a negative one, and want nothing to do with religion one way or the other. They don't want to join a group or a movement; they want simply to be left alone. We might label this position indifferent atheism. Others remain silent concerning their unbelief because they worry that expressing their opinion would harm relationships with family members or perhaps limit their professional opportunities for advancement. They find it easier simply to say that they aren't religious. One of the things that I have learned from countless conversations in the last year with atheists, humanists, freethinkers, and so forth is that there is a very real sense on their part of being a marginalized group in contemporary American culture. I think they overestimate the degree to which atheists are stigmatized in our culture, but regardless this perception is still a factor in some choosing to remain anonymous. The result, again, is that it is difficult to get a clear picture of how many atheists there actually are at this time.

Is atheism growing? The safest answer is yes—and no. There seem to be more atheists today than at any other time in history. Yet it also appears to be the case that as a percentage of the world's population, atheism is declining. In their book, *Sacred and Secular*, political theorists Pippa Norris and Ronald Inglehart note: "The world as a whole now has more people with traditional religious views than ever before—and they constitute a growing proportion of the world's population."[1] One reason for this may be the fact that the birthrates in those nations that are among the more religious typically are higher than in those nations that are more atheistic. (My look-around-town epistemology tells me that the same is true of individual families, but this is clearly a subjective and nonscientific measurement.) If this is so, and if belief is simply a matter of what culture one is born into, or from what family one comes—or even if those factors play a major but not necessarily determinative role in belief formation—then the future of atheism appears bleak. But I reject the idea that belief formation is simply the result of historical or geographical or familial accident. Rational people can and do choose what to believe based upon evidence and argument. And they can and often do choose to go against the flow of their own culture.

On the other hand, Phil Zuckerman notes that atheism fares best in those nations that are the wealthiest, best educated, and experience the greatest degree of political and personal freedom. In fact, nations with a higher instance of atheism tend to rate more highly in most of the categories that make for a secure and comfortable lifestyle (the lone exception being suicide—the suicide rates for nations with higher degrees of atheism are consistently higher than they are in highly religious nations).[2] Nevertheless, one cannot infer that atheism brings about a better or more comfortable life than does belief in God. Accordingly Zuckerman insists that one cannot conclude that "high levels of organic atheism *cause* societal health or that low levels of organic atheism *cause* societal ills. Rather, societal health seems to cause widespread atheism, and societal insecurity seems to cause widespread belief in God . . ."[3]

This is consistent with the testimony of Christian Scripture. The Bible warns of the negative influence of prosperity upon belief. Jesus warns that it is harder for a rich man to enter the kingdom of God than for a camel to go through the eye of a needle—but he also says that with God all things are possible (Matt. 19:23-26). The apostle Paul warns that the love of money is a root of all sorts of evil (1 Tim. 6:9-10). But again I believe that one goes too far in concluding that societal, or even personal, conditions determine belief or unbelief. Certainly they are a contributing factor one way or the other—but they are not determinative. There are wealthy individuals with deep faith in God and individuals in poverty equally entrenched in their unbelief. At most, one can conclude that the tendency to belief or unbelief is greater in one context than the other.

Granting this conclusion, however, is not insignificant in that one can predict the direction of a society economically and socially. It is safe to say that a greater percentage of the world enjoys greater creature comforts today than was the case at the turn of the last century or at the turn of the nineteenth century. Barring a massively destructive world war, or a cataclysmic climate change, or some incredibly large environmental disaster, there is no reason to think that this trend to financial well-being will not continue. Therefore, it is perhaps the case that the conditions for atheism to flourish are increasing. Nevertheless, there are always other factors to consider. Economic factors definitely play a role in belief formation but so do political, philosophical, and scientific factors, to name but a few of the relevant conditions. These are less simple to predict. Finally and most importantly, none of this says anything about whether theism or atheism is *true*, or whether one should or should not believe in God. This is the truly important question. Some beliefs will survive despite being false, but true beliefs must survive. Accordingly, the question of the future of either atheism or theism often reduces to which one is believed to be true.

A further complicating issue is the fact that religious belief and unbelief are always contextual, whether one is a believer or an unbeliever. Exactly what God or god(s) is believed in—or denied—is always a contextual issue related to one's historical/cultural setting and personal background and makeup. Jan Bremmer, writing in *The Cambridge Companion to Atheism* on the difficulty of drawing historical conclusions concerning atheism in the ancient world, notes that the term *atheist* was sometimes used as a labeling device, often pejoratively so. For example, in the Roman period "Christians were called *atheoi* by the pagans and vice versa."[4] But clearly neither the monotheistic Christians nor the polytheistic Romans were atheists by today's standards. Equally clear is the fact that each group rejected the other group's ideas concerning the divine. It may also be that some who were not identified as atheists in their own day would properly qualify as such today. Knowing just who actually is an atheist has thus always been a difficult task.

We live in a world that has been affected by modernity. This is not a matter for debate, it is a fact. Although we often speak of our own age as postmodern, consider the fact that even the term *postmodern* is dependent, both linguistically and conceptually, upon modernity. "Postmodern" makes sense—whatever sense it makes—only in light of modernity. *In one sense* it is what follows modernity: if there is no modernity, then there can be no postmodernity. But it is also *something other* than modernity, whether it is the variety that reflects modernism taken to its logical end or the rejection of modernism's certainty. Like everything else, the atheism-theism debate has been influenced by modernity.

One will note that the Bible is neither a modern nor a postmodern book. The Bible does not present one with a formal argument for God's existence, instead it *presumes* that God exists and is a personal being, who is active in the world he has created and has a plan for its history. The bulk of the Bible is dedicated not to a philosophical demonstration of God's existence but to a description of the Judeo-Christian God throughout the Old Testament and to a presentation of the Christian gospel in the New.

Indeed, the Bible presents the interaction between Christianity and other worldviews as one in which the primary question is not, "Should I believe in God?" but rather, "Who is the God in whom I should trust?" Please recognize the essential difference between belief *that God exists* and *trust in God.* The God presented in the Bible calls for more than a theoretical or even a matter-of-fact recognition of his existence—God demands an existential commitment on our part, an abandoning of ourselves into his care.

Nevertheless, belief in God is entailed in the Christian gospel and Christians began early on to argue for the existence of God, if only to show the reasonableness of their beliefs. Consider Anselm's ontological argument for God's existence. That it was not intended for a skeptical academy is obvious: it is found in the form of a prayer in *Proslogion,* a work consciously modeled after Augustine's *Confessions.*[5] It was written for Christians; and, indeed, Anselm's chief critic, Guanilo, was himself a Christian monk. Thomas Aquinas, as well, working at least in part within the context of the rediscovery of Aristotle and Arab belief in God, offered five proofs of God's existence by which one could through the use of reason alone know that there is a God. It is important to note, however, that Aquinas did not come to faith in God via rational proofs, nor did he address his proofs primarily to non-Christians. His audience was Christian, and his intention was to demonstrate to them that the faith they had was a rational faith.[6]

It was not until René Descartes in the seventeenth century that rational arguments for God's existence became the basis by which one would try to prove to skeptics that God does certainly exist. The upshot, whether or not Descartes himself held to such a view, was that Western intellectuals began to think that religious conviction is based *primarily upon rational beliefs.*[7] This made sense in a historical context in which knowledge had to be based upon either logic or empirical verification via the scientific method. In other words, this makes sense only within the modern world.

The novelty was not so much in the arguments for God's existence—they had a long and distinguished history—but in their new purpose, and the new criteria by which they were assessed. With Descartes, and modernity, such arguments—based either upon a priori logic or scientific empiricism—became the only acceptable foundations for belief in God. No longer was divine revelation to be allowed its day in court, or at best one could consider the testimony of Scripture only after the reasonableness of the case had been decided. The effect was that claims of revelation were relegated to a lower class of evidence—even by those who believed Scripture to be the very words of God. In other words, prior to the Enlightenment, what we take today to be commonplace in the theism-atheism debate was virtually unknown.

One can thus go so far as to say that today's atheism-theism debate is largely a product of modernity. Gavin Hyman, in his contribution to *The Cambridge Companion to Atheism*, concurs: "Atheism, it seems, is a feature or symptom of the modernity that is traumatically coming to birth. . . . In this sense, atheism is an inescapable aspect of modernity, atheism and modernity seem to be inextricably linked."[8] Michael Buckley goes even further, asserting that modern atheism came to pass as a reaction to a type of modern belief that attempted to base belief in God upon either philosophical or scientific bases. When such arguments were rejected, so was the Christianity that they were intended to prove. He concludes: "Religion was not undermined by science; the religious assent was undermined when theologians excised the specifically religious and came to rely upon scientific evidence and procedure as foundational. The more that theologians insisted upon such a foundation, the more they discredited belief."[9]

Post-Enlightenment atheism has taken several forms. A representative but by no means all-inclusive list would include the projection theories of Ludwig Feuerbach and Sigmund Freud, the dialectical materialism of Karl Marx, the nihilistic perspectivism of Friedrich Nietzsche, the existentialism of Martin Heidegger, Jean-Paul Sartre, and Albert Camus, and the objectivism of Ayn Rand, to say nothing of various types of linguistic positivism that have tried to marginalize talk about God as nonscientific. Each of these positions has had and continues to have its devotees, although with the possible exception of Nietzsche's thought as reflected in postmodern skepticism, none of these schools of thought seems to be in vogue today. Nevertheless, atheism is still a viable option for many.

Why belabor this point in a book on the future of atheism? Because in order to understand the atheism of the present day one must understand the historical context out of which it arose. Just as context determined the meaning of the word *atheist* in the ancient and medieval worlds, so it determines meaning today—regardless of whether one considers our culture to be modern or postmodern, or something else altogether. Before we can frame an opinion concerning any belief system, we must understand the context in which it was birthed. The contextual nature of unbelief also means that before one can make predictions as to the future of atheism one must also understand its present context.

The first decade of the third millennium has witnessed an increase of interest in atheism in North America and Europe. The release of several high-profile books touting the benefits of atheism, such as *The God Delusion* by Richard Dawkins, *Breaking the Spell: Religion as a Natural Phenomenon* by Daniel Dennett, and *The End of Faith* and *Letter to a Christian Nation* by Sam Harris, have captured the attention of the media and the reading public. One could add to these Christopher Hitchens's *God Is Not Great*, Victor Stenger's *God: The Failed Hypothesis*, and Michel Onfray's *Atheist Manifesto*. In addition to being best sellers, these books bring to the fore an aggressive atheist message, which Gary Wolf, contributing editor to *Wired* magazine, has termed the New Atheism. The consistent message of the New Atheists is: (1) that belief in God is irrational in an age of science; and (2) that religion is dangerous. Simply put, the New Atheists are issuing a call to action "to help exorcise this debilitating curse: the curse of faith."[10]

What is the context of the New Atheism? What has prompted such an outpouring of atheistic treatises? Two factors in contemporary Western culture, especially in America, are especially significant in this regard. The first is the denial of evolution on the part of Christian conservatives, whether they are young-earth creationists or old-earth intelligent design advocates—although the popularity of intelligent design seems to be the more troubling of the two to the New Atheists. The fact that a large number of Americans have doubts as to all or parts of the theory of evolution, coupled with the fact that some school districts have allowed for—or even mandated—the teaching of intelligent design in science classes, disturbs them. That those pushing for "equal time" for the teaching of intelligent design generally seem to be motivated by religious belief leads the New Atheists to the conclusion that belief in God is contrary to the pursuit of "good science."[11] They thus see themselves as the guardians of science, truth, and progress. Conversely, they view the proponents of intelligent design as biased, ideologically driven, and occasionally as willing to stoop to any level to achieve their goals, which not surprisingly is often how intelligent design advocates view those who affirm Darwinism.

The second contextual factor is the specter of religious violence. Our world was changed forever by the events of September 11, 2001. On at least a surface level Al Qaeda is a religiously motivated organization. The New Atheists typically insist that contemporary religious terrorism is no mere historical accident. It is nothing more than the latest example of religious violence throughout history, the best-known examples of which are the Crusades and the Spanish Inquisition. Accordingly, religion is seen as poisoning everything, to use Hitchens's phrase. Simply put, they believe this would be a better world, certainly a safer world, without religion.

One of the first things one notes when reading many of the New Atheists is the strident tone that characterizes much of their rhetoric. That I was not the only one who noticed this was confirmed to me during a recent postoperative conversation with my physician, a well-educated man (graduate of Tulane University and Harvard medical school) who carefully guards his thoughts on religion. When he asked me what I was working on this year, I said I was editing a book on the future of atheism. He replied: "I tried to read *The God Delusion* but I gave up. It was just too shrill." Dawkins's assessment of those who deny evolution serves as an example of this shrillness: "It is absolutely safe to say that if you meet somebody who claims not to believe in evolution, that person is ignorant, stupid or insane (or wicked, but I'd rather not consider that)."[12] I must add here that though Daniel Dennett's writings are certainly full of atheistic conviction—and he is held in high esteem by the New Atheists and rightfully takes his place among them—I do not find his tone as shrill or his statements as combative in nature as those of Dawkins, Harris, Hitchens, and Onfray. No doubt this is in part because he is a philosopher and thus more careful with his use of language. I suspect it has more to do with his not joining Dawkins and others in calling for an end to religion: "Neither Dawkins nor I believe in God, but whereas Dawkins is convinced that belief in God, and religion in general, does far more harm than good, I have not yet made up my mind about that. I can see that a lot of good comes from believing in God, and it might still outweigh all the harm."[13] Wolf opines that this stridency is because the New Atheists are not really trying to convert believers but to mobilize agnostic fence-sitters. He writes of Dawkins: "His true interlocutors are not the Christians he confronts directly but the wavering nonbelievers or quasi believers among his listeners—people like me, potential New Atheists who might be inspired by his example."[14] Accordingly, Wolf understands the New Atheism as a social movement as well as an intellectual position.

Charles Darwin looms large for contemporary atheists. Concerning the impact of Darwin on atheism, Dawkins declares:

> An atheist before Darwin could have said, following Hume: "I have no explanation for complex biological design. All I know is that God isn't a good explanation, so we must wait and hope that somebody comes up with a better one." I can't help feeling that such a position, though logically sound, would have left one feeling pretty unsatisfied, and that although atheism might have been *logically* tenable before Darwin, Darwin made it possible to be an intellectually fulfilled atheist.[15]

On the first page of *The Selfish Gene* Dawkins informs his readers that Darwin has forever altered our situation:

> We no longer have to resort to superstition when faced with deep problems: Is there a meaning to life? What are we here for? What is man? After posing the last of these questions, the eminent zoologist G. G. Simpson put it thus: "The point I want to make now is that all attempts to answer that question before 1859 are worthless and that we will be better off if we ignore them completely."[16]

Similarly, Dennett insists that Darwin's theory is a type of "universal acid" that "eats through just about every traditional concept, and leaves in its wake a revolutionized worldview, with most of the old land-marks still recognizable, but transformed in fundamental ways."[17]

The idea that Darwinian evolution (or the neo-Darwinian synthesis)[18] is incompatible with belief in God is not new. In fact, numerous evangelical Christians—though certainly not all—have insisted that the two are mutually exclusive. Still more to the point, many Christians have agreed that Darwinism and Christianity, or at least a literal biblical doctrine of creation, are incompatible. Dennett recognizes that some Christians feel similarly when he states:

> Almost no one is indifferent to Darwin, and no one should be. The Darwinian theory is a scientific theory, and a great one, but that is not all it is. The creationists who oppose it so bitterly are right about one thing: Darwin's dangerous idea cuts much deeper into the fabric of our most fundamental beliefs than many of its sophisticated apologists have yet admitted, even to themselves.[19]

But the idea that Darwinism and Christianity are mutually exclusive is not accepted by all who endorse evolution—or all who reject it. Consider the comments of the late Stephen Jay Gould, himself an agnostic, on the claim that Darwinism denies that the world, including humankind, was designed and exists for a purpose:

> To say it for all my colleagues and for the umpteenth millionth time . . . science simply cannot (by its legitimate methods) adjudicate the issue of God's possible superintendence of nature. We neither affirm nor deny it; we simply can't comment on it as scientists. . . .
> . . . Either half my colleagues are enormously stupid, or else the science of Darwinism is fully compatible with conventional religious beliefs—and equally compatible with atheism, thus proving

that the two great realms of nature's factuality and the source of human morality do not strongly overlap.[20]

Natural selection, the Darwinian mechanism that works with random mutations to retain genetic changes that are beneficial for the survival of a species—and by which new species evolve—is the primary reason that the New Atheists believe God is no longer required. Natural selection provides an instrumental cause for the form and order of life that a scientist, operating as a *methodical naturalist*, observes. But natural selection coupled with random mutations does not prove there is no designer; it shows only that the designer does not need to work directly. Natural selection may tell us—in an instrumental sense—*how* living organisms came to be as they are but it cannot tell us *why*—in a teleological sense— they came to be, or even why natural selection came to work—instrumentally—as it does. (No effect can be its own cause. Accordingly, natural selection cannot be the answer for why natural selection works as it does.) Therefore, an investigator could not, on the basis of natural selection, correctly infer that there is no God, just as one could not logically infer that Henry Ford had never lived simply by observing the production of cars in an entirely automated automobile plant.[21] There is therefore no logical reason to see the relationship between biological evolution and Christian faith as disjunctive.

There is a subtler claim, however, that the New Atheists may make in this regard that merits close attention. The claim is that though Darwinism may not *require* atheism it nevertheless makes belief in God unnecessary. The nontheist will thus argue that natural selection coupled with Ockham's razor, the general scientific dictum that the simpler solution is to be preferred, leads to the conclusion that though atheism is not required, it is still a more likely explanation than is theism. This seems a bit simplistic, however. It may be the case that God is not needed to make sense of biological life as we know it, or to understand the nature of DNA. This, however, has nothing to do with the larger metaphysical question of whether God is needed to make sense of why there is something rather than nothing, or even whether a supremely intelligent and powerful being is the best explanation of the complexity and design that one finds when considering cosmology. Clearly, something like Darwinism is necessary for atheism to be true, but it does not seem to be the case that Darwinism alone is sufficient to determine that God does not exist.

The second premise of most of the New Atheists, that religion is dangerous, seems again to overstate the case. Certainly there have been examples in history of cases where religious beliefs have led to conflict, and even horrible injustices. But can one correctly infer from these that all religion is dangerous, or that on the whole society would be better off without religion than with it? As noted above, Dennett is not so sure. Dinesh D'Souza argues forcefully against this idea in part two of his *What's So Great About Christianity?* In fact, he concludes that Christianity is responsible for history's greatest idea of justice, one that almost all atheists affirm: the equality of all human beings.[22] Even Nietzsche seems to agree with D'Souza: "Another Christian concept, no less crazy, has passed even more deeply into the tissue of modernity: the concept of the 'equality of souls before God.' This concept furnishes the prototype of all theories of equal rights: mankind was first taught to stammer the proposition of equality in a religious context, and only later was it made into morality."[23]

Reasoning via analogy, Keith Ward offers a somewhat different sort of rebuttal to the idea that religion is dangerous by asking if society might be better off without politics and/or science.

> But consider a parallel case: politics could also be said to be one of the most destructive forces in human life. In Russia and Cambodia, millions of people have been killed in the name of socialist political ideologies. In Latin America, millions of people "disappeared" in ruthless campaigns of violence propagated by right-wing politicians. Deception, hypocrisy and misrepresentation are commonplace in political life. Might we not be better off in a world without politics too?
>
> Even science, often thought of as an uninterested search for truth, produces terrifying weapons of mass destruction, and the most advanced technology is used to destroy human lives in ever more effective and brutal ways. Would we be better off without science as well?[24]

Ward concludes that society needs all three: religion, politics, and science—yet all three can go very wrong and turn destructive. Still, he concludes that on the whole society is better off with religion than without.

There is yet another contextual factor to consider when discussing the future of atheism, namely, the health of Christianity. Alister McGrath argues persuasively that atheism flourished in the Enlightenment period not only because of modernism's reliance upon reason and experience but also because established Christianity was widely perceived to be in league with dictatorial powers while atheism was seen as a liberating force.[25] Simply put, the church at the dawn of the Enlightenment was not healthy. There is a correlation between the health of the Christian church and the health of unbelief. When the church follows the example of Jesus, her Master, and serves those who are most needy in this world, and speaks to corrupt powers rather than joining them in their attempts to dominate, the Gospel of Jesus is particularly attractive. It was thus in the first three centuries of Christianity, it has been thus for the past three centuries, and it will continue to be so. Atheism, however, is especially attractive when the dominant expression of Christianity is out of step with the message of Jesus.

Atheism has always posed certain challenges to Christianity. Today, the New Atheism raises certain challenges for Christians. One of these is to give more attention to science—and to philosophy of science in particular. Many conservative Christians do not understand the claims of Darwinism and thus reject something other than the theory itself. Similarly, they do not understand what is meant when a scientist claims that a scientific theory is proven. This is because many conservative Christians do not understand the nature of scientific paradigms or the pragmatic criteria by which a scientific paradigm is tested. This explains why working scientists often appear baffled when non-scientists, whether Christian or non-religious, confidently declare that "Darwinism is *only a theory*." True enough, as far as the statement goes. But what sort of theory is it? Is it a theory that is testable, fruitful, from which we can make predictions, and that has explanatory power or is it simply something Charles Darwin thought up after being too long away from home on a sea voyage? In other words, is it a theory that fares well by the standards of contemporary science? The answer to this question is that according to the standards by which scientific paradigms are generally judged Darwinian evolution has been a hugely successful theory of biological development.

This does not mean that a believer must accept Darwinism. There are challenges, both religious and non-religious in nature, which can be raised against Darwinism. But one should understand the issues involved in order to hold a position in a legitimate fashion. This is also true for atheists as well. One often gets the feeling that there are many on both sides of the issue who hold their position because someone from their respective camp has told them quite confidently that there is really no good evidence for the other position. One should always respect informed and sincere differences of opinion; such is not the case with an opinion rooted in ignorance or bias.

The New Atheism also challenges Christians to live according to higher ethical standards. Christians need to deal in a responsible manner with claims of past and present abuse by Christians. Sometimes fringe positions are portrayed as being either representative of Christian faith or the logical result of Christian teaching. When this is done, believers must point out the specious nature of such claims. Other times there is a more legitimate claim to be made. There have been instances of abuse—and shocking evil—that have taken place in the name of Christianity. Sometimes the extent of these abuses is exaggerated, but this does not mean that Christians have nothing for which to answer. In such cases the appropriate response is repentance and censure. One must understand, however, that Christianity teaches that even Christians are subject to sin and to fall back into the old life lived according to the flesh. The Bible teaches as much—without condoning such behavior. Yet violence, intolerance, hypocrisy, hubris, and denial are not merely Christian problems—they are human problems. Still, the Christian response to moral failure, whether that failure is individual or corporate, is repentance and reparation. Christians should lead the way in setting right what is wrong in our culture, and seek to do so with humility as servants, rather than in arrogance as conquerors.

The New Atheism also poses a hermeneutical challenge for Christians. One strategy employed by the New Atheists in insisting that religion is dangerous is to highlight passages in both the Old and New Testaments that are difficult to interpret. Among these are passages such as Lot offering his virgin daughters to the men of Sodom or God ordering the death of entire communities, including women, children, and livestock. Sometimes one is faced with a situation where a particular atheist writer has not really grappled with the text of Scripture in a serious fashion, and has thus failed to consider the best scholarship on the issue. Other times there are difficult interpretive issues to be addressed. Christians need to address these "hard passages" forthrightly and be honest as to their challenging nature. In this regard, believers need to espouse a well-informed doctrine of Scripture and practice proper interpretive methods.

There are also challenges that arise for nontheists in connection with the New Atheism. Many of these challenges flow out of the purely material nature of reality that they espouse. Among these challenges are how to account for human rationality, freedom, and consciousness. In other words, how are we to account for certain phenomena of human life—that all of us experience—if human beings are the result of physical and social forces alone?

Consider rationality. How is it that we all think that we can generally trust our mental faculties to provide us with reliable beliefs? We know that sometimes we are mistaken but for the most part we trust our minds and senses to guide us reliably upon reflection. Yet if naturalism is true, why should we do this? Naturalist Patricia Churchland puts it thus:

> Boiled down to essentials, a nervous system enables the organism to succeed in the four F's: feeding, fleeing, fighting and reproducing. The principle chore of nervous systems is to get the body parts where they should be in order that the organism may survive. . . . Improvements in sensorimotor control confer an evolutionary advantage: a fancier style of representing is advantageous *so long as it is geared to the organism's way of life and enhances the organism's*

chances of survival. Truth, whatever that is, definitely takes the hindmost.[26]

Richard Rorty put it this way: "The idea that one species of organism is, unlike all the others, oriented not just toward its own uncreated prosperity but toward Truth, is as un-Darwinian as the idea that every human being has a built-in moral compass—a conscience that swings free of both social history and individual luck."[27] Alvin Plantinga has formulated a much-discussed argument against naturalism in which he argues that the probability of our minds producing rational beliefs is either low or inscrutable given the conjunction of naturalism and evolution, precisely because natural selection prefers beliefs that are advantageous to those that are true.[28]

A second challenge for the atheist is explaining human consciousness if the material is all there is. Consciousness is a mystery if physicalism is true. Richard Dawkins agrees:

> There are aspects of human subjective consciousness that are deeply mysterious. Neither Steve Pinker nor I can explain human subjective consciousness—what philosophers call qualia. In *How the Mind Works* Steve elegantly sets out the problem of subjective consciousness, and asks where it comes from and what's the explanation. Then he's honest enough to say, "Beats the heck out of me." That is an honest thing to say, and I echo it. We don't know. We don't understand it.[29]

Daniel Dennett has worked mightily to address this question. In several books he offers a third-person account of human consciousness.[30] He also argues that the idea of qualia does not provide a basis for refuting naturalism, in that the concept of qualia is a thoroughly confused idea that cannot be put to use in any noncontradictory way. Simply put, Dennett is a type of functionalist. Accordingly, he has encountered stern opposition from those philosophers of mind who do not affirm functionalism, such as John Searle, who quips: "If you are tempted to functionalism, I believe you do not need refutation, you need help."[31] Suffice it to say that Dennett's writings on this point are both creative and controversial. They merit close attention from theists as they are skillfully written, serious attempts to spell out an evolutionary approach to these issues.

Human free will is also a challenge for the materialist. How do we account for the fact that all of us believe that we make meaningful choices, that we could have chosen otherwise had we preferred to do so? Consider this statement from Naturalism.org, a Web site associated with the Center for Naturalism.[32]

> From a naturalistic perspective, there are no *causally privileged* agents, nothing that causes without being caused in turn. Human beings act the way they do because of the various influences that shape them, whether these be biological or social, genetic or environmental. We do not have the capacity to act outside the causal connections that link us in every respect to the rest of the world. This means we do not have what many people think of as *free will,* being able to cause our behavior without our being fully caused in turn.[33]

But if we do not have free will, how can we be responsible for our decisions? Why should we applaud Mother Teresa and condemn Jeffrey Dahmer if they both behaved as they did because of "the various influences that shape[d] them, whether these be biological or social, genetic or environmental"? Naturalists certainly attempt to answer these questions, but I personally find none of their answers fully satisfying.[34] It is one thing to show that there is a possible way that such-and-such phenomena could be so given physicalism, and an entirely different matter to demonstrate that the proposed physicalist solution is actually the case. More to the point in this discussion is the fact that those who are religious typically have their beliefs reinforced by personal religious experience. The fact that others do not share their religious experiences does nothing to render them meaningless in this regard because they are *personal religious experiences.* They may be reinforced by the personal testimonies of the same sort from others but they are not undermined by the lack of such testimonies.

Another materialist challenge is how to explain human relationality. Just how do we make sense of this thing we call love? If our actions are the result of physical causes, then why does your husband or wife, boyfriend or girlfriend, love you? Why do you love your significant other? Do you do so freely? Does he or she? It is hard to see how in a naturalist world. Love, it would seem, is simply a by-product of our biology and upbringing. In a very real sense, then, in a naturalist world we can say that love is the fruit of our genes and our experiences—but so is mental illness.

These challenges highlight the fact that, at least for most people, *atheism is counterintuitive.* It *seems* as though we decide issues based on rational reflection, that we choose to act, to love, and that we are more than our bodies—this includes being more than our brains. Intuition, however, is not a perfect guide. Many propositions *seem* to be true that are actually false. Nevertheless, it is generally foolish to disregard one's intuitions without strong evidence to the contrary.

Perhaps the most controversial feature of much contemporary atheism is the concept of a *meme.* Richard Dawkins first introduced the concept in his book *The Selfish Gene.*

We need a name for the new replicator, a noun that conveys the idea of a unit of cultural transmission, or a unit of *imitation*. "Mimeme" [that which is imitated] comes from a suitable Greek root, but I want a monosyllable that sounds a bit like "gene". I hope my classicist friends will forgive me if I abbreviate mimeme to *meme*. If it is any consolation, it could alternatively be thought of as being related to "memory", or to the French word *même*. It should be pronounced to rhyme with "cream".[35]

Simply put, a meme is a cultural replicator. Suggested examples of memes include such disparate things as thoughts, ideas, theories, practices, habits, songs, dances, and languages. Accordingly, memes propagate themselves and can move through a culture in a manner similar to the behavior of a virus. But what exactly does a meme resemble, a gene or a virus? This highlights the fact that there is a substantial amount of disagreement—on many levels—as to the nature and working of memes among those who accept the general concept.[36] Concerning this lack of agreement Susan Blackmore opines, "Perhaps a new word is needed to describe the replication of memes with variation and selection. . . ."[37] But of course, *meme itself is a new word.* She continues, "but we probably need to understand the process much better before inventing one."[38] Indeed.

Several other challenges arise related to memetic theory. One is to show how memetics is truly an empirical discipline. When asked to give evidence for memes at the 2007 Greer-Heard Point-Counterpoint Forum in Faith and Culture, Dennett responded that it was an accepted scientific belief and offered his article, "The New Replicators"[39] in the *Encyclopedia of Evolution,* as one line of evidence supporting his position. But what kind of *empirical* evidence is this? It certainly is not the sort of evidence brought forward in support of general Darwinian theory, such as the fossil record, vestigial organs, embryology, geographic distribution of species, contemporary observation of evolution (for example, bacteria becoming disease-resistant), and so on. Simply put, while encyclopedia articles are sufficient to explain a theory, they are not sufficient to establish a scientific theory—and with good reason.

Another issue is that memes can frequently appear to be nothing more than an ad hoc theory, that is, they are not so much an explanation discovered as a solution created to solve an intractable problem. One must remember that the concept of memes began as an analogy with genes. An analogy is a type of supposal, a way of likening one thing to another—analogies are not evidence that something *is so*, but rather illustrations of how something *could be so.* Analogies are tremendously useful tools in philosophy, science, and history. Positing them often allows us to make progress. Unfortunately, analogies can also distort our view of reality and lead us down many dead-end paths. Remember that scientists in the late nineteenth century routinely posited the luminiferous ether—the hypothetical substance that was rigid in relationship to electromagnetic waves but completely permeable to matter—based upon the supposed analogy between light and sound. The idea was analogically plausible but mistaken. Worse, the idea of ether actually held back scientific progress. Fortunately, Albert Einstein built upon the work of Albert Michelson and Edward Morley and disproved it in his special theory of relativity. Beyond this, there is also the question of whether memes are genuinely "scientific," that is, can memetics be tested and falsified, and so on.

Contra Dennett, Blackmore, herself a staunch advocate of meme theory, writes that "Memetics is a fledgling science engaged in lively and largely constructive controversy. . . ."[40] It may be the case that memes will become routinely accepted scientific theory. It may not be. On this point Blackmore concludes: "but the most important open question is just how useful it [memetics] will prove to be."[41]

One must note, however, that the case for atheism does not depend upon memetics. A case can be made for atheism without appealing to memetic theory; in fact, historically such has been the case.

I am well aware of the fact that there are many fair-minded, intelligent people who embrace some form of nontheism, many of them more intelligent than I. I also know that much scholarship and research is being conducted in the attempt to answer these challenges to naturalism. Most importantly, I am well aware of the fact that I am not neutral in this matter; I am a theist and a Christian. I have endeavored, however, to highlight issues that challenge both perspectives and to do so fairly, although I can only be certain that I *tried* to be fair, not that I have actually succeeded.

The debate between theists and nontheists, between Christians and atheists, is not new. This book will not resolve it; in fact, it may raise as many questions as it answers. I am grateful, however, that we can address this issue in print rather than through physical conflict or political manipulation. My own Christian tradition (Baptist) has always affirmed the right of the individual to believe or not to believe, based upon the dictates of his or her conscience. I know that all of the contributors to this volume agree with me that such freedom of opinion is a good thing—and treasure it. I thank all the contributors to this volume for their unique perspectives on this issue. I hope that you enjoy reading these offerings as much as we enjoy having the opportunity to bring them to you.

1

The Future of Atheism: A Dialogue

Daniel Dennett and Alister McGrath

Opening Remarks
Daniel Dennett

First of all, I'm delighted to be here, and honored that you all came out here for this event, and I'm grateful for Mr. Heard and the New Orleans Baptist Theological Seminary for creating this occasion. I'm particularly happy to hear the opening remarks by President Kelley. I think, as you'll see, at the end of my brief presentation, I'm going to be seconding those in a very strong way.[1]

So I'm *the* atheist. (*The audience laughs.*)

I'm going to start with a very brief film by somebody that in a way you know. How many of you know Homer Simpson? Well, Homer Simpson's creator is Matt Groening. Matt Groening's father is Homer Groening, now deceased. His father made films among other things, and at the [2006] TED Conference a year ago[2] Matt showed a two-minute film that his father made in 1967. And I was thrilled with this film because it so perfectly expressed what to me was a very important idea. I actually have Matt's permission to show it here. I'm going to share that film with you now, so if we could just run the video.

Here's Matt Groening, introducing the film . . .

The short film shown by Dennett is introduced by Matt Groening, creator of The Simpsons. *The experimental film begins with the title card reading, "The following is a public service announcement from Homer Groening." The camera cuts to a close-up of a dingy old soccer ball being kicked around in the dirt. The camera pans out to reveal three or four young men, presumably in an African setting, playing with the ball. Told entirely through title slides, Homer Groening's text is a sort of naturalist hymn:*

> There are millions of years in the past
> There are millions of years yet to come
> And here we are
> right in the middle
>
> There's also space
> there are miles and miles of universe in all directions
> And here we are
> right in the middle
>
> Sort of makes your eyes water
> We'd never find this moment again in a million years
> This is a big deal
> Being in the middle of time and space
> Man, this is our world
> Let's not blow it

(The audience applauds.)

I find that that message is, in its own way, both deep and beautiful, and it responds to a question that I'm sure many of you have. And that is, Can you possibly have a morality, can you have a sense of life's meaning without religion? The answer is, yes, yes. You just saw a very succinct and, in its own way, beautiful version of that. Here we are, with time and space going off unimaginably in all directions, and here we are in the middle. This is our world; let's not blow it. It's not the St. Matthew Passion, but it's a beautiful piece of art in any case. And I wanted to share that with you.

So now, let me get down to my talk. My title, "Taming the Wild Memes of Religion," will be clear enough as we go along. Leaving off where Homer Groening stopped, I want to give you another perspective. Let's go back ten thousand years. This was after the dawn of agriculture, but thousands of years before the beginning of Christianity, thousands of years before the beginning of Judaism. At that point, the human population of the globe, plus their livestock and pets, amounted to a very small fraction of the terrestrial vertebrate biomass. The terrestrial vertebrate biomass does not include the invertebrates, the bugs, and what is in the ocean. But we were a minor primate, maybe a major primate, but that was a tenth of one percent. Would anybody hazard a guess at what percentage of the terrestrial vertebrae biomass—human beings plus their livestock and pets today—that it is today? Would anybody make a guess? Fifty? Do I hear any raise on fifty? Seventy? Do I hear any raise on seventy? Ninety-eight percent. What a huge change in a biological instant—in ten thousand years! This is calculated by the visionary engineer Paul MacCready, and he came up with a really rather remarkable thing to say about it:

> Over billions of years, on a unique sphere, chance has painted a thin covering of life, complex, improbable, wonderful, and fragile. Suddenly, we humans—a recently arrived species no longer subject to the checks and balances inherent in natures—have grown in population, technology, and intelligence to a position of terrible power. We now wield the paintbrush.[3]

To appreciate how amazing this is, that we have inherited this earth in this way, it sometimes helps to take an alien perspective. So let's pretend we're Martians and we're coming to the planet, and we're wondering what we're going to find on this planet. What would happen if Martian scientists came to earth? Well, here's a picture of something that might amaze them. This is approximately one million human beings gathered for Maha Kumbh Mela in 2001 on the banks of the Ganges River, one of the largest convocations of bipedal mammals ever. That would impress Martian biologists. They would say, "Goodness, me! What an amazing event! This is a very remarkable gathering of animals."

Here's another. That's Mecca, of course. Another: St. Peter's Square. *The Martians would want to know what on earth explains these patterns.* This is a pie graph that shows as of a few years ago what the breakdown of the populations of the world are. You see that Christianity has about 33 percent. Hinduism has about 16 percent, the same as nonreligious. Islam has about 18 percent. The fastest growing of these is probably Islam, mainly because of birth rate. The second fastest growing, or maybe fastest growing, is *nonreligious*. According to the *World Christian Encyclopedia*, the only major religion that is growing worldwide is Islam. Secularism and nonreligion are growing even faster. Southern Baptists are now baptizing about 300,000 a year according to the figures that I was able to get. That's about the same as you were doing in the 1950s. You're not growing any faster than you were then, but the population has doubled.

I mention these facts because one often sees in the press the claim that there's a tremendous upsurge in religion in the United States and around the world, and it's not really true. Religions are making a lot of noise, and they're getting a lot of attention, but if you go and look for the facts, if you do a careful study of the demographics, you'll find out that some of those claims are very misleading. Right now, there are roughly 749 million atheists in the world, and that's a very conservative estimate. That is, there are twice as many atheists as Buddhists, forty times more atheists than Jews, more than fifty times as many atheists as Mormons. (That's from Zuckerman, 2006.)[4]

In an October piece that many of you may have read in *The New York Times*, Laurie Goodstein wrote about the notorious "4 percent problem" that many people are worried about. Quoting her, "If current trends continue, only 4 percent of teenagers will be Bible-believing Christians as adults."[5] It was this calculation that led the National Association of Evangelicals to pass a resolution deploring the epidemic of young people leaving the evangelical church.

So it is simply not the case that religion is booming and that atheism is on the wane. Those are just facts. What to make of them, whether to deplore them or to be thrilled by them is another matter. First, we have to understand what the facts are. Gregory Paul, in a recent article in the *Journal of Religion and Society*, draws our attention to some interesting facts, because many people are very concerned that if a nation becomes more secular, family values will go down the drain. Well, let's compare the homicide rate in the United States, which is not a very secular state, with European secular states. The homicide rate is much higher in the United States than in any secular democracy. But sexually transmitted disease rates, teen pregnancy, and abortion rates are also much higher in the United States than in "godless Europe."[6]

Now, our Martian scientists see this and say: "Well, these are interesting facts, what explains them? What accounts for all these patterns in the world?" Now this is the question that interests me. I'm a philosopher by training, but I work in and on the edges of science and evolutionary biology, evolutionary theory, cognitive science, and psychology. I'm interested in knowing what happens when you put on your Martian glasses, which are the same as scientific glasses, and you look at these phenomena. They are fascinating phenomena; they are unmistakably important phenomena. They are deeply important, amazing phenomena, and they are going to become more important as the century progresses. What do we make of them?

To help us think about this, I want to draw a comparison. Here's a cow, a nice cow (not, I think, a sacred cow, but maybe for some). Here's a question: "Who designed this cow?" You're going to say: nobody designed this cow. Well, actually, a lot of people have spent a lot of time in the last few hundred years redesigning cows. This is a domesticated species, and they have tried to make the cow just right for us. Let's consider its ancestor, the aurochs. About ten thousand years ago, people started keeping aurochs and they began to domesticate them, but who designed the aurochs? The answer is evolution. Evolution by natural selection designed the aurochs over millions of years. No intelligent designer was responsible for the aurochs. What were aurochs for? They were for making more aurochs. They were a wild species, and that's all they were for. But now, we have domesticated the aurochs, and we've reverse-engineered it. We figured out how the parts work, and we've figured out how to optimize the parts and revise the parts. We've basically redesigned the auroch to serve our purposes. Who designed the cow? Well, natural selection designed the cow for millions and millions of years, and now, for about ten thousand years, we've been sometimes inadvertently and sometimes very deliberately redesigning the cow. The same thing is true of religion.

Religions are brilliantly designed systems. They are tremendously robust, efficient, powerful, long-lived institutions. We can reverse-engineer them. They have an evolutionary history. They started off wild and then were domesticated. And many of the features of organized religions today are very different from the features of their wild ancestors, only some thousands of years ago. And this we can study with the tools of science. We can reverse-engineer religion the same way we can reverse-engineer cows and television sets and just about any complex thing you see. Reverse-engineering is the intellectual exercise, the scientific exercise, that intelligent design (if it were a real science) would use to come up with proofs to show that you just couldn't have this design without an intelligent designer. They haven't yet come up with any good evidence that that's true, but they are at least trying to do that. If you want to disprove evolutionary theory, that's what you want to look for. You want to look for something that couldn't have evolved. The process of studying these questions is really a variety of reverse-engineering.

So, the Martians want to know how all this originated and when. What is it for? How does it perpetuate itself? Well, we know that there have been hundreds of thousands of religions since the first religions. Hundreds of thousands of religions and almost all are extinct. But religions are being born now so fast that the web site on new sects can't keep up with them. Most of them have a life of only a few weeks or months, sometimes a generation or two. Most religions that are started go extinct in short order. That's also true, of course, of biological species. Much more than 99 percent of all the species that have ever existed on this planet have gone extinct. Those that go extinct, however, often pass on a few themes to competitors that survive. So if we study the evolution of religions—seeing what's around today and where it came from—we can learn a lot about the sources of themes that we find in organized religions today.

Well, what is it about the survivors that helps them survive? That is the question that you always want to ask. And one possibility is that one of them is simply the truth. And that presumably is what most of you believe—and it may be true. But you don't know it's true. Scientifically, we can explore the question. We can look at the history of religion and see if there might be in fact some other, better explanation of why this particular religion or these religions have survived. Notice, there are a lot of survivors out there still, and they can't all be true. So if your religion has survived because it is true, the other religions that are robust and healthy today have survived for other reasons. What might those reasons be? These are the questions—factual questions—that we can explore. And that's the point of my book *Breaking the Spell.* The "spell" I want to break is the taboo or prohibition against studying that very question. It's the idea that we shouldn't look so closely and intensely at religion, that we should avert our eyes from these phenomena. According to the taboo, it's not nice and it's not appropriate; there is something blasphemous or just immoral about studying religions. I say no. Religions can be studied as natural phenomena just fine. Let's look at them. Let's see what we can make of them. Now, some people are afraid of what they might learn. Maybe they're right to be afraid, or maybe they're not.

My book is not a "virulent attack" on religion—as some critics have said. I do not hate religion. I am not an enemy of religion. I'm a student of religion. I'm an atheist, but that does not mean that I hate religion. If I were a Jew it would not mean that I hate Buddhism. I hope you agree.

Here's something else that might really amaze a scientist from Mars, or it might amaze you. You go out in the field and you find an ant climbing a blade of grass. And it climbs and it climbs and it climbs to the top of the blade of grass, and if it falls, it climbs again. And you think, What is this ant doing? Why is it wasting all this energy climbing to the top of the blade of grass? What's in it for the ant? What good is it for the ant to climb to the top of the blade of grass? Is it lost? Is it showing off? Is it looking for food? What is it doing? What good accrues to the ant? And the answer is: no good accrues to the ant at all. Is it just a fluke? Yes, it's just a fluke. It's a lancet fluke. A lancet fluke is a little parasitic worm. Now lancet flukes (*Dicrocoelium dendriticum*), in order to complete their life cycle, have to get into the belly of a ruminant—a cow or a sheep. And they improve their chances of getting into the belly of a cow or sheep by commandeering a passing ant, climbing into its brain, and driving it up a blade of grass like an all-terrain vehicle, there the more likely to be eaten by a cow or a sheep. Incredibly smart. Of course the lancet fluke is stupid, but the strategy is brilliant. The lancet fluke doesn't even have a brain, really. It has the IQ of a carrot, roughly, I'd say. But the strategy that it engages in is very devious and very clever, and it's sort of spooky. Here we have a hijacker. We have a parasite that infects the brain and induces suicidal behavior on behalf of a cause other than one's own genetic fitness. Spooky. Gee, I wonder if anything like that happens to us!

Well, let me remind you that the Arabic word *islam* means submission, surrender of one's self to the will of Allah. Built right into the name of Islam is this idea that the individual should surrender his or her interests to the interests of Allah. And it's not just Islam; it's Christianity, too. This is a page from a music manuscript that I found in a Paris bookstall about fifty years ago. It says, *Semen est verbum Dei; sator autem Christus.* "The Word of God is a seed, and the Sower of the seed is Christ." And it goes on to say that all who hear this shall have eternal life; that is the *quid pro quo.* The idea of spreading the word, even at the risk of one's own life, of surrendering one's own life to the will of God, is just as much in Christianity as it is in Islam.

"The heart of worship is surrender."[7]

"Surrendered people obey God's word, even if doesn't make sense."[8]

Now where did I get those quotes? I got those quotes from Pastor Rick Warren, from his book *The Purpose Driven Life,* which many of you, I hope, know. It's an interesting book. It's sold over twenty-three million copies. It's an immensely influential book, and it is extremely well designed. And it can be reverse-engineered. And if you're interested in the reverse-engineering of that book, there's a talk I did at the conference where Matt Groening spoke where I reverse-engineered Rick Warren's book.[9] Warren was not amused. But as I say, it's brilliantly designed, and we can figure out what makes it work. In a way, I'm taking it very seriously.

Well, here are some ideas to die for: Islam, Christianity. But many people have died for communism, and many people have died for democracy. Many people have killed for communism. Many people have killed for democracy, for justice, for freedom. This is the New Hampshire license plate: "Live free or die!" Great sentiment. I'd like to point out something. The moose pictured on that license plate cannot share this sentiment. It is beyond the capacity of the moose's brain to appreciate this idea. We are the only species on the planet that has ever existed which can decide that an idea is more important than having more grandchildren than your neighbor. That sets us apart from all other species, but is itself a biological fact and one that has a biological explanation.

Question: Is maximizing your progeny your highest goal, your *summum bonum?* Now, I'm a father and a grandfather. I love having grandchildren. My second grandchild is going to be born any day now, and I'm thrilled. Many of you are parents or grandparents, or you want to be parents. Hands up those of you who think that the most important thing in life is having more offspring than your neighbor. I do not see a single hand up. That makes us entirely different from the other species on this planet. For every other species, that's their highest imperative. Making more aurochs or making more ants. That's all. Every act they take is aimed at that purpose.

But not us, because we have minds that can have ideas and we can decide to die for an idea.

It's ideas, not worms, that hijack our brains—replicating ideas. Ideas that we rehearse and think about, and decide that we like, pass them on to somebody else, who passes them on to somebody else. They make copies; they spread like a virus. These themes are what Richard Dawkins calls *memes*. Dawkins, who wrote *The Selfish Gene* in 1976, introduced the idea that cultural items had an evolutionary history too. They could replicate. They could differentially replicate, and the fittest were the ones that would get us to make the most copies. He pointed out that they are analogous to genes or to viruses. What's a virus? It's not alive. It's just a big crystal, a macromolecule. It's a string of DNA with attitude. That is to say, it's got a shape that permits it, when it gets in the right place, to provoke its own reproduction by the replicating machinery of a cell.

And Dawkins's brilliant idea was that ideas can do that too. They can go inside a mind and get that mind to make a copy of them and another copy and another copy and then send that copy out into the world where it makes more copies still. That's the idea behind "the Word of God is a seed and the sower of the seed is Christ." It's not an ugly idea; it's a beautiful idea. The idea that ideas themselves have their own fitness and that we are their hosts.

The theologian Hugh Pyper said in 1998: "If 'survival of the fittest' has any validity as a slogan, then the Bible seems a candidate for the accolade of the fittest of texts."[10] There are more copies of it in more languages all over the world than any other book, by a wide margin, but the Qur'an is picking up. These are fit cultural items. Independent of whether they are good for us, whether they are true, whether they are false, they are fit in the biological sense because they have lots of offspring that have lots of offspring that have lots of offspring. Human culture is itself one of the fruits on the Tree of Life.

Culture is composed of symbionts that are either good for us, neutral, or fitness-reducing. But remember, none of you cares about your biological fitness. There wasn't a person in this room who thought their biological fitness was the most important thing in life. So the fact that a particular idea in your brain might be fitness-reducing is neither here no there. Some of them, no doubt, are fitness-enhancing. The idea for making a better mousetrap, a better fishhook, a better plow, these give you more powers. But lots of ideas may be along for the ride, and some of them may even be detrimental.

When I started working on my book on the evolution of religion, people said very often, "Oh, you're working on the evolution of religion. That's an interesting question. What do you think religions are for? Because after all, every human group that's ever been studied has some form of religion, so it must be good for something."

And I said, "Well, yeah, that's a possibility, but that's a false inference."
"Well, why?"

And I said, "Well, every human group that's ever been studied also has the common cold. What's that good for?" It's good for itself. It replicates because it can. I'm not saying religion is like the common cold; I'm saying it *might* be. I'm saying that some religious ideas could be like the common cold; they spread because they can spread. They are fit, and we can't get rid of them any more than we can get rid of the common cold. It is one of the possibilities you have to bear in mind if you are going to be objective in studying this scientifically. You must not assume at the outset that "Gosh, it's got to be wonderful" or that some particular aspect has to be wonderful. The fact that it's still here only shows that it is benefiting the fitness of something, but it might be only itself.

How did human culture get started? If I had more time, I would go into that. It's in my book, but I'm not going to because I want to move ahead to one more idea.

Here's a riddle: How are spoken words and folk songs like squirrels, rats, pigeons, and barn swallows? The answer is: these species are not domesticated species, but they have evolved to fit the human environment. They've evolved to coexist with us. They are beautifully adapted to live with human beings. Some of our ideas are like that too. They're not domesticated—they're wild—but they live with human beings. Now sheep, for instance, were very clever to acquire shepherds. They got to outsource all their problems. But it wasn't the sheep's cleverness, it was evolution's. Sheep are stupid. They're a little smarter than *Dicrocelium dendriticum*, but not much. The fitness move is evolution's move, not the sheep's. Sheep are fortunate to get themselves domesticated, and similarly the wild memes of religion were fortunate to get themselves domesticated because they acquired stewards—people who were prepared to devote their lives to the health and spreading of those very ideas.

Now, there I might end, but I want to go to my final point. Religions are powerful forces in people's lives. Religions are brilliantly designed. When we understand their design, we can see better what we might do or should do to revise their design or improve them. Many of the attempts to reform religion have been misguided; they've been under-informed, and they have done more harm to their religions than good. If you want to save your religion, if you want to improve your religion, you better understand how it works. You better reverse-engineer it.

In the meantime, I have one policy proposal. It surprises a lot of people, but I don't think it's going to surprise you. I think education on the world's religions for all of our children—homeschooled, private school, public school—should be required. We have the three Rs; we should have the fourth R. What am I talking about? I'm talking about the history, the

creeds, the rituals, the music, the symbols, the ethical commands and prohibitions of all the major religions and, for that matter, of atheism. Just
facts, no values, no spin. Just lots of geography, basically.

I'm completely *laissez-faire* about the rest of what you teach your children. If you teach them this, you can teach them whatever else you want.
Whatever else you want, with one little proviso: as long as it doesn't disable
them from informing themselves further through, for instance, hatred or
fear. That's child abuse if you do that. But if you teach them these facts,
then you can teach them anything else you want. Why? Because when religions do go toxic—and we all know every religion has its toxic, fanatical
forms that go off the rails and become lamentable human phenomena—
this depends always on the enforced ignorance of the young. So if you
simply prevent that ignorance, you more or less guarantee as sort of a
public health measure that only the benign, good religions can survive.
A religion that can flourish in a world of mutual knowledge of the facts
about world religions is a benign religion. So I think you can see why I'm
not really an enemy of religion. I think we should study religions carefully, scientifically, objectively, so that we learn what makes them tick. Once
we've reverse-engineered them, first of all, we'll understand better why
they're good at what they're good at and how to make them better.

Thank you very much for your attention.

Opening Remarks
Alister McGrath

Let me begin by saying what a great pleasure it is to be with you here
in New Orleans tonight. And it is a special privilege to be able to have
this dialogue with Professor Daniel Dennett. Although recovering from
an operation, Professor Dennett is able to be with us tonight, and I am
delighted to be able to engage in this provocative and important topic.
There is so much that could be said on this topic, and so little time in
which to say it. So where shall we start?

I'm going to begin with the failure of prophecy—the great secular
prophecies of the 1960s that religion was on its way out globally, as humanity entered a new, secular phase of its existence. Religion was meant to
have disappeared years ago. For more than a century, leading sociologists, anthropologists, and psychologists have declared that their children
would see the dawn of a new era in which the "God delusion" would be left
behind for good. Back in the 1960s, we were told that religion was fading
away, to be replaced by a secular world.

For some of us, that sounded like a great thing. I was an atheist back
in the late 1960s, and remember looking forward to the demise of religion
with a certain grim pleasure. I had grown up in Northern Ireland, and had

known religious tensions and violence at firsthand. The solution was obvious to my freethinking mind. Get rid of religion, and such tensions and violence would be eradicated. The future was bright—and godless.

Two things have changed since then. In the first place, religion has made a comeback. It is now such a significant element of today's world that it seems strange to think that it was only a generation ago that its death was foretold with such confidence. The humanist writer Michael Shermer, perhaps best known as the director of the Skeptics Society and publisher of *Skeptic* magazine, made this point forcefully back in 1999,[11] when he pointed out that never in history have so many, and such a high percentage of the American population, believed in God. Not only is God not "dead," as the German philosopher Nietzsche prematurely proclaimed; God never seems to have been more alive.

Second, and rather less importantly, my own attitudes have changed. Although I was passionately and totally persuaded of the truth and relevance of atheism as a young man, I subsequently found myself persuaded that Christianity was a much more interesting and intellectually exciting worldview than atheism. I have always valued freethinking and being able to rebel against the orthodoxies of an age. Yet I never suspected where my freethinking would take me.

I arrived at Oxford from school a Marxist, believing that religion was the cause of all the world's evils. As an intellectual Darwinian, it seemed perfectly clear to me that the idea of God was on its way out, and would be replaced by fitter and more adapted ideas—like Marxism. I was a "bright," to use Dennett's language.

But it didn't work out like that. At Oxford—to my surprise—I discovered Christianity. It was the intellectually most exhilarating and spiritually stimulating thing I could ever hope to describe—better even than chemistry, a wonderful subject that I had thought to be the love of my life and my future career. I went on to gain a doctorate for research in molecular biophysics from Oxford, and found that immensely exciting and satisfying. But I knew I had found something better—like the pearl of great price that Jesus talks about in the Gospel, which is so beautiful and precious that it overshadows everything. It was intellectually satisfying, imaginatively engaging, and aesthetically exciting. So I guess I became dim.

But this discovery raised questions for me. I had been taught that science disproved God. That all good scientists were atheists. That science was good, religion evil. It was a hopelessly simplified binary opposition, not unlike George Orwell, in *Animal Farm*: Four legs good, two legs bad. But it suited me just fine then.

Yet my newfound Christian faith brought a new sense of fulfillment and appreciation to my studies and later my research in the natural sciences. I saw nature as charged with the grandeur and majesty of God.

To engage with nature was to gain a deeper appreciation of the divine wisdom. I gave up the sciences to read theology, but I still love the sciences, and follow the literature, especially in evolutionary biology. And above all, I have a passion for relating Christian theology to the natural sciences. Hence, my presence tonight.

The first point that got me nodding my head in agreement comes very early in the book. People sometimes feel very defensive about religion. Religious people often get extremely defensive when challenged about the basis of their beliefs, which hinders any serious debate about the nature of their faith. I know what he means. The issue, I suspect, is that a challenge to faith often threatens to pull the rug from under the values and beliefs that have sustained someone's life. But this is a general problem with any significant worldview, not just a religion.

Since the publication of my book *Dawkins' God* in 2004, I am regularly asked to speak on its themes throughout the world. In these lectures, I set out Richard Dawkins's views on religion, and then give an evidence-based rebuttal, point by point.

After one such lecture, I was confronted by a very angry young man. The lecture had not been particularly remarkable. I had simply demon-strated, by rigorous use of scientific, historical, and philosophical argu-ments, that Dawkins's intellectual case against God didn't stand up to critical examination. But this man was angry—in fact, I would say he was furious. Why? Because, he told me, wagging his finger agitatedly at me, I had "destroyed his faith." His atheism rested on the authority of Richard Dawkins, and I had totally undermined his faith. He would have to go away and rethink everything. How *dare* I do such a thing!

As I reflected on this event while driving home afterwards, I found myself in two minds about this. Part of me regretted the enormous incon-venience that I had clearly caused this person. I had thrown the settled assumptions of his life into turmoil. Yet I consoled myself with the thought that, if he was unwise enough to base his life on the clearly inadequate worldview set out by Dawkins, then he would have to realize someday that it rested on decidedly shaky foundations. The dispelling of the delusion had to happen sometime. I just happened to be the historical accident that made it happen at that time and place.

Now I do not intend to imply that the very weak arguments I find in Dawkins's works recur in Dennett's. Let me put on record my belief that *Breaking the Spell* is a well-argued, thoughtful, and interesting work, which shows no signs of the rambling and ranting I fear I find, for example, in Dawkins's *The God Delusion*. Dennett is right—beliefs are critical. We base our lives upon them; they shape our decisions about the most fundamental things. I can still remember the turbulence that I found myself experienc-ing on making the intellectually painful (yet rewarding) transition from atheism to Christianity. Every part of my mental furniture had to be rearranged. Dennett is correct—unquestionably correct—when he demands that we examine our beliefs—especially if we are naïve enough to think that we don't have any in the first place.

So how, I wondered, would Dennett clarify the distinction between a worldview and a religion? The dividing line is notoriously imprecise, and, many would say, is constructed by those with vested interests to defend. Here I must confess some puzzlement. In *Breaking the Spell*, Dennett tells us that "a religion without God or gods is like a vertebrate without a backbone."[12] Now if I were leading a sixth form discussion[13] about how to define religion, this would be the first definition to be considered—and the first to be rejected, precisely because it is so inadequate. What about nontheistic religions? Vertebrates *by definition* have backbones. The concept of religion simply does not entail God.

So why this unworkable definition? I initially thought that it was because Dennett seems to have American Protestant fundamentalism in his gunsights. (This is, if I might say so, a very American book.) After I had finished the book, I could see why he took this line. Dennett wants to explain religion in terms of evolutionary theory. The existence of God is, he asserts, a fantasy that once carried some kind of survival advantages. So religions that don't believe in God don't really fit the bill.

I have to say that I was simply not persuaded by his account of what religion is, which most religious people will regard as unrecognizable. Perhaps it tells us a lot about what leading figures in America's political and intellectual left think about religion, which is a rather different matter.

So let me turn now to what I think is the most interesting aspect of this book—its appeal to science. This is an area that excites me, and Dennett's earlier book *Darwin's Dangerous Idea* shows that he has mastered some of the intellectual issues that he needs to address in this book. Dennett suggests that that there is some kind of taboo against the scientific study of religion. The historian of ideas within me was puzzled by this, in that this has been going on—at least in Europe—since about 1780, with the emergence of comparative mythology. But it's good to welcome a newcomer to the conversation.

I would place Dennett in the broad tradition of naturalist explanation of religion, which includes Ludwig Feuerbach, Karl Marx, and Sigmund Freud. Whatever the benefits of religions, Dennett and these writers believe that they arise entirely inside human minds. No spiritual realities exist outside us. Natural explanations may be given of the origins of belief in God. Now I hesitate to mention this, but this is clearly a rather circular argument, which presupposes its conclusions.

So what models does Dennett propose for the origins of faith in God? I was delighted to find a rich range of explanatory approaches in this book. I read the first—the "sweet tooth" theory. On this approach, just as we have evolved a receptor system for sweet things, so in a similar way we might have a "god center" in our brains. Such a center might depend on a "mystical gene" that was favored by natural selection because people with it tend to survive better.

Just a moment, I thought. Where's the science? What's the evidence for this? Instead, I found mights and maybes, speculation and supposition, instead of the rigorous evidence-driven and evidence-based arguments that I love and respect. These theories are evidence-free and wildly speculative. We are told, for example, that—I quote from the jacket blurb—religious "ideas could have spread from individual superstitions via shamanism and the early 'wild' strains of religion." There's no credible evidence for this. There's no serious attempt to engage with the history of religions. It reminds me of those TV ads, "This could help you lose weight as part of a calorie-controlled diet." *Could.* The TV ad writers would love to be able to say their product was "clinically proven" to do these things. But they can't. There's no evidence.

Now I wish I had time to engage with each of the major models that I noted in working through this book. Sadly, I do not have time. I therefore propose to deal with what I consider to be the strongest of these models in detail. This is the "meme"—a hypothetical cultural or intellectual replicator. On this model, religions might be memes that infect our brains. They are not necessarily parasitic, but could be symbiotic, conferring advantages on those who are infected. It's an idea that Dennett put forward back in *Darwin's Dangerous Idea*, and needs exploration. So let's do that.

Is belief in God a meme? It's an idea that Dawkins floated back in 1976, and it lingers to this day. When I first came across the idea of the meme back in 1977, I was excited by it. I was beginning my career as an intellectual historian, fascinated by cultural development and the history of ideas. I thought that Dawkins's idea of the meme might explain some things far better than other models. And I know that others felt the same. Yet as I—and those others—began to check this idea out, we began to realize it just didn't work.[14] I abandoned the concept as unworkable about ten years later, after detailed work on intellectual developments in the Renaissance.

But the real problems lie deeper than this. First, the meme is just an hypothesis—one that we don't need, as there are better models available, for example, in economics, but also in anthropology. If genes could not be seen, we would have to invent them—the evidence demands a biologically transmitted genetic replicator. *Memes can't be observed, and the evidence can be explained perfectly well without them.* As Maurice Bloch, professor of anthropology at the London School of Economics, commented recently, the "exasperated reaction of many anthropologists to the general idea of memes" reflects the apparent ignorance of the proponents of the meme-hypothesis regarding the discipline of anthropology, and its major successes in the explanation of cultural development—without feeling the need to develop anything like the idea of a "meme" at all.[15]

And what about the cognitive model that underlies the meme? I would welcome some clarification here, as it seems to me that Dennett seems to buy into Dawkins's curious idea, set out in 1976, of memes "leaping from brain to brain." This seems to posit cognition as an essentially passive reception of these memes. But cognition is an active process.

Anyway, has anyone actually seen these things, whether leaping from brain to brain, or just hanging out? The issue, it must be noted, has nothing to do with religion. It is whether the meme can be considered to be a viable scientific hypothesis, when there is no clear operational definition of a meme, no testable model for how memes influence culture and why standard selection models are not adequate, a general tendency to ignore the sophisticated social science models of information transfer already in place, and a high degree of circularity in the explanation of the power of memes.

At this stage, the issue is simply whether memes exist, irrespective of their implications for religion. I say, and most active scientists say with me, that there is no evidence for these things. As Simon Conway Morris, professor of evolutionary paleobiology at Cambridge, points out, memes seem to have no place in serious scientific reflection. "Memes are trivial, to be banished by simple mental exercises. In any wider context, they are hopelessly, if not hilariously, simplistic."[16] Now maybe Simon is playfully overstating things here, just like Dawkins does in *The God Delusion*. (Sure, it's naughty, but it makes for much more interesting reading.) But I cannot help but note that Conway Morris represents the majority report within the scientists I hang out with at Oxford.

I was slightly puzzled that the arguments of such leading critics of memetics were not identified and confronted, point by point. This book, in my view, makes a critique of religion dependent on a hypothetical, unobserved entity, which can be dispensed with in order to make sense of what we observe. Isn't that actually a core atheist critique of God—an unobserved hypothesis that can be dispensed with easily? The evidence for belief in God is far better, in my view, than the evidence for belief in memes.

If I were an atheist, wanting to commend atheism to others on account of its intellectual excellence, I would drop this memetic approach, which merely weakens the case for atheism, and head back to the safer territory of Marxist dialectical reading of history, which is, in my view, much more intellectually rigorous and evidence-driven. But far be it from me, as a lapsed atheist, to tell those of you who still believe how to do your job.

Anyway, what do memes *do*? Dennett tells us that they spread beliefs—like beliefs in God. So are *all* beliefs spread by memes? Or just the ones that anti-religious critics don't like? Is there a meme for atheism? Dennett's "Simple Taxonomy"[17] certainly suggests so. And since there is no compelling scientific evidence for these things, are we to conclude that there is a meme for believing in memes?[18]

This is certainly a problem for the originator of this notion, Richard Dawkins. As many of you will know, Dawkins makes an unsuccessful attempt to evade the trap of self-referentiality by saying that his own ideas are different. God is caused by memes; atheism is not. Anyone familiar with intellectual history will spot the pattern immediately. My ideas are exempt from the general patterns I identify for other ideas, which allows me to explain them away. My fear is that Dennett has fallen victim to this same weakness. So let me ask this question once more: Is it just belief in God that is a meme? *Surely atheism is as well.* And if it is, we seem to end up in the epistemological quagmire in which all theories, worldviews, and beliefs are determined by these mysterious biological drivers.

But the real question is this: How could Dennett and I be able to settle this point *scientifically*? If we are not able to do so, then we have a nonscientific debate about imaginary entities, hypothesized by analogy with the gene. And we all know how unreliable arguments based on analogy can be—witness the fruitless search for the luminiferous ether in the late nineteenth century, based on the supposed analogy between light and sound. That's why the Michelson-Morley experiment was so important—it showed that there was no evidence for this so-called "ether." It was analogically plausible—but nonexistent. Michelson and Morley exposed that analogy as invalid, however attractive or plausible it may have seemed to many at the time. Dawkins tells us that memes are merely awaiting their Crick and Watson, meaning that the clarification of their structure and mechanism is just around the corner.[19] I think they are merely waiting for their Michelson and Morley to deliver the final deathblow to an unsatisfactory and unnecessary theory, of questionable relevance to our debate about God.

Moving on, I was glad to see that Dennett and I share so much in common. We both love democracy, freedom, science, and lots of other good things. We both also abhor violence and oppression. Professor Dennett argued that religion has on occasion encouraged both of those. I agree. That's a fact of history. Yet I have to say that I searched in vain in *Breaking the Spell* for a mention of either Lenin or Stalin, each of whom launched violent programs of repression based on their atheist worldviews against Christianity and Islam. That's a fact of history as well.

Now, Dennett might respond by saying that these are not *typical* of atheism. In fairness, I believe he would be right to do so. But neither, in equal fairness, are the excesses of violence and intolerance that he does mention *typical* of religion. I appreciate the need for a bit of rhetoric and exaggeration to spice up an argument, and have to confess that I do it myself every now and then. But one cannot represent the *pathological* elements of any movement—religious or anti-religious—as if they were *normal* or *typical.* Few of us in this audience tonight are in favor of fanaticism; but it is clearly perfectly possible to be a fanatical atheist, as much as a fanatical religionist. It's fanaticism that's the problem here, not religion or anti-religion. In Oxford at this moment, we are facing a threat from one of the most fanatical groups in British society today: animal rights protestors. They are not religious. They are driven by an ideology—by a worldview. Surely our common enemy is the fanatic, first and foremost. We need to reflect on how to control this phenomenon. But it is a clear factual error to assume that this is limited to, or necessarily characteristic of, religion.

Our topic tonight is the future of atheism, and I fear that I have only begun to scratch the surface of this matter. So I will end by raising a question that I believe to be important. Is science going to sort out the God question for us? I'm sure that at least some of you here tonight remember early episodes of *Star Trek.* Classic *Trek* episodes from the period 1966–1969 were strongly influenced by the humanist philosophy of their creator, Gene Roddenberry. As Roddenberry made clear in a 1991 interview with *Humanist* magazine, religion was simply "nonsense—largely magical, superstitious things." Early *Trek* episodes were saturated with an ethos of the excellence of science, the triumph of logic, and the inevitability of progress. Religion was one of the evils of the past—along with poverty, prejudice, and war—that progress would leave behind. Religious beliefs were to be expected among the primitive alien societies favored by a visit from the crew of the starship *Enterprise.* But there could be no question of these enlightened and thoroughly modern progressives themselves holding such beliefs. Religion was best left to the savages of the more backward parts of the galaxy.

The beginnings of an answer are to be found in a wise book written back in 1984 by Sir Peter Medawar, who won the Nobel Prize for Medicine for his work on immunobiology. In *The Limits of Science,* Medawar reflected on how science, despite being "the most successful enterprise human beings have ever engaged upon," had limits to its scope. Science is superb when it comes to showing that the chemical formula for water is H_2O. Or, more significantly, that DNA has a double helix.

But what of that greater question: What's life all about? This and others like it, Medawar insisted, were "questions that science cannot answer, and that no conceivable advance of science would empower it to answer."[20] They could not be dismissed as "nonquestions or pseudoquestions such as only simpletons ask and only charlatans profess to be able to answer."[21] This is not to criticize science, but simply to calibrate its capacities. Medawar's point is that science is excellent when it comes to exploring the relationships between various aspects of the material universe. But when it comes to questions of meaning or value, it doesn't really get us very far. It's not a controversial point. For example, Dawkins made a very similar point recently, in emphasizing that "science has no methods for deciding what is ethical."[22]

This deft analysis by a self-confessed rationalist, who had little time for religion in his own life, casts light on why scientists hold such a variety of religious beliefs. It makes it clear that scientists are intellectually and morally free to believe (or disbelieve) in God, while at the same time challenging religions to take the findings of science seriously. It also shows that it makes little sense to talk about "proof" of a worldview, whether Christian or atheist. In the end, as Gilbert Harman pointed out decades ago, the real question is which offers the "best explanation" of things. And as there is no general agreement on how to decide which of these explanations is the "best," the argument seems certain to run on and on.[23]

Christians will argue that their worldview represents a superb way of making sense of things, while accepting that this, like its atheist counterparts, is open to challenge by skeptics. "I believe in Christianity as I believe that the Sun has risen—not only because I see it, but because by it, I see everything else," as C. S. Lewis famously said.[24] Christians know that they can't prove that God is there, any more than an atheist can prove that there is no God. The simple fact is that all of us, whether Christians or atheists, base our lives on at least some fundamental beliefs that we know we cannot prove, but nevertheless believe to be reliable and significant—in short, to be the best explanation of this highly complex undertaking and mystery that we call "life."

But that just opens up another question—how on earth can we verify a worldview? But I have run out of time! I'm sure we'll come back to this one!

A Dialogue
Daniel Dennett and Alister McGrath

DENNETT: Thanks, Alister, for very eloquent and interesting comments, and as you pointed out, there's a great deal that we agree about. I'm going to respond to some of the challenges—the ones that struck me as the most important. Maybe I'll leave something out, and then if there is something you want me to respond to particularly, I will.

One of the first things that Alister mentioned was my definition—my working definition—of religion as involving belief in a supernatural agent. He quoted my line, "A religion without a supernatural agent is like a vertebrate without a backbone." Now, when I introduced that, I said, "This is just a working definition." I have to start somewhere, and this strikes me as the most central feature of religions through the ages, that they have believed in gods. Now, there are religions that apparently do not believe in gods or, if they believe in gods, the gods that they believe in are so different that a lot of people wouldn't call them gods. And what are those? Well, they're former religions. Or maybe they're honorary vertebrates. Now what's an honorary vertebrate? Well, in Great Britain, a vertebrate is where they draw the line on the law. You can throw an invertebrate on a hot grill. You can stomp on an invertebrate. You can do whatever you want to an invertebrate. They have no rights at all. You can eat a live oyster. But vertebrates are protected under the law; you can't do whatever you want with a live vertebrate. This gets a bit into the question about animal rights. The British make one exception, and I think it's a very wise one. They have one category of honorary vertebrates: the octopus! Just one species, *Octopus vulgaris*, a mollusk with a large head and prehensile tentacles— basically a smart clam, and it is protected by law even though it's not a vertebrate because it's so much like the vertebrates in so many ways. So it doesn't matter too much where we draw the line. We can have things that are so much like religions that we'll call them religions because they, in some sense, deserve to be called religions. I particularly want to resist Alister's request, but I can't resist quoting him, though: "What is the essence of religion?" What Darwin showed us is that essentialism is a mistake. Don't ever ask for the essence of something because essence is something that's just pre-Darwinian thinking. So if we look at the history of the evolution of religion we see a gradual transition of phenomena. That's not religion; that's just superstition. That's not religion; that's just witch doctoring. And then, well, that's a religion. And then, that's obviously a religion. And then you have things which, well, they're not quite religions anymore, or maybe they're religions because they have the legal status of religion—a good reason to hang onto the term. Scientology is a religion because it says it's a religion, and it gets a tremendous tax break thereby. It's an honorary vertebrate. So the issue has some real practical consequences, but not theoretical ones. In my book, I say that it doesn't make a difference where I draw the line, because I'm going to be looking at both sides of the line in any case, because I don't just have to explain the religions, I have to explain the sort-of-religions and the used-to-be-religions and the quasi-proto-religions, too. If you're going to do the scientific study, you have to study all of them.

Alister suggested that I was begging the question with my naturalism by ignoring the prospect or starting with the assumption that I was going to give a natural explanation of all religious phenomena. That's the subtitle of my book: *Religion as a Natural Phenomenon.* The emphasis is upon *natural* as opposed to *supernatural* phenomena. Now, I want to point out to you that there's nothing illogical or circular in this. This is in fact not just the standard scientific method, it's the standard method of, for instance, the Catholic Church. When somebody is up for sainthood, what do they do? They appoint a devil's advocate. This is the person who is supposed to take the other side and say, "No, no, no miracles here. No miracles here!" That's just the method of finding truth. You start with the assumption of no miracles, of nothing supernatural, and then you try to explain certain phenomena naturally. If you can't explain something, if you're left with a silly grin on your face and the frank admission that you can't explain it, only then do you have any evidence for the supernatural. Now, if you believe in the supernatural but you recognize that it hasn't been proven, you should go with my method, because that's the only way it will ever be proved. The only way anybody will ever prove religions are not a natural phenomenon is by trying to prove that they are natural phenomena and failing. If there are some aspects of religious phenomena that this naturalistic approach is utterly baffled by, then that will be a skyhook, a miracle; that will be something that is real evidence for the supernatural. So there's nothing biased or out of place or illogical in my starting with the assumption that all religious phenomena can be explained naturalistically. I haven't done it yet, but that's the quest.

I'm really pleased that Alister focuses on memes as what he thinks of as the weak point of my book, because I think it's, in fact, the strong point and that Alister's skepticism about memes is seriously misguided. First of all, he doubts the very existence of memes. I want just to check and see how obvious this is to some people. I'm going to ask you, how many of you believe in unicorns? Nobody. How many of you believe in atoms? How many of you believe in words? How many of you don't believe in words, you don't think words exist? *Words are memes.* Words are memes that can be pronounced. They're passed by copying; they spread; they have histories; and they've evolved. The (English) world *table* and the French word *table* both evolved from the Latin word *tabula.* We know the history of the evolution of these words. We know that it wasn't deliberate. We know it wasn't planned, and we know that it happened by differential replication of words. Words are memes. If you're baffled about whether memes exist, just ask yourself if words exist. If you think words exist, then the case for memes is pretty clear.

Now, what about the scientific case, though? Well, we have some sciences of words. We have linguistics—both historical and theoretical. And so, it's quite possible to do science with those memes at least, but maybe not memetic science. It's still an open question just how much memetic science is going to prove useful. But he mentions two, he thinks, eminent critics: Maurice Bloch, the anthropologist, and Simon Conway Morris, the evolutionary paleontologist. He's right. I don't mention them in my book, because I don't think they're serious critics. They're opposed, but that is not enough. Maurice Bloch is certainly haughty in his dismissal of memes but he doesn't actually offer any arguments against them. Now, I do include in my book responses to all the good criticisms that I know of from such anthropologists as Dan Sperber and Scott Atran and some biologists, too. And if you're really pretty sure that the concept of memes is scientifically disreputable, which is the suggestion that Alister gives you, I'd just like to point out to you that the *Encyclopedia of Evolution*—the two-volume encyclopedia published by Oxford University Press—has a chapter called "The New Replicators" about memes, which I wrote—peer-reviewed by evolutionary biologists. This is *the* encyclopedia of evolutionary biology, and I include the chapter as an appendix in my book. So I really do take memes seriously scientifically. There's a lot of good evidence, and in fact, there's more good work just since I've written my book. There are new articles by evolutionary biologist David Haig, and by philosopher of biology Kim Sterelny, who has authored a wonderful new piece called "Memes Reconsidered." There's new work by cultural anthropologists Peter Richerson and Robert Boyd.[25] There's a lot of work on memes, finally. It's taken a few years. It's been thirty-one years since Dawkins published *The Selfish Gene*, but the idea of memes is being taken more and more seriously by the relevant sciences all the time. That doesn't mean it's yet established, but it means that it's in pretty good shape.

One more point, and then I'm going to turn it over to Alister. Is atheism a meme? Of course it's a meme. And so is science. I mean, it's not as if memes are just the irrational, bad ideas. I don't know where Alister gets this. He's pushing on an open door here. Memes are information packets that replicate whether they are true or false, sane or ridiculous, benign or toxic. The memes of calculus, you will notice, do not travel very well. They are domesticated. I don't know about you, but I've never found myself walking down the street thinking, "I just can't get those second differentials out of my head!" Unlike, say, a popular tune, or an advertising jingle, some memes only reproduce with effort. They really depend on their stewards; others we can't get out of our heads. Peter Medawar says that science can't answer deep, important, ultimate questions about meaning, and he's right; I agree. That's why there's philosophy. We pick up where science leaves off. My definition of philosophy is, "That's what you're doing when you don't even know what the right questions are." Once you know what the right questions are, then you can turn them into scientific questions. And in fact, that's why it was a philosopher who wrote *Breaking the Spell*. I'm trying to sort out the questions to help turn it into science. Alister's right. There's a lot of speculation. There are claims and hypotheses put forward without much evidence. And I say these are just a sketch, composed because I want people to see what a scientific theory of religion would look like. I want to give people something to fix. This is the best we can do now. Notice how the pieces work. Notice what we don't know yet. I'm trying to help people see which questions we need to answer next so that we can do a proper scientific study of religion. And I think we can do it. And I think, actually, that Alister agrees. And I agree with him that I don't do it in the book. It is not a book triumphantly announcing the results of a scientific theory of religion. It is a book saying, "Let's try to create a good scientific explanation of religion. Here are some of the problems. Here are some of the questions we can answer; here are some of the questions we can't."

He's particularly concerned with my suggestions about whether there might be a gene involved in making our response to say, shamanic ritual, more prevalent. This is actually a very nice scientific idea because it's parallel to ideas we have now confirmed. How many of you are lactose intolerant, you get sick to your stomach if you drink raw milk? Most of you are lactose tolerant. That makes you remarkably unlike other mammals. We're the only mammal that is lactose tolerant in adulthood after weaning. In general, mammals can only digest milk when they're babies. We know the genetics involved. We know how human beings who are lactose tolerant—like most of us who can eat ice cream, whipped cream, milk, and so forth—can eat this without getting ill. We know which genes have adjusted to create the proteins that permit lactase, which is the enzyme involved, to be expressed in adulthood. We also know that this was a genetic response to a culturally transmitted practice of dairy herding, and that people who are not lactose tolerant are descendants of people that did not have dairy herding in their cultures. That's a slight oversimplification, but it's good hard science and it's well done. Could we do something similar with regard to the apparently wide variability and susceptibility to ritual? For some people, ritual really makes their hair stand on end; it gives them the heebie-jeebies; and it fills them with joy and love. Other people have a sort of tin ear for ritual; you may have noticed this. Could there be a genetic basis for this? There could. Do we know yet? No. Can we find out? Yes. And if we find it, we will probably find the areas of the brain involved. (Dean Hamer thinks he's found them; I don't think he has, but he's written about this in *The God Gene*.) If we find the areas in the brain, and the neuromodulators, that are responsible for this difference, then we will have a question that needs answering, and that is, Why are there these differences? Why are there some people deeply moved by ritual and other people not? We can get to the bottom of these questions. I do not purport to prove what the answers are, but I think I've articulated the questions quite clearly.

McGRATH: Well, thank you very much, Dan. Let me begin by saying how much I appreciate not only the questions Dan has raised but also the very gracious way in which he has put them. So I had some questions that I was going to ask him, but they all seem to have been raised by Dan himself. I'll respond directly to him, which will make it more interesting for you, but also it means we will have a genuine dialogue.

The first point is, "What is religion?" I think Dan's point is good. He wants a "working definition" that can be more finely tuned as he goes along. The point that I was trying to make, though, is that this is extremely difficult to do. And the real difficulty is that there is a barrier, a dividing line, between what I'm going to loosely call a "religion" and a "worldview." Actually, it's difficult to make that distinction rigorously. And the difficulty is that sometimes people import preconceptions about what distinguishes a "religion" from the larger category of "worldview." Now, Dan has made some very kind comments about the United Kingdom; let me make one that may not enhance his esteem which he holds in my Kingdom. During the 1970s, some sectors of British religious education stipulated that atheism should be studied as a religion. Now, many protested about that, arguing that it was clearly not a religion. But those responsible for the decision said, "Look, it seems to have a creed; it seems to have a set of ethical values that derive from that; there seems to be some practices. Therefore, operationally, in terms of how it functions, it seems to be a religion." Now, I think they were wrong, and I think maybe you think they were wrong as well. But it's interesting how for some people, atheism paradoxically could almost be treated in that way. Now, I think that was a wrong adjudication on their part, but it does emphasize this important point of definition. So what is religion? Well, I earlier used the word *essence*. Dan rightly raised some objections to that. But it's still fair to ask, What is it that makes a religion a religion? My point is that this is a very difficult and somewhat subjective judgment. And it does raise some questions for Dan's use of the meme elsewhere. If I could just give one very obvious example, is the essence of religion "belief in God" or "religiosity"? Is it something cognitive or is it something behavioral? Those of you who know different kinds of religious people will be aware that this is actually quite a significant issue. For example, I am an evangelical Protestant, which means that for me, the ritualistic side of things has relatively little importance. But to others, as Dan was saying, it matters quite a lot. Therefore, if one is going to try and develop a memetic approach, there is a perfectly fair question here as to whether the religion meme has to do with belief in God, or certain patterns of behavior. And that seems to me to be an important point which really does need to be followed through. I think there is a very good case to be made for the evolution of human culture, of which religion is a part, and above all—and I think this is where I value Dan's work—the cultural shaping of religion. Yet again, this rests on some very difficult discriminations. When does something stop being "cultural" and start being "religious"? There is a really interesting issue here for me as a theologian—the extent to which various forms of Christianity are shaped by their cultural context. I think this may be an area in which Dan's approach is helpful. There's a serious issue here if you're a theologian, because one of the big problems is that sometimes Christianity morphs into its culture and has to be (I don't know what the opposite is) "unmorphed" to try to recover its identity, which is what you see, for example, in the Protestant Reformation of the sixteenth century. So I think there's a very interesting issue there indeed.

And so we come back to memes again. Dan is right, there are many who still support the idea of memes in some way or another, and therefore you could argue clearly that this is an idea which has survival potential. And certainly, Dan has given us some very interesting, illuminating examples: words, ideas, and others. I also believe in the power of words and ideas, but I don't feel the need to generate a portmanteau concept called a meme to embrace them. I think one can manage perfectly well without it. There is clearly a difference of opinion between us here, as indeed there is in the broader scientific community. In the end, one of the key scientific criteria is whether taking this away renders things unintelligible. Is this hypothesis necessary? My feeling is, it is not. And, therefore, I'm just nervous that as I read Dan, he seems to place a lot of weight on this. I think the research program he suggests we explore is actually a very, very good one, and I certainly would want to encourage that. One of the things that really interests me is why different people respond in different ways. And in a point that is maybe more psychological than cultural, why it is, for example, that in different forms of worship, different people find different modes of worship elicit a different response. That's a very interesting question and I think it may well be a question about human nature that needs to be explored. So I think there is potentially a very interesting line of arguments here.

Our conference is called "The Future of Atheism," and so I find myself asking how Dan's approach helps evaluate the future of atheism. So I'm going to reflect back, if I may, some ideas just to take us on a little further before our time of questions. And certainly, Dan said (and I think that's entirely consistent with what I've read in his book *Breaking the Spell*), that atheism is a form of a meme, if indeed you believe in memes. And so, if there are memes (now obviously, I'm stepping over to his position for a moment) then, yes, atheism is one of them, and I'm sure you're right about that. I find that interesting because if Richard Dawkins was standing here and if I've understood him correctly, I think his view would be that belief in God is a meme whereas the belief that there is not a god is so self-evidently true that it doesn't actually require memetic explanation. So if atheism, religion, and belief in God and so on are all memes, where does this take us in terms of considering what the future of atheism may be? Dan made a point that I think is very true. Maybe science isn't going to give us the answers there. Maybe we do come back to philosophy—and in saying that I'm not in any way degrading or devaluing the sciences. I'm simply saying that there are questions that science generally has difficulty with. It may clarify many points by helping us understand how the human condition works, but in the end it doesn't tell us what's right and what's wrong. And therefore, I find myself in agreement with him that we need something over and above the sciences which might help us make these adjudications, some of which are philosophical, some of which are ethical, and some of which are also religious. Science may help us clarify things, but in the end, we have to go somewhere else to find those "big answers." And while Dan and I think we'll probably disagree about what that source might be, I think nevertheless that the general point is fair. Recognizing that there are general limits to science does not leave us defenseless or without any guidance, it simply means that we realistically and rightly begin to look somewhere else, but hoping that the science will help us as we try and wrestle with that. So I find Dan a very interesting dialogue partner who has many interesting things to say to us in this context.

DENNETT: I agree with Alister that the question of what's a religion and what is religiosity and what's spirituality and so forth, these are very interesting questions, and I talk about them in the book. Of course, on some accounts of religiosity or religion, one of the most powerful religions in America is the NFL. Well, for other reasons we might want to rule it out. It certainly inspires a sort of passion and devotion and large expenditures of energy. We could have a Super Bowl crowd right up there with that crowd in St. Peter's Square as something that the Martians would take note of and say, "Whoa, this is interesting. I wonder what the explanation of that is." And there might be some important similarities between the explanation of the NFL religion and other religions. The important thing about memes is not whether there is a religion meme or an atheism meme. The interesting memes are smaller, more specific ideas. They are, in this regard, like words, but more specific words. Let me tell you in response to Alister's skepticism, the simple argument that convinces me. I'm going to restrict it here to religion, but I could apply the argument to some other topics, too. Manifestly, religions are brilliantly designed. They repay attention from reverse engineers on many, many levels: the music, the rituals, the creeds, the prohibitions, the size of congregations, the hierarchies. The ones that are successful are not successful by accident; they have been beautifully designed to do what they do. Now, that's premise one. Premise two: you never get design for free. Some process has to do the designing. If your only two candidates are genetic evolution—you know, the "religion gene"—and let's say, clever priests, intelligent designers, you are missing a major trick. Many of the features of religion are much older than any deliberate redesigner. Yes, we have the Council of Trent, the Council of Nicaea, Vatican II. We have occasions when people sit down and ask very deliberately how best to design their religions. And I would guess that something like 5 percent of the evolution we've seen in religion in the last two thousand years is due to those conscious, deliberate, foresighted, "intelligently designed" decisions. Most of the revision—and notice how very different Christianity today is from what it was five hundred years ago or one hundred years ago or certainly two thousand years ago—most of the change is so gradual and unheralded that you cannot find an author of that change. Christianity has changed in the Darwinian way, by differential replication of ideas. For that, you need the memetic perspective. You also need the memetic perspective because you want to be neutral as a scientist among all the possibilities for who is the beneficiary of this replicative process. Is it good for the host or is it good for the symbiont? If you don't have that role for the symbiont, you're left having to concoct bogus benefits for the hosts. And believe me, there are theories of cultural evolution, theories of religious evolution, that make the mistake of not adopting the memetic approach, and then they're left with many inexplicable features of religions. They think of cultural evolution as simply an adjunct to genetic evolution, where it's basically a matter of parents teaching their children things. Instead of passing on the wisdom through the genes, they pass it on through early upbringing. Such theories can be very good at explaining adaptations that are good for you, but they can't explain all the things that probably aren't good for you. And they have to treat a great deal of cultural difference as just noise. Scientifically, it's called noise because they can't explain it on their theory. If you have a theory which can treat that noise as signal and say there's pattern in here, that's a scientific advance. And in order to find that advance, you have to take the memetic approach. It's still in its infancy, but it's going somewhere.

One last point: Alister says he's glad that I agree with him that science doesn't give all the answers. Indeed not. He says we have to look somewhere else and that we may not agree. I think we can even agree on that if he'll agree to one more thing. I would say that where we look when we want to answer those deep questions that science doesn't answer, the answer to that was found in that film I showed at the beginning: where we look is to each other. We look to the community, to use the old-fashioned word *man*, to the community of human beings. And it's ultimately not just a philosophical issue, but in a deep sense, in a nonpejorative sense, it's a political issue. What can *we*, by informing each other and persuading one another, agree is right? Morality has changed a lot in the last two thousand years, and in every case, it's because people became better informed and looked around and just decided either this act wasn't as bad as we used to think or it's worse than we used to think. And they've adjusted their ethical views. Nobody here would be comfortable living under the ethical prohibitions and requirements of the Old Testament. Nobody. Now, we the people have worked out in open conversation what we think makes the most sense morally. That's not science. And if you agree, then there's only one more thing we have to agree on that matters here, and that is, when we do that, religious beliefs come very much into the fray. And I agree and I welcome them and think there's a tremendous amount of wisdom to be found in the texts and traditions of religions. If we're going to have a genuinely open forum, we have to agree on the rules. And there's one rule I would insist on, and that's, there's one card you cannot play, the faith card. The faith card is when you say, well, no, we don't talk about that, that's a matter of faith. I'm a Hindu and Hindus don't believe that, and that's all there is to it. If you say that—and I talk about this in the book—if you play the faith card, if you say, "I am sorry, my religion does not permit me to discuss this," you are actually declaring your disability for this political discussion. You are saying, "I am sorry, my mind is closed on that. I am not able or I am not willing to give you reasons." Because it's always about giving reasons. If you will agree not to play the faith card, then you can use all the wisdom in your religious tradition and support it and spread it to others and get them to see why that's right. And if you say, "No, no, I have no obligation to defend or explain it. It's in the book, and that's it," you're basically letting your religion down. You're saying, "I can't defend this. I can't explain this. I'm just going to take my marbles and leave the game; I'm not going to play." Don't play the faith card, but join the conversation.

McGRATH: To respond very briefly because we need time for questions. The last point is a good point, but if you think Alasdair MacIntyre is right in his analysis of faith and of tradition-mediated rationalities, then we all reflect these, whether we are secular or religious. The important thing is to identify these and try to make sure that we don't have unacknowledged taboos that we bring into the discussion. Some are religious, some are cultural.

Then you made some interesting point at the beginning about religions being designed, which I found intriguing. If you look at the way certain forms of Christianity have emerged, there is no doubt that they are now recognized to have certain benefits that I do not believe were recognized at that time at all. I think, therefore, one has to say that if one does use the language of design, it has to be used in a very cautious, very restrained way. That's a bigger discussion, and I'm afraid that time has rather run out. But thank you anyway.

Questions and Answers

ROBERT STEWART: You may make your way to the microphones now. I'm very confident that due to time restrictions some of you will be left standing at the microphone. Let's run over the procedure again very quickly: thirty seconds to frame your question, make sure your question *is* a question, and after you've asked your question, sit down and let our speakers reply. We don't have time for follow-up questions. This will ensure that we allow as many questions as possible in the time we have left.

KEITH PARSONS: I'd like to address a question to Professor Dennett. I notice that you've said that atheism and unbelief is one of the most rapidly growing of the various worldview positions that you had in your powerpoint slide. But how could that be, if indeed religion is a natural phenomenon and explicable in scientific/naturalistic terms as you say? It seems to me that the number of unbelievers vis-à-vis believers would always be low and quite constant. For instance, I would imagine that the number of adult human beings who are uninterested in sex is quite small and remains quite small by comparison. So how then could it be that the number of unbelievers as in fact your evidence indicates is growing? Thank you.

DENNETT: Well, things that are natural are natural because they are maintained by differential replication in the conditions that exist. And when conditions change, they either go extinct or they evolve. And if the world has evolved—think of the difference between the world ten thousand years ago and the world now—there's a tremendous difference—and if the conditions in the world today are no longer hospitable for certain religious ideas, then it's not surprising that they don't replicate very well. Either they go extinct entirely or they get replaced by others. I think that *natural* doesn't mean in everybody. As you say, the love of sex is normal—and there is no mystery as to why that should be because its role in reproduction is quite clear—but aside from things that are that directly related to fitness—genetic fitness—we see variation arising in all sorts of ways. And so it should not surprise us that there are differences and similarities between people when it comes to the religious phenomena that they participate in. I don't know if that answers your question.

QUESTION: I've enjoyed hearing both of you. I have a question. I've always been under the understanding that if you have an opinion you need to understand the opposing opinion also. It's obvious that both of you do this. I have one question, and that is, "Is there a future of atheism?" That was what we were here for. I haven't heard that. And what I'd like to do is have you (*addressing McGrath*) say "No" and answer it *emotionally* without science, memes, or anything. And I'd like you (*addressing Dennett*) to say "Yes" and answer it *emotionally*. I have not heard emotion from either one of you. (*The audience laughs.*)

DENNETT: Emotionally?

QUESTION: Emotionally. Not scientifically, not statistics, but from emotion in your heart. No, there's no future, and yes, there is a future.

DENNETT: Oh, that's easy. No, there's no future for atheism because we're going to destroy the planet before the future arrives.

MCGRATH: I would wickedly say yes, because people don't know a good thing when they see it.

QUESTION: I've been reading your book, Professor Dennett, and I haven't quite finished it, but I get the sense that Professor McGrath's question about the definition of religion might be there in your book. You seem to have a number of phases or stages of religion that you've traced through the natural process. Can you speak to the development of religion, is that possible as a definition for religion?

DENNETT: Well, there's a straight-man question. He's invited me to give another lecture, but I'm not going to do that. Well, very briefly, before there were domesticated religions—when they were just wild religions—they were just responsive to the design (and perhaps I should use the word *design* very cautiously) of natural selection itself. And indeed, as Alister says, features could persist although people had no idea why they were good because they weren't even thinking about it. Sometimes people were the beneficiaries of them, but they hadn't worked out why. We find these things all the time. Then when religions became domesticated, people began to meddle. And when they meddled, they had their reasons. And although their reasons were often very good reasons, sometimes their reasons were very selfish reasons. And so, just as when the cow was domesticated, some of the things that were adjusted were really not good for the cow at all but made life easier for the cowboy or the dairyman or the farmer. And similarly, when religions started getting adjusted, very often, for instance, it was the good of the priests, for instance, that was really being served. And we can trace that. Or it was good for the political rulers of the day. Once people started using religion for ulterior motives, all sorts of pressures were introduced that simply hadn't been there when religions were wild.

WILLIAM LANE CRAIG: Professor Dennett, as I listened to your opening address, it struck me as an attack upon human rationality itself. On the view as I understood it, we don't adopt our ideas as a result of free, rational reflection and adjudication, but acquiring ideas is rather like catching a disease. You use the example of the common cold. In which case these are ultimately the product of nonrational factors. So my question is, Are you a determinist? And second, isn't this then self-defeating since your own ideas would then be the result of these arational processes? You've caught this disease from Richard Dawkins (*audience erupts in laughter*), and as a result, you hold to these views.

DENNETT: Well, first, let me answer your question, Am I determinist? Oh yes, I'm a determinist. And I've written two books on free will and determinism and I've tried to show how free will and determinism are completely compatible. Free will in the sense that you mean, in the sense that it shows that *we* have the power to judge ideas, to evaluate ideas, to choose ideas, to make decisions, all of this is compatible with determinism. There is no magical exemption from causality in our brains. There is no little part of our brains which is somehow undetermined, but that doesn't mean that we don't have free will. I know that's a hard idea for many people to understand. That's why I've taken two whole books—*Freedom Evolves*—surprise, surprise, and *Elbow Room*, which I wrote back in 1984. Now, if you read *Origin of Species*, (and I hope if you haven't, you will—we atheists read the Bible as literature; you should read the *Origin of Species* as literature. It's simply a great read. It's wonderful. He's a brilliant writer.) In the early going, he distinguishes three processes. First, he talks a lot about artificial selection. He calls it *methodical* selection. And he points out that all the animal breeders—the pigeon fanciers, the dog fanciers, the cattle breeders—are making deliberate, conscious, thoughtful decisions about which of their animals they are going to breed. Then he points out as a segue that there was an earlier period (and it's still going on in some regards) when we had *unconscious* selection, by which he means people are favoring some of the dogs in the litter and not others. They are not trying to do anything, it just happens. It's not a rational choice but it leads to selection. He has some wonderful examples of this—the King Charles spaniel, which had grown much larger at the time of his day from what it had been in the days of King Charles. And this was not a deliberate process. And then there's natural selection. Notice what we have here is the gradual diminution of free, rational interference with the process. Eventually, he's showing how natural selection can do without the intelligent decision altogether, but in fact, all three processes are instances of natural selection. The dachshund is just as much an instance of natural selection as the weasel is. It's just that the selection has been focused through the mind of a particular evolved biped, namely human beings. And I want to say that the same thing is true of memes. There are memes that can only replicate by making it through ferocious filters that have been established in the brains of, let's say, biologists. And if they can't get through those rational filters they are not going to be copied or passed on. That's called science. Scientific memes have to pass some very big tests of rationality before they get passed on. It doesn't mean that they're not memes, but it just means that they are memes that have been through the mill of rational evaluation. Then we have memes that are unconsciously selected and we have memes that were completely wild—we didn't even know we were doing it. So there's no contradiction. And indeed, it's not self-contradictory to say that scientific ideas are memes. Did I catch the meme meme from Dawkins? Yes I did. But did I put it through the rational mill before I caught it? I'd like to think I did. At least I show some evidence of that in that I have now written something like a dozen papers in the last twenty years on problems with memetics and whether or not they are soluble. It's rational evaluation that's the filter.

QUESTION: Professor McGrath, in the discussion of Peter Medawar's obvious statement that there are things that science cannot answer for us-purpose and meaning—you know, Professor Dennett mentions philosophy and you mentioned philosophy, ethics, and religion. And I'm wondering if there's kind of like a god of the gaps—science can't do it. Why is religion in this argument besides the fact that it might be the eight-hundred-pound gorilla in the room? Thank you.

McGRATH: Well, I think the first point is just to say that there is widespread agreement that science does have limits. I say that not in any way because I'm a critic of science, but because I think it's simply important to calibrate it. In other words, if you are using any instrument, the first point is to establish the conditions under which it works well. And if it doesn't work well under certain conditions, you don't use it there. And I think that Medawar is just articulating a generally held consensus, that when science works it is very, very good. When it doesn't work it can't be relied upon. So the question that you were asking me is, Why should I then move on and try to bring religion or belief in God into this? Now, you have some American tax benefits here that we don't have in the U.K. but obviously it's an important point to make. One of the classic debates which lies unresolved but it is still extremely interesting is this—namely, whether there is something from which we can infer from looking at the world. I'm going to refer to this as God. In other words, we say we observe this, we observe this, we observe this, and we draw a conclusion and ultimately in order to make sense of what we do observe we posit a god. Now, of course, some would rightly want to challenge that. And I'm very open to that. One of the key points here is that Christians—and I certainly speak here for myself—don't just simply rush and say, "There's a gap in the argument here, let's stick God in there." That is not what Christians are saying at all. I think one of the key points here is if we look at what science does do, we find that it has a remarkable capacity to explain what may be observed. But the key point here is that explicability itself requires explanation. John Polkinghorne, in a very interesting recent article in *Science and Religion* published in 2005, just makes the point that there are many basic understandings of the epistemic virtues. You could make a very good case for saying that God is a very good explanation of what we observe in the world and culture and human experience. But of course, it could be a challenge. And that's why Christians would then begin to want to talk about the whole importance of divine revelation, not as a way of weaseling out of intellectual difficulties, but rather as a statement about the kind of God that we believe we are involved with. In other words, not a God who leaves us on our own, wandering around, but rather tries to make himself known in ways that can really transform and transfigure the human experience. So the question's point really was that I seemed to be saying that science explains this and that it leads to gaps and let's just fill the gaps with God. That certainly isn't what I want to do. Maybe some others do. If they do, then I would want to critique that. But for me I think a very good rational case could be made for arguing that the invocation of God is actually an extremely important explanatory agent. Again, if I could just briefly end my response with a quote I love from C. S. Lewis. He writes, "I believe in Christianity as I believe that the sun has risen. Not just because I see it but because by it I see everything else." So he's offering this vision of an intellectual sun that illumines the landscape and enables us to make sense of things.

STEWART: This will be the final question. I'm very sorry that we do not have time for more but we do have a book signing, so Dan and Alister will be around for you to question.

QUESTION: Professor Dennett, I just wanted to start by saying that I am eagerly anticipating your book on reverse-engineering of atheism. And on that line, I would like you to put yourself in the position of a thousand years in the future and atheism has grown and it is 90 percent of the population. Their goal is to reverse-engineer atheism and explain it. Could you take that position?

DENNETT: I'm sorry, I don't know . . .

QUESTION: To reverse-engineer atheism? In the same way you reverse-engineer religion, could you do the same for atheism?

DENNETT: Absolutely. Certainly. We reverse-engineer atheism and we see what is it about the tenets of the atheism that you are imagining a thousand years in the future—when atheism goes without saying. And we see what is it that convinces people in that day that atheism makes sense. And also, what is it about those who are still not atheistic? Have they got some special insight, or special experiences, or do they have different genes? That is one remote possibility. Certainly. We can reverse-engineer anything complex. Now, Alister ended with a quote from C. S. Lewis. I'm going to end with a paraphrase—I can't quote it exactly—from my friend and his *bête noire* Richard Dawkins, who points out, we're all atheists about Baal, about Thor, about Zoroaster, so some of us just go one god more.

2

Atheism: Twilight or Dawn?

Keith M. Parsons

According to Professor Alister McGrath, atheism is an ideology with a great past. At one time it blazed across the intellectual firmament like a comet, a harbinger of doom for established churches and orthodoxics. Hume, Kant, Voltaire, Strauss, Feuerbach, Darwin, Huxley, Marx, Freud—all the great names struck mighty blows against the intellectual and social foundations of religion. The theistic "proofs" were left in tatters; Scripture was assailed as a repository of myth and legend; the Creator was replaced by natural selection; the comforts of religion were debunked as puerile illusions or opiates for the masses. To capture the mid-nineteenth-century's perception of the retreat of religion in the face of atheist attack, McGrath quotes Matthew Arnold's famous lament that the Sea of Faith once was full:

> But now I only hear
> Its melancholy, long, withdrawing roar,
> Retreating, to the breath
> Of the night-wind, down the vast edges drear
> And naked shingles of the world.

These days, says McGrath, it is not faith's but atheism's withdrawing roar that we hear. Now, early in the twenty-first century, atheism is in decline and religion is resurgent.

How odd, in that case, to find atheist books recently heading up the best-seller lists and atheists showing up on the TV talk shows to make the case for unbelief. Is atheism becoming *chic?* The public response to Sam Harris's *The End of Faith* and *Letter to a Christian Nation* as well as Richard Dawkins's *The God Delusion* and Daniel Dennett's *Breaking the Spell* appears to indicate a swelling interest in arguments for unbelief. A best-selling atheist book is really quite a novelty. Speaking from my own personal experience, an atheist book typically sells in the dozens, and its author will die of old age long before seeing a royalty check. But perhaps the current rash of atheist best sellers is an anomaly, an exception to an overall downward trend. Perhaps interest in these books is a transient response to current events. Maybe people are presently outraged at terrorism perpetrated by sectarian fanatics or disgusted when politicians of even worse than usual mendacity and hypocrisy pose as the Lord's anointed. At any rate, though, McGrath cannot be refuted by displaying a copy of the *New York Times* best-seller list.

McGrath states his case with clarity, erudition, and style. His book is a pleasure to read, with a wealth of deftly delivered historical detail. It is hard to be harsh with so congenial a book. However, as I regard many of McGrath's major conclusions as poorly supported, I would do a disservice to the author and everyone else if I offered a less than candid evaluation.

As a percentage of the population, those who believe in no God or gods always have been and, almost certainly, will remain in the minority (though, I hasten to add, if, as the 2006 survey by the Pew Forum on Religion and Public Life indicates, 11 percent of Americans list themselves as atheists, agnostics, or without religion, then, the number of unbelievers will exceed that of all Christian denominations except Roman Catholicism). But McGrath's claim is not about numbers or percentages, but about the intellectual status of atheism. So we need to ask two questions: (1) Has the intellectual clout, stature, or influence of atheism declined in recent years? and (2) Should it have? The first question asks whether, as a matter of fact, the *Zeitgeist* has turned against atheism; the second asks whether, despite the association with great names, the intellectual credentials of atheism have been overstated.

McGrath answers both of these questions in the affirmative, asserting, first, that in the marketplace of ideas, atheism's stock has plummeted, and second, that atheists have failed to make their case for unbelief. I partially agree with his first answer. Prior to the publication of the recent best sellers, it had been quite some time since atheism had been a hot topic of intellectual debate. But if philosophical atheism has declined in salience among the topics most urgently discussed in intellectual forums, this is chiefly because it is, paradoxically, a victim of the success of secularization. "Atheism" may be defined "positively" as the doctrine that denies the existence of God or asserts the incoherence or inconsistency of the God concept, or "negatively" as the claim that there is no good reason for belief in God.[1] Either way, atheism as a doctrine is largely oppositional in nature. It thrives when religion is culturally important but has lost its coercive power to physically suppress dissent. Where religion has become largely culturally irrelevant, as in modern-day Sweden or the Netherlands (except in their immigrant Muslim communities), atheist advocacy is also seen as irrelevant, and an atheist polemic elicits yawns. Practically speaking, in most of the developed world, business, education, the arts and sciences, and (outside the United States) even politics and the law are pursued with no deference to or even recognition of religious tenets. When, in the most important fields of human endeavor, a practical atheism reigns, theoretical atheism is regarded as otiose.

I shall argue that McGrath has failed to substantiate his claim that the intellectual case for atheism fails. Chiefly he relies on an argument of guilt by association. Atheism, he claims, hitched its wagon to the once-rising stars of Marxism and Freudianism, but the wreckage of those ideologies has also dragged down atheism. He fails to answer and, indeed, hardly even addresses the real intellectual case for atheism. McGrath briefly notes Bertrand Russell's *Why I Am Not a Christian,* and J. J. C. Smart gets a single mention, as does Adolf Grunbaum, but the other major defenders of philosophical atheism of the last half-century do not even merit a nod. His index contains no listings for Antony Flew, Wallace Matson, Kai Nielsen, Richard Gale, William L. Rowe, Michael Martin, J. L. Mackie, Daniel Dennett, Evan Fales, Michael Tooley, Quentin Smith, Jordan Howard Soble, Robin Le Poidevin, Theodore Drange, Walter Sinnott-Armstrong, Nicholas Everitt, J. L. Schellenberg, or Graham Oppy.

On the other hand, the late atheist agitator Madelyn Murray O'Hair gets fourteen pages. What would thoughtful theists make of a book attacking theism that ignored the arguments of, for instance, Alvin Plantinga, Richard Swinburne, William Lane Craig, or William P. Alston while devoting fourteen pages to Jim Jones and the People's Temple cult?

So, since McGrath does not undertake to rebut or even to address the major recent defenders of atheism and their arguments, it is hard even to ascertain the basis of his polemic. Chiefly, I think he is trying to do to atheism what the social constructivist sociologists and historians like Bruno Latour, Steve Woolgar, David Bloor, and Steven Shapin tried to do to science.[2] That is, he tries to show that atheism is a social construct, a historically contingent by-product of larger social and political forces, and that atheism lost its impetus when these forces eventually played out. Like the would-be constructivist debunkers of science, McGrath offers a historical account intended to spell out the particular local circumstances that account for the one-time popularity and subsequent decline of a set of ideas. According to social constructivist analysis, ideas grow and spread because they serve larger political and cultural agendas, and so the fate of those ideas depends upon the success or failure of those agendas.

Let us turn, then, to McGrath's account of the connection between atheism and Marxism. It is a familiar story but he tells it well: Marx was a metaphysical materialist who regarded doctrinal systems as epiphenomena, wholly determined in their nature and content by underlying economic and material conditions. Why, then, did Marx think that religion existed? For Marx religion was caused by unjust economic conditions and the consequent alienation of the victims of injustice. In turn, religion serves to support the system of exploitation that creates it. A proletariat narcotized with assurances of ethereal bliss will be less resentful of mundane oppression. Small wonder, then, that the established churches enjoyed the enthusiastic support of kings and capitalists; and small wonder, also, that atheism became a corollary of Marxist theory.[3]

According to McGrath's analysis, though, atheism's partnership with Marxism became a deal with the devil when communism, and hence atheism, became the established, and exclusive, ideology of repressive regimes: "The appeal of atheism to generations lay in its offer of liberation. It promised to liberate the enslaved and exploited masses from their cruel oppression by the state and church. Yet wherever atheism became the establishment, it demonstrated a ruthlessness and lack of toleration that destroyed its credentials as a liberator. The Promethean liberator had turned nasty."[4] Indeed, McGrath says, the collapse of Soviet communism forced the world to confront the genuine nastiness of atheism:

> The fall of the Berlin Wall in 1989 did more than allow inhabitants of the Soviet bloc access to the West; it also paved the way for Western scholars to inspect the archives of the Soviet Union and its allies. The opening of the Soviet archives led to revelations that ended any notion that atheism was a gracious, gentle, and generous worldview. . . . Communism was a "tragedy of planetary dimensions" with a grand total of victims variously estimated . . . at 85 and 100 million—far in excess of those murdered under Nazism.[5]

But, of course, precisely the same sort of argument could cite the actions of the 9/11 hijackers to discredit theism. The 9/11 hijackers were, to a man, devout theists, but the obvious reply would be that the impetus behind their atrocious acts was not theism per se, but their adherence to a particularly fanatical brand of Islamic fundamentalism. Precisely the same kind of retort could be given to McGrath's argument. Unless he shows, which he hasn't, that the communists committed their atrocities *qua* atheists, that is, that it was their atheism that inspired their murderous rancor, the argument fails. In fact, of course, Marxism/Leninism and Maoism were irrational ideologies that became objects of fanatical, indeed, "religious" devotion for many of their adherents. If theism can take on poisonous and destructive forms without thereby discrediting theistic belief in general, precisely the same should be said of atheism.

McGrath errs in identifying atheism as a "worldview." From the mere fact that one is an atheist very little else can be inferred. Atheists can be political fascists, conservatives, libertarians, liberals, communitarians, anarchists, or radicals. Their philosophical views can be pragmatist, empiricist, rationalist, idealist, existentialist, postmodernist, feminist, or almost anything else. As cases in point, Antony Flew and Kai Nielsen have been two of the most outspoken atheists among recent analytical philosophers. Their critiques of theism often are nearly identical in content. Yet Flew was a staunch Thatcherite Tory and Nielsen is a dedicated Marxist. Atheism, whether it is taken as the claim that belief in God is false or incoherent or unjustified, just does not have sufficient content to constitute a worldview.

Naturalistic humanism *is* a worldview, and most present-day atheists are probably naturalistic humanists. Humanists claim no more affinity with Joseph Stalin than do Southern Baptists. Indeed, some of the most damning indictments of Stalinism were written by humanists such as George Orwell and atheists like Arthur Koestler. Bertrand Russell is just as emphatic in *Why I Am Not a Communist* as in *Why I Am Not a Christian.* Humanist intellectuals and activists have a long and honorable record of opposing dictatorships of the left and the right, standing against oppression whether conducted by ayatollahs or commissars. Christian churches, let us recall, have far too often winked at right-wing autocrats, just as long as they were friendly to the interests of the church hierarchy. To mention just one of many possible examples, during his long dictatorship over Spain, Franco enjoyed the support, or at least the acquiescence, of the Roman Catholic Church.

But would McGrath say that—though atheists are not *necessarily* intolerant—disbelief does tend toward intolerance? If anything, the shoe seems to be on the other foot. It is plausible that theism, with its insistence upon the existence of single, all-important deity who demands the exclusive devotion of his followers, has a natural and spontaneous tendency to develop into intolerant and exclusionist forms. This was eloquently argued by David Hume in *The Natural History of Religion:*

> While one sole object of devotion is acknowledged, the worship of other deities is regarded as absurd and impious. Nay, this unity of object seems naturally to require the unity of faith and ceremonies, and furnishes designing men with a pretence for representing

their adversaries as profane, and the objects of divine as well as human vengeance. For as each sect is positive that its own faith and worship are entirely acceptable to the deity, and as no one can conceive that the same being should be pleased with different and opposite rites and principles, the several sects fall naturally into animosity, and mutually discharge on each other that sacred zeal and rancour, the most furious and implacable of human passions. . . . The intolerance of all religions, which have maintained the unity of God is as remarkable as the contrary principle of polytheists.[6]

Hume's argument has at least prima facie plausibility. *Any* ideology, theist or atheist, can become repressive and intolerant when it is allied with coercive power and with the determination to exclude competing views. But if, as Hume charges, theism has an inherent tendency to develop into intolerant and repressive forms—and if atheism does not, or not nearly so much—then McGrath's claim that atheists are hypocritical in attacking religious intolerance[7] is unfounded.

Could McGrath argue that atheism does in fact have a natural propensity to grow into intolerant and repressive forms? Roger Scruton, in a 1986 essay published in the *Times Literary Supplement*, makes precisely this argument:

It seems to me that the morally defective feature of the death camp—and of the totalitarian system which engenders it—is the impersonal, cynical and scientific approach to the victims. Systematic torture and murder become a bureaucratic task, for which no one is liable and for which no one is particularly to blame. . . . I do not offer to prove, what nevertheless has been vividly impressed on me by my own study and experience, that this impersonal (and therefore ungovernable) evil is the true legacy of the naturalistic view of man. Those very philosophies which enjoin us to place man upon the throne from which God was taken away for burial, have been most influential in creating a new image of man as an accident of nature, to whom nothing is either forbidden or permitted by any power beyond himself. God is an illusion; so too is the divine spark in man.[8]

But respect for other persons does not arise from detection of some "divine spark," whatever that might be, but from the experience of shared humanity. Recognition that another has thoughts, feelings, dreams, hopes, and fears like one's own naturally promotes empathy toward that person, while campaigns of dehumanization, like that conducted against

Jews in Nazi Germany or against the "Kulaks" in Stalinist Russia, almost always precede genocidal campaigns. In fact, the impersonal, reductive view of persons that characterizes totalitarianism is more reasonably seen as a pathological outgrowth of a religious rather than a humanistic world-view. Characteristic of totalitarianism is the exaltation of ideological purity and the enforcement of strict conformity in action and belief. But belief systems that insisted upon doctrinal purity, and enjoined obedience in thought, word, and deed did not enter the world with the rise of natural-ism and humanism. Such systems are the legacy of belief in One God, One Creed, One Church, and One Law. Paganism had no concept of heresy or apostasy for the simple reason that it had no creed. A classical Greek could join any number of mystery cults without raising questions about his or her devotion to the recognized Olympian deities. Pagan Rome tolerated associations devoted to the worship of Isis, Mithras, Cybele, Jehovah, and—except for highly sporadic and often half-hearted persecutions—Christ.

Perhaps all that McGrath aims to accomplish by recounting the atroci-ties of communism is to rebut an attitude of messianic atheism, the uto-pian hope that atheism, if universally adopted, will usher mankind into a new world of tolerance and progress. Will atheism save mankind? No, but neither will anything else. Religion has been trying for thousands of years now, and so far has achieved a record of less than complete success. Besides, just who are these messianic atheists? Among the major defend-ers of atheism, which ones have said that atheism is the gate to utopia? Some may have seen the spread of atheism as *necessary* for progress, or as a reform that, in conjunction with other changes, will *contribute to* intel-lectual enlightenment and social amelioration, but I know of no major atheist thinker who has said that the general adoption of atheism, even if feasible, would per se be *sufficient* to deliver mankind from oppression and ignorance. Unless McGrath can supply us with some substantiating names and claims here, it is hard not to suspect that he is tilting at windmills.

McGrath does not rest his entire case against atheism on the claim that it backed the wrong ideological horses. He also, very succinctly, directly attacks the intellectual credentials of atheism in arguing that the intellec-tual case for atheism has "stalled."[9]

The section of his seventh chapter, called "The Stalled Intellectual Case against God," begins with a considerable overstatement: "It is increas-ingly recognized that philosophical argument about the existence of God has ground to a halt."[10] Really? Dozens of academic books and hundreds of peer-reviewed articles published in the last twenty years would seem to belie that claim, but, for the sake of argument, let us grant that debates over natural theology and natural atheology do not feature as prominently in today's intellectual milieu as in some past times. What follows? Certainly not McGrath's next claim: "The matter [the existence of God] lies beyond rational proof, and is ultimately a matter of faith, in the sense of judgments made in the absence of sufficient evidence."[11] What "lies beyond rational proof" is not thereby "a matter of faith." Much, indeed most, of what we rationally believe is insusceptible of "proof," on any reasonably strict construal of that term, but nevertheless is open to evaluation in the light of various rational and evidential considerations. McGrath is certainly right to assert that neither the theist nor the atheist has conclusive arguments: "Knockdown and foolproof arguments are simply not available to us. It is for this reason that polemicists on both sides of the argument are so often reduced to rhetorical devices, bludgeoning their audiences into submission by crude verbal bullying rather than by careful evidence-based reasoning."[12] But the lack of proof or knockdown arguments does not imply, as McGrath claims, that "The belief that there is no God is just as much a matter of faith as the belief that there is a God."[13] Justifying such a claim would require a careful examination of the best *arguments* for atheism, and, as we have seen, McGrath's treatment is seriously deficient in that respect.

In various writings, McGrath does respond in detail to one prominent defender of atheism, Richard Dawkins, so let us turn to his response to Dawkins's attack. McGrath identifies four charges made by Dawkins against religion:

1. A Darwinian worldview makes belief in God unnecessary or impossible . . .
2. Religion makes assertions which are grounded in faith, which represents a retreat from a rigorous, evidence-based concern for the truth. For Dawkins, truth is grounded in explicit proof; any form of obscurantism or mysticism grounded in faith is to be opposed vigorously.
3. Religion offers an impoverished and attenuated vision of the world. . . . In contrast, science offers a bold and brilliant vision of the universe as grand, beautiful, and awe-inspiring . . .
4. Religion leads to evil . . .[14]

At one time, particularly in the heyday of natural theology in the eighteenth and early nineteenth centuries, there was a broad consensus that divine design was apparent in the natural world. The most common argument was an appeal to analogy, as eloquently expressed by Cleanthes, the defender of natural theology in Hume's *Dialogues Concerning Natural Religion*:

> The curious adapting of means to ends, throughout all nature, resembles exactly, though it much exceeds, the productions of human contrivance; of human designs, thought, wisdom, and

intelligence. Since, therefore, the effects resemble each other, we are led to infer, by all the rules of analogy, that the causes also resemble; and that the Author of Nature is somewhat similar to the mind of man; though possessed of much larger faculties. . . .[15]

In books like *The Blind Watchmaker* and *Climbing Mount Improbable*, Dawkins argues that the appearance of design, the "curious adapting of means to ends" in organic nature has now received a naturalistic explanation, namely, natural selection. Natural selection, the "blind watchmaker," operates when natural variability endows some organic variants with traits that enhance their odds of survival and reproduction vis-à-vis competitors, and then, since such advantageous traits are heritable, leads to the accumulation and improvement of adaptations in successive populations. This process operating across geological time, says Dawkins, accounts for the appearance of design in living things, and so the blind watchmaker displaces the divine watchmaker.[16]

> If Dawkins is right, it follows that there is no need to believe in God to offer a scientific explanation of the world. Some might draw the conclusion that Darwinism encouraged agnosticism, while leaving the door wide open for a Christian or atheist reading of things—in other words, permitting them, but not necessitating them. But Dawkins is not going to leave things there; for Dawkins, Darwin impels us to atheism.[17]

McGrath challenges the assumption, which he attributes to Dawkins, that the scientific method is capable of adjudicating the God hypothesis. He argues:

> The scientific method is incapable of delivering a decisive adjudication of the God question. Those who believe that it proves or disproves the existence of God press that method beyond its legitimate limits, and run the risk of abusing or discrediting it. Some distinguished biologists . . . argue that the natural sciences create a positive presumption of faith; others . . . that they have a negative implication for theistic belief. But they *prove* nothing, either way. If the God question is to be settled, it must be settled on other grounds.[18]

Again we see the idea of proof doing the heavy lifting in McGrath's argument, and we need to note that "proof," if too strictly construed, is too great an onus for the methods of the natural sciences to bear. However, if "proof" means a decisive empirical test then, if Scripture is any guide, a scientific test, or something very much like one, could indeed adjudicate the "God question." 1 Kings 18 provides as good an example of a crucial experiment as one could wish for: Elijah challenged the priests of Ba'al to a contest. They would erect an altar to Ba'al and he one to Jehovah. The priests of Ba'al would implore their god to send fire to consume their sacrifice, and Elijah would call upon Jehovah to do likewise. According to the story, the fire fell from heaven, consuming Elijah's sacrifice. Jehovah was vindicated as the true god, and Elijah led the people in a celebratory massacre of the priests of Ba'al. Whatever one's opinion of the historicity of this narrative, it certainly shows that, in principle at any rate, there could be a decisive empirical test of religious claims. Had fire instead consumed the sacrifice to Ba'al this would have been strong confirmation of the Ba'al hypothesis and strong disconfirmation of the Jehovah hypothesis.

Even if we set aside such histrionic scenarios as the story in 1 Kings, it still certainly seems that the findings of science could offer strong evidence confirming or disconfirming hypotheses postulating creators or designers. For instance, if, contrary to fact, the fossil record revealed no unambiguous examples of transitional fossils between higher taxa—birds and reptiles, say—this would indeed support a hypothesis postulating piecemeal creation, that is, that over geological time there had been a series of creation-events. On the other hand, since there *are* indisputable instances of transitional fossils between higher taxa, this fact counts heavily against any hypotheses of intermittent special creation-events.[19] That is, any hypothesis that rejects macroevolutionary explanations and invokes the occasional direct creative activity of a Creator or Designer to account for the appearance of new higher taxa will be seriously undermined by the presence of undeniable instances of transitional fossils.

Clearly, then, the results of science can have considerable bearing on hypotheses postulating deities, designers, and creators. What about Dawkins's specific claim, as stated by McGrath, that Darwinism "impels us to atheism"? If "impels us to atheism" is taken to mean "proves that there is no God," or "makes atheism the only rational option," then Darwinism does not impel us to atheism. However, Dawkins is entirely correct that the burgeoning explanatory success of Darwinian and other naturalistic explanations does threaten at least some theistic hypotheses.

The real danger that science poses for theism is not that it can "disprove" God's existence, but that, as science progresses, God seemingly becomes increasingly irrelevant and God's role in the universe is diminished. Scientific explanations inevitably end with an *explanans* that, for the time being at least, must be treated as a brute fact. Therefore, there is always the option of inviting God to take over the explanatory labor left unfinished by science. One problem with this "God of the gaps" option, however, is that it tends to relegate God to an ever-more marginal or distant role, one more appropriate for a deistic rather than a theistic Creator.

To be of any *religious* interest, a deity has to have something important to do; there has to be a domain for divine activity in the world that advancing science cannot seal off, marginalize, or supplant with naturalistic explanations. "Intelligent design" (ID) theorists such as Michael Behe and William Dembski owe their fame to their claim, backed by clever but controversial arguments, to have identified such distinct domains for direct, intelligent, creative input into the natural world.[20] Whatever one thinks of the efforts of the ID theorists (I regard them as total failures), such theories are clearly a response to precisely the kind of threat that Dawkins articulates.[21]

The upshot is that McGrath's criticism of Dawkins's first charge has force only if Dawkins is making an unreasonably strong claim of disproof. But if Dawkins is making a weaker claim—perhaps something akin to Dennett's argument that Darwinism is "universal acid," that is, that Darwinian explanations tend over time to drive all rival explanations from the field[22]—then, McGrath's criticism fails. Further, Dawkins correctly points out that as the realm of naturalistic explanation broadens, gaps for God narrow.

What about Dawkins's second charge, that, though they are held with great tenacity and often asserted vehemently, religious beliefs are based merely upon faith and not upon evidence? McGrath correctly points out that a dichotomy between faith and evidence is grossly simplistic.[23] Faith need not be blind and science is not always quite as evidence-driven as simple stereotypes imply.

Here again, though, Dawkins's argument is refuted only in an extremely simplistic form. Perhaps the gravamen of Dawkins's contention can be restated as the charge that there is a great disparity between the assurance with which major religious claims are generally asserted and the actual epistemic credentials of those claims. Creedal claims are often presented as so manifestly true that those who willfully reject them are regarded as deserving of temporal or eternal punishment, or perhaps as invincibly ignorant. In this case we might expect that those creedal propositions are as well-established, as irrefragable and apodictically certain as claims can be. Yet this seems not to be the case. Every such set of tenets is doubted by many ostensibly rational, intelligent, and well-informed people. This alone is reason to think that the strength of the claims of religion is often overblown. Further, if creedal claims are manifestly true, it must be the case that each of the propositions constituting those claims is (*a*) clear, coherent, internally consistent, and compatible with other creedal claims; (*b*) either obviously true or established beyond a reasonable doubt; and (*c*) such that if established by reasons, those reasons should be readily apparent to any serious inquirer, since if the reasons for believing a proposition are too obscure, abstruse, or arcane, this could be a legitimate reason for not accepting it. However, it is highly doubtful that conditions *a*, *b*, and *c* are met with respect to the creedal claims of any religion.

So, however rhetorically overblown and simplistic Dawkins's statements might be, at their core they make a legitimate complaint, namely, that their adherents often represent the creedal claims of religion as possessing a far greater degree of certainty or obviousness than is warranted. When this happens, the consequences are bad. Claiming more for your beliefs than is their due not only debases rationality, but is conducive to intolerance, fanaticism, and obscurantism.

Dawkins's third charge is that religion diminishes our appreciation for the richness, mystery, majesty, and beauty of the universe, and instead gives us a diminished and impoverished view of reality. McGrath responds, "A Christian reading of the world denies nothing of what the natural sciences tell us. . . ."[24] Therefore, whatever majesties the atheist finds in the natural world may be equally if not more deeply appreciated by the theist. Well, this may be an apt answer for those who adhere to a Christian "reading" of the world like McGrath's. However, I fear that the Christian "reading" of an Oxford don might bear little relationship to that which prevails, in, say, Pine Bluff, Arkansas. What about those persons, and they number in the many millions, who adhere to a strict, literal, inerrantist view of Scripture? "God says it, I believe it, and that settles it," as one bumper sticker puts it. The fundamentalist's universe is indeed quite small. For one thing, it is less than ten thousand years old. Needless to say, this crowds the events of prehistory, resulting, for instance, in the dinosaurs being pushed onto the ark with Noah.[25] Further, it is a world that is ending quite soon. No exact date is given for the events of the "end time," such as the "rapture," but clearly they are at most just a few years away.

Now, McGrath may think that I mention such views to ridicule them or to embarrass sophisticated believers such as himself, but that is not my intent at all. We Americans must face the fact that multiple millions of our fellow citizens are Christian fundamentalists. This is simply a demographic fact. Further, over the last few decades fundamentalist cadres have been quite aggressive in seeking political power and cultural clout. Again, this is simply a fact. We are therefore fully justified in being interested in what fundamentalists believe, that is, in the contents of their little universe. As a critique of the constricted fundamentalist worldview, if not of religion in general, Dawkins's charge has relevance and significance.

Finally, McGrath considers Dawkins's accusation that religion is a bad thing that has led to much evil and suffering. McGrath replies that Dawkins again indulges in overblown rhetoric, that he carefully selects certain notorious episodes and treats them as typical rather than aberrant, that he ignores the facts mentioned earlier about the suffering inflicted by atheists, and that he overlooks the evidence of benefits of religion.[26]

Is it fair for a critic such as Dawkins to adduce the evils committed in the name of religion? Yes, because of the claims that religion makes for itself. The Christian church, according to its own account, was charged by its Founder to be the Light of the World and the holder of the keys to the kingdom of God. The church, again as it presents itself, is the Bride of Christ, and as such its behavior is to be holy and chaste. When so much is expected of an institution, or an individual, moral lapses are going to stand out with particular vividness. This is inevitable. Consider the case of the former high public official, the author of several books promoting personal virtue, and the self-appointed spokesman for public morality, who was discovered to be a compulsive gambler who had lost several million dollars. When such things happen, it is not at all unfair to hold the guilty individuals or institutions up to their own standards. Defenders of those individuals or institutions who respond by directing a *tu quoque* at critics are missing the point. It cannot be enough to be *no worse* than others when you are supposed to be *setting the standard*. If that is what you settle for, then you have relinquished any claim to moral authority.

In all fairness, of course, no human institution could exist for nearly two thousand years without numerous lapses, abuses, and excesses having been committed in its name. But there are evils that are woven into the very fabric of Christian belief and practice, so that it is hard to imagine Christianity ever changing so much as to be entirely free of them. For instance, James Carroll, a Roman Catholic layman, in his book *Constantine's Sword*, recounts the Catholic Church's two-thousand-year war against Judaism. Of all the Church's sins, this one is the most bizarre.

After all, Jesus was a Jew—born of a Jewish woman, he worshiped in the Temple and observed Jewish holidays. Two of the four Gospels provide lengthy genealogies to establish Jesus' descent from King David. In fact, Christianity began as a reform movement *within* Judaism. Yet, by the late first century, the church was largely Gentile, and these Gentile Christians saw the Jews as perversely stiff-necked in their rejection of Christ. The Gospels themselves begin the demonization of the Jews. John 8:44 literally calls Jews the children of the devil because they will not believe in Jesus. Matthew 27:25 depicts the Jews as saying that the blame for Jesus' crucifixion should fall on them and their children. Thus did the inflammatory charge of deicide—the murder of God—become Christians' excuse for the persecution of the Jews.

Carroll carefully shows how the church "fathers," the most important theologians of the early church, vilified the Jews, sometimes in the crudest terms. For instance, St. John Chrysostom, Bishop of Antioch in the early fifth century, said "a place where a whore stands on display is a whorehouse. What is more, the synagogue is not only a whorehouse and a theater; it is also a den of thieves and a haunt of wild animals."[27] Small wonder that after such calumny riots broke out against the Jews and the great synagogue at Antioch was demolished. St. Augustine, the most influential of the church "fathers," argued that Jews should not be killed, because, he said, their own Scriptures testify to the truth of Christianity. Yet, they should be scattered throughout the earth, to live as exiles everywhere, and to have a home nowhere. In the thirteenth century, St. Thomas Aquinas, perhaps the preeminent philosopher of the Christian church, wrote the *Summa Contra Gentiles*, a compendium of Christian apologetic. His aim was to make the case for Christianity rationally compelling, and therefore to deny Jews any excuse for their unbelief. Henceforth, Aquinas held, their rejection of Christianity must be seen not as "invincible ignorance," but as willful defiance of the truth. At the beginning of the Protestant Reformation, Martin Luther expressed sympathy for the Jews, but he erupted into rabid denunciation when they proved no more receptive to Lutheranism than to Catholicism. Here is one of his gems: "Know, my dear Christian, and do not doubt that next to the devil you have no enemy more cruel, more venomous and virulent, than a true Jew."[28] Carroll leaves no doubt that the hatred sown by such diatribes was abundantly harvested at Auschwitz.

The upshot is that critics such as Dawkins do not have the burden of proving that religion is always bad, or even that it is, on balance, more often bad than good. It is sufficient to show that religion is human, all too human. You ought not to be regarded as the Light of the World when even your most eloquent defenders can say only that your record is not quite as bad as that of the greatest monsters or most pernicious ideologies of history.

So, how effective is McGrath's critique of Dawkins? Well, he correctly notes the instances where Dawkins indulges in overstatement and oversimplification. Professional philosophers and other scholars whose vocation requires them to put a premium on precisely stated and rigorously argued claims often cringe when less careful controversialists enter the fray, firing off rhetorical broadsides, and reducing complex issues to slogans and sound bites. Because the issue evokes so much passion, popular apologists on both sides of the "God question" all too often offer overheated polemic and propaganda instead of logical argument. For instance, philosopher John Beversluis, in his book *C. S. Lewis and the Search for Rational Religion*,[29] carefully documents how the author of such classics of popular Christian apologetics as *Mere Christianity* often employs straw men to characterize opponents and makes claims far too large for his evidence. Unsurprisingly, authors of popular atheist apologetics often do likewise. Once the overstatement is trimmed back, however, we have seen some serious problems lurking in the neighborhood of Dawkins's charges. I have argued that McGrath's critique of Dawkins is inadequate to address these deep problems that may be articulated by qualifying, refining, or restricting Dawkins's accusations.

Has *The Twilight of Atheism* said anything to show that the intellectual case for atheism is deficient or that atheism is not, in fact, capable of raising very serious problems for religion? I do not see that it has. The strategy of associating atheism with defunct and pernicious ideologies does not work, and McGrath's intellectual engagement with atheist arguments stays at a superficial level. Well, then, should we at least agree with the claim that the intellectual prominence of atheist advocacy has declined since its heyday in the mid-nineteenth century? Yes, I think, but, paradoxically, the reason for this decline is the fact that the developed world is a far more secularized place than it was in the mid-nineteenth century. Who needs atheist agitators when the day-to-day impact of the church on people's lives is so small? For instance, Italy, one of the most Roman Catholic of countries, has the lowest birthrate in Europe. Either the church's strictures against artificial birth control are being widely ignored or Italians have lost interest in sex.

On the other hand, if McGrath is right that we are now in the midst of a spiritual and religious revival,[30] then we may soon be hearing more about atheism, too. In fact, I will go out on a limb and say that the recent crop of atheist best sellers is the first wave of the atheist revival. The two go hand in hand: if we are experiencing a widespread renewal of interest in traditional religions, and we can expect more and more public recognition of this fact, then we shall soon be hearing more from atheists. The problem is that religion has a Janus face. It represents the best and the worst in humanity; for every St. Francis there is a Torquemada.[31] Religion will therefore always be controversial and divisive. There will always be those who encounter its ugly, hateful face instead of its benevolent one. Therefore, there will always be an audience for atheism, and the bigger religion gets, the bigger that audience will get. So is atheism facing a twilight? To answer that question we need to ask: Is religion enjoying a dawning? If so, I think that McGrath will find that the rising sun shining on religion will shine on atheism as well.

3

In Defense of Theistic Arguments

William Lane Craig

The most important philosophical event of the twentieth century was undoubtedly the collapse of the verificationism that lay at the heart of the then-prevailing philosophy of scientific naturalism. The demise of verificationism has been accompanied by a resurgence of metaphysics, along with all the other traditional questions of philosophy that had been suppressed by the verificationists. With this resurgence has come something new and altogether unanticipated: the birth of a new discipline, philosophy of religion, and a renaissance in Christian philosophy.

Since the late 1960s Christian philosophers have been coming out of the closet and defending the truth of the Christian worldview with philosophically sophisticated arguments in the best scholarly journals and professional societies. The face of Anglo-American philosophy has been transformed as a result. Theism is on the rise; atheism is on the defensive.

To gain some feel of the impact of this revolution in Anglo-American philosophy, we have only to turn to an article by philosophy professor Quentin Smith that appeared in the fall of 2001 in the secularist journal *Philo*, lamenting what the author called "the desecularization of academia that evolved in philosophy departments since the late 1960s." He complains,

> Naturalists passively watched as realist versions of theism . . .
> began to sweep through the philosophical community, until today

perhaps one-quarter or one-third of philosophy professors are theists, with most being orthodox Christians . . . in philosophy, it became, almost overnight, "academically respectable" to argue for theism, making philosophy a favored field of entry for the most intelligent and talented theists entering academia today.[1]

Smith concludes, "God is not 'dead' in academia; he returned to life in the late 1960s and is now alive and well in his last academic stronghold, philosophy departments."

The change has not gone unnoticed even in popular culture. In 1980 *Time* magazine carried a major story entitled "Modernizing the Case for God," in which it described the movement among contemporary philosophers to refurbish and defend the traditional arguments for God's existence. *Time* marveled, "In a quiet revolution in thought and argument that hardly anybody could have foreseen only two decades ago, God is making a comeback. Most intriguingly, this is happening not among theologians or ordinary believers, but in the crisp intellectual circles of academic philosophers, where the consensus had long banished the Almighty from fruitful discourse."[2]

Indeed, the rise of analytic philosophy of religion has been accompanied by a resurgence of interest in natural theology, that branch of theology which seeks to prove God's existence apart from the resources of authoritative divine revelation. *Time* cites the late Roderick Chisholm to the effect that the reason that atheism was so influential a generation ago was that the brightest philosophers were atheists; but today, in Chisholm's opinion, many of the brightest philosophers are theists, using a tough-minded intellectualism in defense of their belief.

Now atheists like Daniel Dennett are hitting back. Dennett believes that there are no good arguments for the existence of God. But insofar as we mean by a "good argument" an argument which (1) is formally and informally valid, (2) consists of true premises, and (3) has premises that are more plausible than their negations, there do appear to be good arguments for God's existence, and there are on the contemporary scene plenty of philosophers who think so. I shall examine four of the most important of these arguments.

The Cosmological Argument

The cosmological argument is a family of arguments that seek to demonstrate the existence of a Sufficient Reason or First Cause of the existence of the cosmos. One version of the argument, defended, for example, by Leibniz, is the argument from contingency.

The Argument from Contingency

A simple statement of the contingency argument might run as follows:

1. Anything that exists has an explanation of its existence, either in the necessity of its own nature or in an external cause.
2. If the universe has an explanation of its existence, that explanation is God.
3. The universe exists.
4. Therefore, the explanation of the existence of the universe is God.

Is this a good argument?

Premise (1) is a modest version of the Principle of Sufficient Reason which circumvents the typical objections to strong versions of that principle. For (1) merely requires any existing *thing* to have an explanation of its existence. This premise is compatible with there being brute *facts* about the world.[3] What it precludes is that there could exist things which just exist inexplicably. According to (1) there are two kinds of being: necessary beings, which exist of their own nature and so have no external cause of their existence, and contingent beings, whose existence is accounted for by causal factors outside themselves. Numbers might be prime candidates for the first sort of being, while familiar physical objects fall under the second kind of being.

This principle seems quite plausible, at least more so than its contradictory. One thinks of Richard Taylor's illustration of finding a translucent ball while walking in the woods.[4] One would find the claim quite bizarre that the ball just exists inexplicably; and increasing the size of the ball, even until it becomes coextensive with the cosmos, would do nothing to obviate the need for an explanation of its existence.

Crispin Wright and Bob Hale, while recognizing that explicability is the default position and that exceptions to the requirement of an explanation therefore require justification, nonetheless maintain that an exemption is justified in the case of the contingent universe. For the demand for an explanation of the contingent universe is preempted by the restrictive principle that *the explanation of the obtaining of a (physical) state of affairs must advert to a causally prior state of affairs in which it does not obtain.*[5] This principle would require that any explanation of the existence of the universe must advert to a causally prior state of affairs in which the universe does not exist. But since a physically empty world would not cause anything, the demand for an explanation of the universe becomes absurd and thus the demand for an explanation is preempted. This line of reasoning, however, plainly begs the question in favor of atheism. For apart from that assumption, there is just no reason to think that a causally prior state of affairs must be a physical state of affairs. The theist will regard Wright and Hale's principle as not at all restrictive, since the explanation of why the physical universe exists can and should be provided in terms of a causally prior nonphysical state of affairs involving God's existence and will.

Premise (2) is, in effect, the contrapositive of the typical atheist response to Leibniz that on the atheistic worldview the universe simply exists as a brute contingent thing. Atheists typically assert that, there being no God, it is false that everything has an explanation of its existence, for the universe, in this case, just exists inexplicably. In affirming that if atheism is true, then the universe has no explanation of its existence, atheists are also affirming the logically equivalent claim that if the universe has an explanation of its existence, then atheism is not true, that is to say, God exists. Hence, most atheists are implicitly committed to (2).

Moreover, (2) seems quite plausible in its own right, for if the universe, by definition, includes all of physical reality, then the cause of the universe must (at least causally prior to the universe's existence) transcend space and time and therefore cannot be physical or material. But there are only two kinds of things that could fall under such a description: either an abstract object or else a mind. But abstract objects do not stand in causal relations. Therefore, it follows that the explanation of the existence of the universe is an external, transcendent, personal cause—which is one meaning of "God."

Finally, premise (3) states the obvious, that there is a universe. Since the universe exists, it follows that God exists.

Although I have not read all that Dennett has written, I have not been able to find in his writings any response to this version of the cosmological argument apart from the following sentence: "If 'why something exists rather than nothing' is intelligible, the answer 'because God exists' is probably as good an answer as any; but look at its competition: 'why not?'."[6] This is an amazingly conciliatory response. Dennett says nothing to show that the question is unintelligible, and if the theistic answer is as good as any answer that can be given to the question, then the theist will find himself so far forth as justified in his views as any atheist.

But what about the atheistic competition? Look at it. The counterquestion is ambiguous. Is the atheistic answer the claim that the universe just exists as a brute contingent? Then it runs afoul of the plausible version of the Principle of Sufficient Reason stated in premise (1).

Or is the atheist answer the claim that the universe exists by the necessity of its own nature? This would be an extremely bold suggestion that atheists, including Dennett, have not been eager to embrace. We have, one can safely say, a strong intuition of the universe's contingency. A possible world in which no concrete objects exist certainly seems conceivable. We generally trust our modal intuitions on other matters with which we are familiar; if we are to do otherwise with respect to the universe's contingency, then the nontheist needs to provide some reason for such skepticism other than a desire to avoid theism.

Moreover, I think we have good argumentative grounds for thinking that the universe does not exist by a necessity of its own nature.[7] It is easy to conceive of the nonexistence of any and all of the macroscopic objects we observe in the world; indeed, prior to a certain point in the past none of them did exist. As for fundamental particles or the building blocks of matter, be they quarks or strings, it is easy to conceive of a world in which all of the present microscopic constituents of macroscopic objects were replaced by other quarks or strings. A universe consisting of a totally different collection of quarks, say, seems quite possible. If that is the case, then the universe does not exist by a necessity of its own nature, since a universe composed of a wholly different collection of quarks is not the same universe as ours.[8] This is the case whether we think of the universe as an object in its own right, just as a block of marble is not identical to a block of the same shape constituted of different marble, or as an aggregate or group, just as a flock of birds is not identical to a similar flock composed of different birds, or even as nothing at all over and above the quarks themselves. Since quarks are the fundamental building blocks of material objects, one cannot say, as one might of macroscopic objects, that while they are contingent, the stuff of which they are made is necessary, for there is no further stuff beyond them. No atheist will, I think, have the temerity to suggest that some quarks, though qualitatively similar to ordinary quarks, have the special occult property of being metaphysically necessary. It is all or nothing here. But no one thinks that every quark exists by a necessity of its own nature. It follows that neither does the universe composed of such quarks exist by a necessity of its own nature.

Perhaps it will be said, as Bede Rundle has in fact said,[9] that while nothing exists by a necessity of its own nature, nevertheless it is necessary that something or other exist. Rundle agrees with the theist (albeit for different reasons) that it is broadly logically impossible that nothing exist; but the proper conclusion to be drawn from this fact is not that a necessary being exists, but that, necessarily, some contingent being or other exists. In short, premise (1) is, on Rundle's view, false after all.

Alexander Pruss has pointed out that Rundle's view has an extremely untoward consequence.[10] It is plausible that no conjunction of claims about the nonexistence of various things entails, say, that a unicorn exists. After all, how could the fact that certain things do not exist entail that some other thing does exist? But on Rundle's view the conjunction, "There are no mountains, there are no people, there are no planets, there are no rocks, . . . [including everything that is not a unicorn]," entails that there is a unicorn! For if it is necessary that contingent beings exist, and none of the other contingent beings listed exist, then the only thing left is a unicorn. Hence, a conjunction about the nonexistence of certain things entails that a unicorn exists, a most implausible consequence.

Moreover, on Rundle's view there is nothing that would account for *why* there exist contingent beings in every possible world. Since there is no metaphysically necessary being, there is nothing that could cause contingent beings to exist in every possible world and no explanation why every world includes contingent beings. There is no strict logical inconsistency in the concept of a world devoid of contingent beings. What accounts for the fact that in every possible world contingent beings exist? Given the infinity of broadly logically possible worlds, the odds that in all of them contingent beings just happen inexplicably to exist is infinitesimal. Hence, the probability of Rundle's hypothesis is effectively zero. Rundle cannot avoid this difficulty by asserting that the reason why contingent beings exist is that matter necessarily exists, for none of the fundamental building blocks of matter does seem to exist by a necessity of its own nature, so that matter itself is contingent. The probability that matter inexplicably happens to exist in every world is vanishingly small.

So the atheistic answer to the question as to why anything at all exists strikes me as less plausible that the theistic answer. The premises of this Leibnizian version of the cosmological argument thus all seem more plausible than their negations. It therefore follows logically that the explanation for why the universe exists is to be found in God.

The *Kalam* Cosmological Argument

Another version of the cosmological argument, which I have called the *kalam* cosmological argument, constitutes an independent argument for a transcendent Creator of the universe. The *kalam* cosmological argument may be formulated as follows:

1. Whatever begins to exist has a cause.
2. The universe began to exist.
3. Therefore, the universe has a cause.

Conceptual analysis of what it means to be a cause of the universe then aims to establish some of the theologically significant properties of this being.

Premise (1) seems obviously true—at the least, more so than its negation. It is rooted in the metaphysical intuition that something cannot come into being from nothing. To suggest that things could just pop into being uncaused out of nothing is to quit doing serious metaphysics and to resort to magic. Furthermore, if things could really come into being uncaused out of nothing, then it becomes inexplicable why just anything and everything does not come into existence uncaused from nothing. Finally, the first premise is constantly confirmed in our experience. Atheists who are scientific naturalists thus have the strongest of motivations to accept it.

Dennett, in his all-too-brief critique of the cosmological argument, misstates the first premise as "Everything that exists must have a cause," which occasions his obvious retort, "What caused God?"[11] This is merely to caricature the argument. In fact, apart from certain Enlightenment rationalists, who by "cause" meant merely "sufficient reason," no orthodox theist has ever asserted that everything has a cause or that God is self-caused, a notion rightly rejected by Aquinas as metaphysically impossible.

Nevertheless, it is noteworthy that Dennett does not think that the universe popped inexplicably into being, uncaused out of nothing. On the contrary, he affirms the first premise, stating that a being "outside of time . . . is nothing with an *initiation* or *origin* in need of explanation. What does need its origin explained is the concrete Universe itself. . . ."[12] Dennett rightly sees that a being which exists eternally, since it never comes into being, has no need of a cause, as do things that have an origin. So Dennett affirms the first premise, which will lead him, as we shall see, to the remarkable position that the universe must have caused itself to come into being.

Premise (2) may be supported by both deductive, philosophical arguments and inductive, scientific arguments. Since the latter are apt to be more appealing to Dennett as a scientific naturalist and since he never discusses the philosophical arguments for the finitude of the past, and, most of all, since I am short on space, let me focus on the scientific arguments.

A principal empirical argument for the beginning of the universe is based on the expansion of the universe. In 1917, Albert Einstein made a cosmological application of his newly discovered gravitational theory, the General Theory of Relativity (GTR). In so doing he assumed that the universe exists in a steady state, with a constant mean mass density and a constant curvature of space. To his chagrin, however, he found that GTR would not permit such a model of the universe unless he introduced into his gravitational field equations a certain "fudge factor" in order to counterbalance the gravitational effect of matter and so ensure a static universe. Unfortunately, Einstein's static universe was balanced on a razor's edge, and the least perturbation would cause the universe either to implode or to expand. By taking this feature of Einstein's model seriously, the Russian mathematician Alexander Friedman and the Belgian astronomer Georges Lemaître were able to formulate independently in the 1920s solutions to the field equations that predicted an expanding universe.

In 1929, the astronomer Edwin Hubble showed that the red-shift in the optical spectra of light from distant galaxies was a common feature of all measured galaxies and was proportional to their distance from us. This red-shift was taken to be a Doppler effect indicative of the recessional motion of the light source in the line of sight. Incredibly, what Hubble had discovered was the isotropic expansion of the universe predicted by Friedman and Lemaître on the basis of Einstein's GTR.

According to the Friedman-Lemaître model, as time proceeds, the distances separating galactic masses become greater. It is important to understand that as a GTR-based theory, the model does not describe the expansion of the material content of the universe into a preexisting, empty space, but rather the expansion of space itself. The ideal particles of the cosmological fluid constituted by the galactic masses are conceived to be at rest with respect to space but to recede progressively from one another as space itself expands or stretches, just as buttons glued to the surface of a balloon would recede from one another as the balloon inflates. As the universe expands, it becomes less and less dense. This has the astonishing implication that as one reverses the expansion and extrapolates back in time, the universe becomes progressively denser until one arrives at a state of "infinite density" at some point in the finite past. This state represents a singularity at which spacetime curvature, along with temperature, pressure, and density, becomes infinite. It therefore constitutes an edge or boundary to spacetime itself. The term *big bang* is thus potentially misleading, since the expansion cannot be visualized from the outside (there being no "outside," just as there is no "before" with respect to the big bang).

The Standard Big Bang Model, as the Friedman-Lemaître model came to be called, thus describes a universe that is not eternal in the past, but that came into being a finite time ago. Moreover—and this deserves underscoring—the origin it posits is an absolute origin *ex nihilo*. For not only all matter and energy, but space and time themselves, come into being at the initial cosmological singularity. There can be no natural, physical cause of the big bang event, since, in Quentin Smith's words, "It belongs analytically to the concept of the cosmological singularity that it is not the effect of prior physical events. The definition of a singularity . . . entails that it is *impossible to extend the spacetime manifold beyond the singularity. . . .* This rules out the idea that the singularity is an effect of some prior natural process."[13] Sir Arthur Eddington, contemplating the beginning of the universe, opined that the expansion of the universe was so preposterous and incredible that "I feel almost an indignation that anyone should believe in it—except myself."[14] He finally felt forced to conclude, "The beginning seems to present insuperable difficulties unless we agree to look on it as frankly supernatural."[15]

Sometimes objectors appeal to non-Standard models of the expanding universe in an attempt to avert the absolute beginning predicted by the Standard Model. But while such theories are possible, it has been the overwhelming verdict of the scientific community than none of them is more probable than a model with an absolute beginning. Indeed, the history of twentieth-century cosmology can be viewed as one failed attempt after another to avert the absolute beginning predicted by the Standard Model. According to Stephen Hawking, "Almost everyone now believes that the universe, and *time itself*, had a beginning at the Big Bang."[16]

Moreover, a watershed of sorts appears to have been reached in 2003 when Arvind Borde, Alan Guth, and Alexander Vilenkin successfully formulated a theorem which establishes that any universe which has on average over its past history been in a state of expansion cannot be infinite in the past but must have a past spacetime boundary. This is a theorem of great power that applies alike to inflationary models and to higher-dimensional, brane cosmological models based on string theory, as well to as typical expansion models. Theorists intent on avoiding the absolute beginning of the universe could previously always take refuge in the period prior to the Planck time, an era so poorly understood that one commentator has compared it with the regions on the maps of ancient cartographers marked, "Here there be dragons!"—it can be filled with all sorts of chimeras. But the Borde-Guth-Vilenkin theorem does not depend upon any particular physical description of the universe prior to the Planck time, being based instead on deceptively simple physical reasoning that will hold regardless of our uncertainty concerning that era. It single-handedly sweeps away the most important attempts to avoid the absolute beginning of the universe. Vilenkin pulls no punches: "It is said that an argument is what convinces reasonable men and a proof is what it takes to convince even an unreasonable man. With the proof now in place, cosmologists can no longer hide behind the possibility of a past-eternal universe. There is no escape, they have to face the problem of a cosmic beginning."[17]

We thus have strong empirical grounds for accepting the truth of premise (2) of the *kalam* cosmological argument. It follows from the two premises that the universe therefore has a cause of its existence.

Dennett, as we have seen, agrees. But, he claims, the cause of the universe is itself; the universe brought itself into being! Dennett writes, "What does need its origin explained is the concrete Universe itself, and as Hume's Philo long ago asked: Why not stop at the material world? It . . . does perform a version of the ultimate bootstrapping trick; it creates itself *ex nihilo*. Or at any rate out of something that is well-nigh indistinguishable from nothing at all."[18] Here Dennett spoils his radical idea by waffling at the end: maybe the universe did not create itself out of nothing but at least out of something "well-nigh indistinguishable from nothing." This caveat evinces a lack of appreciation of the metaphysical chasm between being and nothingness. There is no third thing between being and nonbeing; if anything at all exists, however ethereal, it is something and therefore not nothing. So what could this be? Dennett does not tell us. In fact, he seems somewhat impatient with the question. He complains,

> This leads in various arcane directions, into the strange precincts of string theory and probability fluctuations and the like, at one extreme, and into ingenious nitpicking about the meaning of "cause" at the other. Unless you have a taste for mathematics and theoretical physics on the one hand, or the niceties of scholastic logic on the other, you are not apt to find any of this compelling, or even fathomable.[19]

How strange, especially for a man who claims to be among the "brights," to indict an argument because it appeals only to the inquisitive and the intelligent! In any case, the appeal of the argument is irrelevant; if even Dennett's complaint were correct, it constitutes at best a piece of friendly, atheistic advice to theists about the limited utility of the *kalam* cosmological argument in evangelism. We can thank Dennett for his advice, while still demanding an account of the origin of the universe.

The best sense I can make out Dennett's suggestion is to construe it as an endorsement of a model of quantum creation such as is offered by his Tufts University colleague Alexander Vilenkin. Vilenkin invites us to envision a small, closed, spherical universe filled with a false vacuum and containing some ordinary matter. If the radius of such a universe is small, classical physics predicts that it will collapse to a point; but quantum physics permits it to "tunnel" into a state of inflation. If we allow the radius to shrink all the way to zero, there still remains some positive probability of the universe's tunneling to inflation. Now Vilenkin equates the initial state of the universe explanatorily prior to tunneling with nothingness. Unfortunately, this equivalence is clearly mistaken (perhaps Dennett's waffling betrays an understanding of this fact). As Vilenkin illustrates in his recent book *Many Worlds in One*,[20] the quantum tunneling is at every point a function from something to something. For quantum tunneling to be truly from nothing, the function would have to have a single term, the posterior term. Another way of seeing the point is to reflect on the fact that to have no radius (as is the case with nothingness) is not to have a radius, whose measure is zero. Thus, on Vilenkin's model we are still left wondering what caused the initial state of the universe to come into being.

Dennett's answer is: the universe, in the ultimate bootstrapping trick, created itself! Dennett's bold hypothesis would at least help to resolve A. N. Prior's objection that if something can come into being out of nothing, then it becomes inexplicable why anything and everything does not come into being out of nothing. On Dennett's view the coming of the universe into being is causally constrained: it creates itself. Of course, that still leaves us wondering why other things, say, bicycles and hot dogs and uni-corns, do not have the same capacity; but never mind. As Aquinas argued, self-creation is metaphysically absurd, since in order to cause itself to come into being, the universe would have to already exist. One is thus caught in a vicious circle. Aquinas made the point with respect to an eternally existing universe, but his argument is even more forceful with respect to a universe with a beginning. For in the latter case the universe must be not only explanatorily prior to itself but even, it seems, chronologically prior to itself, which is incoherent. Thus, Dennett's imaginative suggestion is wholly implausible.

It therefore follows that the universe has an external cause. Concep-tual analysis enables us to recover a number of striking properties that must be possessed by such an ultra-mundane being. For as the cause of space and time, this entity must transcend space and time and therefore exist atemporally and nonspatially, at least without the universe. This tran-scendent cause must therefore be changeless and immaterial, since time-lessness entails changelessness, and changelessness implies immateriality. Such a cause must be beginningless and uncaused, at least in the sense of lacking any antecedent causal conditions. Ockham's razor will shave away further causes, since we should not multiply causes beyond necessity. This entity must be unimaginably powerful, since it created the universe with-out any material cause.

Finally, and most remarkably, such a transcendent cause is plausibly to be taken to be personal. Three reasons can be given for this conclusion. First, there are two types of causal explanation: scientific explanations in terms of laws and initial conditions, and personal explanations in terms of agents and their volitions. A first state of the universe *cannot* have a scientific explanation, since there is nothing before it, and therefore it can be accounted for only in terms of a personal explanation. Second, as we have already seen, the personhood of the cause of the universe is implied by its timelessness and immateriality, since the only entities we know of which can possess such properties are either minds or abstract objects, and abstract objects do not stand in causal relations. Therefore, the tran-scendent cause of the origin of the universe must be of the order of mind. Third, this same conclusion is also implied by the fact that we have in this case the origin of a temporal effect from a timeless cause. If the cause of the origin of the universe were an impersonal set of necessary and suffi-cient conditions, it would be impossible for the cause to exist without its effect. For if the necessary and sufficient conditions of the effect are time-lessly given, then their effect must be given as well. The only way for the cause to be timeless and changeless but for its effect to originate anew a finite time ago is for the cause to be a personal agent who freely chooses to bring about an effect without antecedent determining conditions. Thus, we are brought, not merely to a transcendent cause of the universe, but to its Personal Creator.

The Teleological Argument

Once thought to have been demolished by Hume and Darwin, the teleological argument for God's existence has come roaring back into prominence in recent years. The explanatory adequacy of the neo-Darwinian mechanisms of random mutation and natural selection with respect to observed biological complexity has been sharply challenged, as advances in microbiology have served to disclose the breathtaking complexity of the micromachinery of a single cell, not to speak of higher-level organisms. The field of origin-of-life studies is in turmoil, as all the old scenarios of the chemical origin of life in the primordial soup have collapsed, and no new, better theory is on the horizon. And the scientific community has been stunned by its discovery of how complex and sensitive a nexus of initial conditions must be given in order for the universe even to permit the origin and evolution of intelligent life.

Undoubtedly, it is this last discovery that has most served to reopen the books on the teleological argument. Due to sociological factors surrounding the neo-Darwinian theory of biological evolution captured most poignantly in the public image of the Scopes trial, biologists have been for the most part extremely loath to so much as even contemplate a design hypothesis, lest they let a creationist foot in the door. But cosmologists, largely untainted by this controversy, have been much more open to entertain seriously the alternative of design. The discovery of the cosmic fine-tuning has led many scientists to conclude that such a delicate balance of physical constants and quantities as is requisite for life cannot be dismissed as mere coincidence but cries out for some sort of explanation.

What is meant by "fine-tuning"? The physical laws of nature, when given mathematical expression, contain various constants, such as the gravitational constant, whose values are not mandated by the laws themselves; a universe governed by such laws might be characterized by any of a wide range of values for such variables. Moreover, there are certain arbitrary physical quantities, such as the entropy level, which are simply put in as boundary conditions on which the laws of nature operate. By "fine-tuning," one means that the actual values assumed by the constants and quantities in question are such that small deviations from those values would render the universe life-prohibiting or, alternatively, that the range of life-permitting values is exquisitely narrow in comparison with the range of assumable values.

Dennett therefore errs when he represents the argument from fine-tuning as based upon the elegance and precision of the laws of nature. The laws of nature may, as he suggests, be metaphysically necessary. But it is the contingent values of the constants appearing in those laws and the contingent boundary conditions on which those laws operate that are incomprehensibly fine-tuned for life and are the focus of interest. For that reason the speculation is irrelevant that in universes governed by different laws of nature, deleterious consequences might not result from varying the values of the various constants and quantities. One need not deny the possibility, for such universes are not germane to the argument. What matters is that among possible universes governed by the same laws (but having different values of the constants and quantities) as the actual universe, life-permitting universes are extraordinarily improbable. John Leslie gives the illustration of a fly, resting on a large, blank area of the wall. A single shot is fired, and the bullet strikes the fly. Now even if the rest of the wall outside the blank area is covered with flies, such that a randomly fired bullet would probably hit one, nevertheless it remains highly improbable that a single, randomly fired bullet would strike the solitary fly within the large, blank area. In the same way, we need only concern ourselves with the universes governed by the same laws in order to determine the probability of the existence of a life-permitting universe.

In a sense more easy to discern than to articulate, this fine-tuning of the universe seems to manifest the presence of a designing intelligence. The inference to design is best thought of, not as an instance of reasoning by analogy (as it is often portrayed), but as a case of inference to the best explanation.[21] Leslie speaks of the need for what he calls a "tidy explanation." A tidy explanation is one that not only explains a certain situation but also reveals in doing so that there is something to be explained. Leslie provides a whole retinue of charming illustrations of tidy explanations at work. Suppose, for example, that Bob is given a new car for his birthday. There are millions of license plate numbers, and it is therefore highly unlikely that Bob would get, say, CHT 4271. Yet that plate on his birthday car would occasion no special interest. But suppose Bob, who was born on August 8, 1949, finds BOB 8849 on the license plate of his birthday car. He would be obtuse if he shrugged this off with the comment, "Well, it had to have *some* license plate, and any number is equally improbable. . . ." But what makes this case different than the other?

A full-fledged theory of design inference has recently been offered by William Dembski in his *The Design Inference*.[22] Dembski's analysis can be used to formalize what Leslie grasped in an intuitive way. What makes an explanation a tidy one is not simply the fact that the *explanandum* is some improbable event, but the fact that the event also conforms to some independently given pattern, resulting in what Dembski calls "specified complexity." It is this specified complexity (high improbability + an independent pattern) that tips us off to the need for an explanation in terms of more than mere chance. An alternative approach to design inferences is offered by Robin Collins, who employs a Bayesian approach to argue that the cosmic fine-tuning is much more probable on the hypothesis of design than on the hypothesis of a single, atheistic universe and that therefore the evidence of fine-tuning strongly confirms design over its rival hypothesis.[23] Regardless of which approach one adopts, the key to detecting design is to eliminate the two competing alternatives of physical necessity and chance. Accordingly, a teleological argument appealing to cosmic fine-tuning might be formulated as follows:

1. The fine-tuning of the universe is due to either physical necessity, chance, or design.
2. It is not due to physical necessity or chance.
3. Therefore, it is due to design.

Since premise (1) seems to exhaust the alternatives, the soundness of this argument will depend on the plausibility of premise (2).

Can the cosmic fine-tuning be plausibly attributed to physical necessity? According to this alternative, the constants and quantities must have the values they do, and there was really no chance or little chance of the universe's not being life-permitting. Now on the face of it this alternative seems extraordinarily implausible. It requires us to believe that a life-prohibiting universe is virtually physically impossible. But surely it does seem possible. If the primordial matter and anti-matter had been differently proportioned, if the universe had expanded just a little more slowly, if the entropy of the universe were marginally greater—any of these adjustments and more would have prevented a life-permitting universe, yet all seem perfectly possible physically. The person who maintains that the universe must be life-permitting is taking a radical line which requires strong proof. But as yet there is none; this alternative is simply put forward as a bare possibility.

Sometimes physicists do speak of a yet-to-be-discovered Theory of Everything (T.O.E.), but such nomenclature is, like so many of the colorful names given to scientific theories, quite misleading. A T.O.E. actually has the limited goal of providing a unified theory of the four fundamental forces of nature, to reduce gravity, electromagnetism, the strong force, and the weak force to one fundamental force carried by one fundamental particle. Such a theory will, we hope, explain why these four forces take the values they do, but it will not even attempt to explain literally everything. For example, the most promising candidate for a T.O.E. to date, superstring theory or M theory, fails to predict uniquely our universe. Stephen Hawking recently addressed this question at a cosmology conference at the University of California, Davis. Notice the alternative answers available to the question he poses:

> Does string theory, or M theory, predict the distinctive features of our universe, like a spatially flat four dimensional expanding universe with small fluctuations, and the standard model of particle physics? Most physicists would rather believe string theory uniquely predicts the universe, than the alternatives. These are that the initial state of the universe, is prescribed by an outside agency, code named God. Or that there are many universes, and our universe is picked out by the anthropic principle.[24]

These represent the three alternatives before us. Hawking shows that the first alternative is a vain hope: "M theory cannot predict the parameters of the standard model. Obviously, the values of the parameters we measure must be compatible with the development of life. . . . But within the anthropically allowed range, the parameters can have any values. So much for string theory predicting the fine structure constant." He wrapped up by saying,

> . . . even when we understand the ultimate theory, it won't tell us much about how the universe began. It cannot predict the dimensions of spacetime, the gauge group, or other parameters of the low energy effective theory. . . . It won't determine how this energy is divided between conventional matter, and a cosmological constant, or quintessence. . . . So to come back to the question. . . . Does string theory predict the state of the universe? The answer is that it does not. It allows a vast landscape of possible universes, in which we occupy an anthropically permitted location.

In fact this idea of a "cosmic landscape" predicted by string theory has become something of a phenom in its own right. It turns out that string theory allows around 10^{500} different possible universes governed by the present laws of nature, so that it is far from rendering the observed values of the constants and quantities physically necessary. Moreover, even though there will be a huge number of possible universes lying within the anthropically favorable boundaries, nevertheless that life-permitting region will be unfathomably tiny compared to the entire landscape, so that the existence of a life-permitting universe is fantastically improbable. There is no reason to think that showing every constant and quantity to be physically necessary is anything more than a pipe dream.

What, then, of the alternative of chance? One may seek to eliminate this hypothesis either by appealing to the specified complexity of cosmic fine-tuning or by arguing that the fine-tuning is significantly more probable on design (theism) than on the chance hypothesis (atheism).

Issues pertinent to the so-called Anthropic Principle arise here. As formulated by Barrow and Tipler, the Anthropic Principle states that any observed properties of the universe which may initially appear astonishingly improbable can only be seen in their true perspective after we have accounted for the fact that certain properties could not be observed by us, were they to be exemplified, because we can only observe those compatible with our own existence. The implication is that we ought not to be surprised at observing the universe to be as it is and that therefore no explanation of its fine-tuning need be sought. The argument is, however, based on confusion. Barrow and Tipler have confused the true claim,

> A. If observers who have evolved within a universe observe its fundamental constants and quantities, it is highly probable that they will observe them to be fine-tuned to their existence.

with the false claim,

> A'. It is highly probable that a universe exists which is finely tuned for the evolution of observers within it.

An observer who has evolved within the universe should regard it as highly probable that he will find the basic conditions of the universe fine-tuned for his existence; but he should not infer that it is therefore highly probable that such a fine-tuned universe exist.

Anthropic theorizers now recognize that the Anthropic Principle can only legitimately be employed when it is conjoined to a Many Worlds hypothesis, according to which a World Ensemble of concrete universes exists, actualizing a wide range of possibilities. The Many Worlds hypothesis is essentially an effort on the part of partisans of the chance hypothesis to multiply their probabilistic resources in order to reduce the improbability of the occurrence of fine-tuning. The very fact that they must resort to such a remarkable hypothesis is a sort of backhanded compliment to the design hypothesis in that they recognize that the fine-tuning does cry out for explanation. But is the Many Worlds hypothesis as plausible as the design hypothesis?

If the Many Worlds hypothesis is to commend itself as a plausible hypothesis, then some plausible mechanism for generating the many worlds needs to be explained. Dennett appeals to Lee Smolin's ingenious suggestion that if we suppose that black holes spawn other universes beyond our own, then universes that produce large numbers of black holes would have a selective advantage in producing offspring, so that a sort of cosmic evolution would take place.[25] If each new universe is not an exact reproduction of its parent universe but varies in its fundamental constants and quantities, then universes that are proficient in producing black holes would have a selective advantage over those that are less proficient. Thus, in the course of cosmic evolution universes whose fundamental parameters are fine-tuned to the production of black holes would proliferate. Since black holes are the residue of collapsed stars, cosmic evolution has the unintended effect of producing more and more stars and hence, more and more planets where life might form. Eventually observers would appear who marvel at the fine-tuning of the universe for their existence.

Unfortunately for Dennett, Smolin's idea proved to be a nonstarter. The fatal flaw in Smolin's scenario, wholly apart from its ad hoc and even disconfirmed conjectures, was his assumption that universes fine-tuned for black hole production would also be fine-tuned for the production of stable stars. In fact, the opposite is true: the most proficient producers of black holes would be universes that generate them prior to star formation, so that life-permitting universes would actually be weeded out by Smolin's cosmic evolutionary scenario.[26]

Dennett also floats the old idea of an eternally oscillating universe in order to secure an infinite past, during which time various combinations of constants and quantities could have been tried ere this present system was struck out. Not only is he apparently unaware of the manifold problems that led to the demise of such models in the late 1970s, but such theories actually require fine-tuning in order to ensure an infinite regress of oscillations, and fine-tuning of a very special sort, since the conditions must be set noncausally at minus-infinity. Moreover, since the thermodynamic properties of oscillating models require that the oscillations increase over time, such a model cannot be extended into the infinite past.

The best shot at providing a plausible mechanism for generating a World Ensemble comes from inflationary cosmology, which is often employed to defend the view that our universe is but one domain (or "pocket universe") within a vastly larger universe, or multiverse. Vilenkin is one who vigorously champions the idea that we live in a multiverse. At the heart of Vilenkin's view is the theory of future-eternal, or everlasting, inflation. In order to ensure that inflation will go on forever, Vilenkin hypothesizes that the scalar fields determining the energy density and evolution of the false vacuum state are characterized by a certain slope which issues in a false vacuum expanding so rapidly that, as it decays into pockets of true vacuum, the "island universes" thereby generated in this sea of false vacuum, though themselves expanding at enormous rates, cannot keep up with the expansion of the false vacuum and so find themselves increasingly separated with time. Moreover, each island is subdivided into subdomains which Vilenkin calls O-regions, each constituting an observable universe bounded by an event horizon. Despite the fact that the multiverse is finite and geometrically closed, the false vacuum will, according to the theory, go on expanding forever. New pockets of true vacuum will continue to form in the gaps between the island universes and become themselves isolated worlds.

As the island universes expand, their central regions eventually grow dark and barren, while stars are forming at their ever-expanding perimeters. We should think of the decay of false vacuum to true vacuum going on at the islands' expanding boundaries as multiple big bangs. From the global perspective of the inflating multiverse, these big bangs occur successively, as the island boundaries grow with time. In the global time of the multiverse, each island is at any time finite in extent though growing. Now at this point Vilenkin executes a nifty piece of *legerdemain*. When we consider the internal, cosmic time of each island universe, each O-region can be traced back to an initial big bang event. We can string together these various big bang events as occurring simultaneously. Big bangs that will occur in the global future are now to be regarded as present. As a result, the infinite, temporal series of successive big bangs is converted into an infinite, spatial array of simultaneous big bangs. Hence, from the internal point of view each island universe is infinite in extent. We see the switch from a temporal ordering to a spatial ordering when Vilenkin says, "any history that has a nonzero probability will happen—or rather has happened—in an infinite number of O-regions!"[27] Viewed globally, these O-regions are in the future and will be infinite in number only in the sense that the island will continue to expand forever and so ceaselessly to generate new O-regions. If tense and temporal becoming are objective features of reality, then the future is potentially infinite only, and future O-regions do not in any sense exist. If there is a global tide of becoming, then there is no actually infinite collection of O-regions after all.

But if an infinite ensemble of simultaneous island universes does not actually exist, the appeal to the multiverse to explain away the fine-tuning of the universe for intelligent life collapses. For if, in fact, an infinite array of island universes does not yet exist, if most of them lie in the potentially infinite future and are therefore unreal, then there actually exist only as many universes as can have formed in the false vacuum since the multiverse's inception at its boundary in the finite past. Given the incomprehensible improbability of the constants all falling randomly into the life-permitting range, it may well be highly improbable that a life-permitting island universe should have decayed this soon out of the false vacuum. In that case the sting of fine-tuning has not been relieved.

The whole multiverse scenario depends, it will be recalled, on the hypothesis of eternal inflation, which in turn is based upon the existence of certain primordial scalar fields that govern inflation. Although Vilenkin observes that "Inflation is eternal in practically all models suggested so far,"[28] he also admits, "Another important question is whether or not such scalar fields really exist in nature. Unfortunately, we don't know. There is no direct evidence for their existence."[29] This lack of evidence ought to temper the confidence with which the Many Worlds hypothesis is put forward.

Wholly apart from its speculative nature, however, the Many Worlds hypothesis faces a potentially lethal problem. Simply stated, if our universe is but one member of an infinite World Ensemble of randomly varying universes, then it is overwhelmingly more probable that we should be observing a much different universe than that which we in fact observe.

By way of background, the nineteenth-century physicist Ludwig Boltzmann proposed a sort of Many Worlds hypothesis in order to explain why we do not find the universe in a state of "heat death" or thermodynamic equilibrium. Boltzmann hypothesized that the universe as a whole *does*, in fact, exist in an equilibrium state, but that over time fluctuations in the energy level occur here and there throughout the universe, so that by chance alone there will be isolated regions where disequilibrium exists. Boltzmann referred to these isolated regions as "worlds." We should not be surprised to see our world in a highly improbable disequilibrium state, he maintained, since in the ensemble of all worlds there must exist by chance alone certain worlds in disequilibrium, and ours just happens to be one of these.

The problem with Boltzmann's daring Many Worlds hypothesis was that if our world were merely a fluctuation in a sea of diffuse energy, then it is overwhelmingly more probable that we should be observing a much tinier region of disequilibrium than we do. In order for us to exist, a smaller fluctuation, even one that produced our world instantaneously by an enormous accident, is inestimably more probable than a progressive decline in entropy to fashion the world we see. In fact, Boltzmann's hypothesis, if adopted, would force us to regard the past as illusory, everything having the mere appearance of age, and the stars and planets as illusory, mere "pictures" as it were, since that sort of world is vastly more probable given a state of overall equilibrium than a world with genuine, temporally and spatially distant events. Therefore, the scientific community has universally rejected Boltzmann's Many Worlds hypothesis, and the present disequilibrium is usually taken to be just a result of the initial low entropy condition mysteriously obtaining at the beginning of the universe.

Now a precisely parallel problem attends the Many Worlds hypothesis as an explanation of fine-tuning. Roger Penrose calculates that the odds of our universe's low entropy condition obtaining by chance alone are on the order of $1:10^{10^{(123)}}$, an inconceivable number. If our universe were but one member of a collection of randomly ordered worlds, then it is vastly more probable that we should be observing a much smaller universe.[30] The odds of our solar system's being formed instantly by random collisions of particles is, according to Penrose, about $1:10^{10(60)}$, a vast number, but inconceivably smaller than $10^{10(123)}$. (Penrose calls it "utter chicken feed" by comparison.) Adopting the Many Worlds hypothesis to explain away fine-tuning would thus result once more in a strange sort of illusionism: it is far more probable that all our astronomical, geological, and biological estimates of age are wrong and that the universe's appearance of age is a massive illusion. Some cosmologists have, in melodramatic language reminiscent of grade-B horror movies of the 1950s, dubbed this problem "the return of the Boltzmann brains."[31] For the most probable state that is adequate to support our ordered observations is a "universe" consisting of a single brain which appears out of the disorder via a thermal fluctuation. Boltzmann brains are much more plenteous in the ensemble of observable universes than ordinary observers, and, therefore, each of us ought to think that he is himself a Boltzmann brain if he believes that the universe is but one member of an ensemble of worlds.

Or again, if our universe is but one member of a World Ensemble, then we ought to be observing highly extraordinary events, like horses popping into and out of existence by random collisions, or perpetual motion machines, since these are vastly more probable than all of nature's constants and quantities falling by chance into the virtually infinitesimal life-permitting range. Observable universes like those are much more plenteous in the ensemble of universes than worlds like ours and, therefore, ought to be observed by us if the universe were but one member of an ensemble of worlds. Since we do not have such observations, that fact strongly disconfirms the multiverse hypothesis. On naturalism, at least, it is therefore highly probable that there is no World Ensemble.

For these reasons the Many Worlds hypothesis is severely disabled as a candidate for the best explanation of the observed cosmic fine-tuning. Since the alternative of chance stands or falls with the Many Worlds hypothesis, that explanation does not commend itself.

It therefore seems that the fine-tuning of the universe is plausibly due neither to physical necessity nor to chance. It follows that the fine-tuning is therefore due to design, unless the design hypothesis can be shown to be even more implausible than its competitors.

The implication of the design hypothesis is that there exists a Cosmic Designer who fine-tuned the initial conditions of the universe for intelligent life. Such a hypothesis supplies a personal explanation of the fine-tuning of the universe. Is this explanation implausible? Detractors of design sometimes object that on this hypothesis the Cosmic Designer himself remains unexplained. It is said that an intelligent Mind also exhibits complex order, so that if the universe needs an explanation, so does its

Designer. If the Designer does not need an explanation, why think that the universe does?

This popular objection is based on a misconception of the nature of explanation. It is widely recognized that in order for an explanation to be the best, one need not have an explanation of the explanation (indeed, such a requirement would generate an infinite regress, so that everything becomes inexplicable). If astronauts should find traces of intelligent life on some other planet, for example, we need not be able to explain such extraterrestrials in order to recognize that they are the best explanation of the artifacts. In the same way, the design hypothesis's being the best explanation of the fine-tuning does not depend on our being able to explain the Designer.

Moreover, the complexity of a Mind is not really analogous to the complexity of the universe. A mind's *ideas* may be complex, but a mind itself is a remarkably simple thing, being an immaterial entity not composed of pieces, or separable parts. Moreover, properties like intelligence, consciousness, and volition are not contingent properties that a mind might lack, but are essential to its nature. Thus, postulating an uncreated Mind behind the cosmos is not at all like postulating an undesigned cosmos. Thus, the teleological argument based on the fine-tuning of the initial state of the universe fares well as a sound and persuasive argument for a Designer of the cosmos.

The Axiological Argument

Many philosophers have argued that if God does not exist, then morality is wholly subjective and nonbinding. On the other hand, if we do believe that moral values and duties are objective, that provides moral grounds for believing in God. We should thus have an axiological argument for the existence of God.

According to classical theism, objective moral values are rooted in God. To say that there are objective moral values is to say that something is right or wrong independently of whether any human being believes it to be so. It is to say, for example, that Nazi anti-Semitism was morally wrong, even though the Nazis who carried out the Holocaust thought that it was good; and it would still be wrong even if the Nazis had won World War II and succeeded in exterminating or brainwashing everybody who disagreed with them. On classical theism God's own holy and perfectly good nature supplies the absolute standard against which all actions and decisions are measured. God's moral nature is what Plato called the "Good." God is the locus and source of moral value. God is by nature loving, generous, just, faithful, kind, and so forth.

Moreover, God's moral nature is expressed in relation to us in the form of divine commands that constitute our moral duties or obligations. Far from being arbitrary, these commands flow necessarily from God's moral nature. On this foundation we can affirm the objective goodness and rightness of love, generosity, self-sacrifice, and equality, and condemn as objectively evil and wrong selfishness, hatred, abuse, discrimination, and oppression.

Now if God does not exist, then what is the foundation for moral values? More particularly, what is the basis for the value of human beings? Although Dennett claims to be a moral realist, it is extraordinarily difficult to discern what foundation exists on his naturalistic worldview for such an affirmation. If God does not exist, then it is difficult to see any reason to think that human beings are special or that their morality is objectively valid. At the conference in New Orleans at which these papers were presented, Dennett opened his lecture by showing a short film that encapsulated what he wanted to convey. It showed a group of young African men playing with a soccer ball, kicking it into the air and adroitly catching it on their feet in quite amazing ways, while never letting the ball touch the ground. Meanwhile a silent narration played across the screen, describing the unfathomable vastness of the cosmos in space and time and contrasting the tininess and brevity of human existence. We are here for a mere twinkling of the eye and then gone forever. The punch line of the film finally came: "We'd better not blow it." That was the end. But what does it mean on a naturalistic worldview to "blow it"? If there is no objective purpose for the human race, then how can one miss that purpose? "Blowing it" is an evaluative notion that finds no foothold in an atheistic universe. The boys' skill and evident joy in playing football is no more valuable a pursuit on atheism than some other kid's staying home and drinking himself into a stupor.

Moreover, why think that we have any moral obligations to do anything? Who or what imposes any moral duties upon us? Philosopher of science Michael Ruse writes,

> The position of the modern evolutionist . . . is that humans have an awareness of morality . . . because such an awareness is of biological worth. Morality is a biological adaptation no less than are hands and feet and teeth. . . .
>
> Considered as a rationally justifiable set of claims about an objective something, ethics is illusory. I appreciate that when somebody says "Love they neighbor as thyself," they think they are referring above and beyond themselves. . . . Nevertheless, . . . such reference is truly without foundation. Morality is just an aid to survival and reproduction, . . . and any deeper meaning is illusory. . . .[32]

As a result of sociobiological pressures, there has evolved among *Homo sapiens* a sort of "herd morality" that functions well in the perpetuation of our species in the struggle for survival. But there does not seem to be anything about *Homo sapiens* that makes this morality objectively binding. If the film of evolutionary history were rewound and shot anew, very different creatures with a very different set of values might well have evolved. By what right do we regard our morality as objective rather than theirs?

If there is no God, then any ground for regarding the herd morality evolved by *Homo sapiens* as objectively true seems to have been removed. Human beings are just accidental by-products of nature that have evolved relatively recently on an infinitesimal speck of dust lost somewhere in a hostile and mindless universe, and that are doomed to perish individually and collectively in a relatively short time. Some action, say, rape, may not be socially advantageous and so in the course of human evolution has become taboo; but on the atheistic view it is difficult to see why there is really anything really *wrong* about raping someone. Crudely put, on the atheistic view human beings are just animals; and animals are not moral agents.

Now it is important that we remain clear in understanding the issue before us. The question is *not*, Must we believe in God in order to live moral lives? There is no reason to think that atheists and theists alike may not live what we normally characterize as good and decent lives. Similarly, the question is *not*, Can we formulate a system of ethics without reference to God? If the nontheist grants that human beings do have objective value, then there is no reason to think that he cannot work out a system of ethics with which the theist would also largely agree. Or again, the question is *not*, Can we recognize the existence of objective moral values without reference to God? The theist will typically maintain that a person need not believe in God in order to recognize, say, that we should love our children. Rather, as humanist philosopher Paul Kurtz puts it, "The central question about moral and ethical principles concerns their ontological foundation. If they are neither derived from God nor anchored in some transcendent ground, are they purely ephemeral?"[33]

Some philosophers, equally averse to transcendently existing moral values as to theism, try to maintain the existence of objective moral principles or supervenient moral properties in the context of a naturalistic worldview. But the advocates of such theories are typically at a loss to justify their starting point. If there is no God, then it is hard to see any ground for thinking that the herd morality evolved by *Homo sapiens* is objectively true or that the property of moral goodness supervenes on certain natural states of such creatures. If our approach to meta-ethical theory is to be serious metaphysics rather than just a "shopping list" approach, whereby one simply helps oneself to the supervenient moral properties or principles needed to do the job, then some sort of explanation is required for why moral properties supervene on certain natural states or why such principles are true. It is insufficient for the naturalist to point out that we do, in fact, apprehend the goodness of some feature of human existence, for that only goes to establish the objectivity of moral values and duties, which just is the second premise of the axiological argument.

Some philosophers seem to suppose that moral truths, being necessarily true, cannot have an explanation of their truth.[34] But the crucial presupposition here—that necessary truths cannot stand in relations of explanatory priority to one another—is not merely not evidently true, but seems plainly false. For example, the proposition *A plurality of persons exists* is necessarily true (in a broadly logical sense) because *God exists* is necessarily true and God is essentially a Trinity. To give a nontheological example, on a nonfictionalist account *2+3=5* is necessarily true because the Peano axioms for standard arithmetic are necessarily true. Or again, *No event precedes itself* is necessarily true because *Temporal becoming is an essential and objective feature of time* is necessarily true. It would be utterly implausible to suggest that the relation of explanatory priority obtaining between the relevant propositions is symmetrical.

We therefore need to ask whether moral values and duties can be plausibly anchored in some transcendent, nontheistic ground. Let us call this view *atheistic moral realism*. Atheistic moral realists affirm that objective moral values and duties do exist and are not dependent upon evolution or human opinion, but they insist that they are not grounded in God. Indeed, moral values have no further foundation. They just exist.

It is difficult, however, even to comprehend this view. What does it mean to say, for example, that the moral value *justice* just exists? It is hard to know what to make of this. It is clear what is meant when it is said that a person is just; but it is bewildering when it is said that in the absence of any people, justice itself exists. Moral values seem to exist as properties of persons, not as mere abstractions—or at any rate, it is hard to know what it is for a moral value to exist as a mere abstraction. Curiously, since the abstract object *justice* is not itself just, it would seem to follow that in the absence of any people justice does not exist—which seems to contradict the hypothesis. Atheistic moral realists seem to lack any adequate foundation in reality for moral values but just leave them floating in an unintelligible way.

Second, the nature of moral duty or obligation seems incompatible with atheistic moral realism. Let us suppose for the sake of argument that moral values do exist independently of God. Suppose that values like mercy, justice, love, forbearance, and the like just exist. How does that result in any moral obligations for me? Why would I have a moral duty, say, to be merciful? Who or what lays such an obligation on me? On this view moral vices such as greed, hatred, and selfishness also presumably exist as abstract objects, too. Why am I obligated to align my life with one set of these abstractly existing objects rather than any other?

In contrast with the atheist, the theist can make sense of moral obligation because God's commands can be viewed as constitutive of our moral duties. As the ethicist Richard Taylor points out, "A duty is something that is owed. . . . But something can be owed only to some person or persons. There can be no such thing as duty in isolation. . . ."[35] God makes sense of moral obligation because God's commands constitute for us our moral duties. Taylor writes,

> Our moral obligations can . . . be understood as those that are imposed by God. . . . But what if this higher-than-human lawgiver is no longer taken into account? Does the concept of a moral obligation . . . still make sense? . . . The concept of moral obligation [is] unintelligible apart from the idea of God. The words remain but their meaning is gone.[36]

As a nontheist, Taylor therefore thinks that we literally have no moral obligations, that there is no right or wrong. The atheistic moral realist rightly finds this abhorrent, but, as Taylor clearly sees, on an atheistic view there simply is no ground for duty, even if moral values somehow exist.

Third, it is fantastically improbable that just that sort of creature would emerge from the blind evolutionary process who corresponds to the abstractly existing realm of moral values. This seems to be an utterly incredible coincidence when one thinks about it. It is almost as though the moral realm *knew* that we were coming. It is far more plausible to regard both the natural realm and the moral realm as under the hegemony of a divine Creator and Lawgiver than to think that these two entirely independent orders of reality just happened to mesh.

Thus, it seems that atheistic moral realism is not as plausible a view as theism but serves as a convenient halfway house for philosophers who do not have the stomach for the moral nihilism which atheism seems to imply.

We thus come to radically different perspectives on morality depending upon whether or not God exists. If God exists, there is a sound foundation for morality. If God does not exist, then, as Nietzsche claimed, we seem to be ultimately landed in nihilism.

But the choice between the two need not be arbitrarily made. On the contrary, the very considerations we have been discussing can constitute moral justification for the existence of God.

For example, if we do think that objective moral values exist, then we shall be led logically to the conclusion that God exists. And surely we do apprehend a realm of objective moral values. I take it that in moral experience we do apprehend objective moral values, just as in sensory experience we apprehend a realm of objectively existing physical objects. Just as it is impossible for us to get outside our sensory input to test its veridicality, so there is no way to test independently the veridicality of our moral perceptions. In the absence of some defeater, we rationally trust our perceptions, whether sensory or moral. There is no more reason to deny the objective reality of moral values than the objective reality of the physical world. The reasoning of Ruse is at worst a textbook example of the genetic fallacy and at best only proves that our subjective perception of objective moral values has evolved. But if moral values are gradually discovered, not invented, then our gradual and fallible apprehension of the moral realm no more undermines the objective reality of that realm than our gradual, fallible perception of the physical world undermines the objectivity of that realm. Most of us think that we do apprehend objective values. As Ruse himself confesses, "The man who says that it is morally acceptable to rape little children is just as mistaken as the man who says, 2+2=5."[37]

Or consider the nature of moral obligation. To all appearances, some moral principles, at least—for example, *It is wrong to torture a child for fun*—are metaphysically necessary, synthetic truths. The international community recognizes the existence of universal human rights, and many persons are willing to speak of animal rights as well. But the best way to make sense of such rights is in terms of agreement or disagreement of certain acts with the will or commands of a holy, loving God.

In summary, we can formulate this argument simply as follows:

1. If God does not exist, objective moral values and duties do not exist.
2. Objective moral values and duties do exist.
3. Therefore, God exists.

The Ontological Argument

The common thread in ontological arguments is that they try to deduce the existence of God from the very concept of God, together with certain other necessary truths. Proponents of the argument claim that once we understand what God is—the greatest conceivable being or the most perfect being or the most real being—then we shall see that such a being must in fact exist.

In his version of the argument, Alvin Plantinga appropriates Leibniz's insight that the argument assumes that the concept of God is possible, that is to say, that it is possible that a being falling under that concept exists or, employing the semantics of possible worlds, that there is a possible world in which God exists. Plantinga conceives of God as a being that is "maximally excellent" in every possible world, where maximal excellence entails such excellent-making properties as omniscience, omnipotence, and moral perfection. Such a being would have what Plantinga calls "maximal greatness." Now maximal greatness, Plantinga avers, is possibly instantiated, that is to say, there is a possible world in which a maximally great being exists. But then this being must exist in a maximally excellent way in every possible world, including the actual world. Therefore, God exists.

We can summarize Plantinga's premises as follows:

1. It is possible that a maximally great being exists.
2. If it is possible that a maximally great being exists, then a maximally great being exists in some possible world.
3. If a maximally great being exists in some possible world, then it exists in every possible world.
4. If a maximally great being exists in every possible world, then it exists in the actual world.
5. If a maximally great being exists in the actual world, then a maximally great being exists.

The principal issue to be settled with respect to Plantinga's ontological argument is what warrant exists for thinking the key premise that maximal greatness is possibly instantiated to be true. It is crucial in this regard to keep in mind the difference between metaphysical and merely epistemic possibility. One is tempted to say, "It's possible that God exists, and it's possible that God doesn't exist!" But this is true only with respect to epistemic possibility; if God is conceived as a maximally great being, then God's existence is either metaphysically necessary or impossible, regardless of our epistemic uncertainty. Thus, the epistemic entertainability of the key premise (or its denial) does not guarantee its metaphysical possibility.

As an intuitively coherent notion, the idea of God as a maximally great being differs from supposedly parallel notions traditionally put forward by the argument's detractors like the idea of a maximally great island or of a necessarily existent lion. In the first place, the properties that go to make up maximal excellence have intrinsic maxima, whereas the excellent-making properties of things like islands do not. There could always be more palm trees or native dancing girls! Moreover, it is far from clear that there even are objective excellent-making properties of things like islands, for the excellence of islands seems to be relative to one's tastes—does one prefer a desert island or an island boasting the finest resort hotels? The idea of something like a necessarily existent lion also seems incoherent. For as a necessary being, such a beast would have to exist in every possible world we can conceive. But any animal that could exist in a possible world in which the universe is composed wholly of a singularity of infinite density just is not a lion. By contrast, a maximally excellent being could transcend such physical limitations and so be conceived as necessarily existent. So Dennett's query, "Could you use the same argument scheme to prove the existence of the most perfect ice-cream sundae conceivable . . . ?" can be answered decisively, "No."

Jordan Howard Sobel, following William Rowe, objects to this appeal to modal intuition by proposing an example of a being that is intuitively coherent but which is in fact impossible if it does not actually exist.[38] He imagines a being that, if it is possible, exists contingently in whichever world is actual. For example, a "dragoon" is a thing which is such that if it is possible, then it exists as a dragon in the actual world. If there are no dragons, then the notion of a dragoon is broadly logically impossible. But we can ascertain that fact only by looking about in the actual world to see if there are dragons. We cannot tell from the concept alone whether dragoons are possible. In the same way, we cannot tell from the concept alone whether a maximally great being is really possible; we can know only a posteriori by seeing if God actually exists.

This objection is crucially ambiguous in its use of the phrase, "in the actual world." When Sobel says that something is a dragoon in a possible world W if it exists in W and is a dragon in the actual world, does he mean by "actual world" (i) whichever world is actual or (ii) this world W^*? If the latter, then W and W^* could both be nonactual. In that case a dragoon seems to be only a notional entity which is just a dragon by a different name. But then it's hard to see the relevance to the ontological argument, for, of course, a contingent being like a dragon exists in more than one, but not every, possible world.

On the other hand, if he means the latter, then I see the relevance to the ontological argument, for a dragoon, if it is possible, will actually exist. But the only way it can be possible is if there are dragons. So we should look around to see. But then I should say that the idea of a being which is such that if it is possible it exists contingently in whichever world is actual, is not as intuitively possible as is the idea of a being that necessarily exists. The latter idea is clear and unproblematic, but the former is not. Indeed, I should say that the idea of a dragoon is intuitively *not* possible. It seems incredible that there should be a contingent being that, so to speak, tracks whichever world is actual so that it exists as a dragon in that world. Only a being that has necessary existence would seem to be such that it exists in whichever world is actual. But the idea of a dragoon seems intuitively not possible.

Dennett objects to the ontological argument simply by asserting, "You can't prove the existence of *anything* (other than an abstraction) by sheer logic. You can prove that *there is* a prime number larger than a trillion. . . , but you can't prove that something that has effects in the physical world exists except by methods that are at least partly empirical."[39] This appears to be sheer arbitrariness on Dennett's part. On a Platonist view mathematical objects like numbers exist, in Plantinga's words, just as serenely as your most solidly concrete object.[40] Dennett himself seems to believe in what he calls "a timeless Platonic possibility of order" which "is, indeed, a thing of beauty, as mathematicians are forever exclaiming. . . . Being abstract and out of time, it is nothing with an *initiation* or *origin* in need of explanation."[41] Dennett insists that *there are* mathematical objects; by Quine's Criterion of Ontological Commitment, at least, Dennett is therefore, like Quine himself, as committed to the existence of mathematical objects as to concrete objects. But if there can be proofs based on "sheer logic" for the reality of mathematical objects, then it is mere arbitrariness to insist that there can be no such proofs of the reality of concrete objects. The point is that such a proof has now been offered in the form of the ontological argument, and it is special pleading on the part of the atheist to allow such proofs for mind-independent abstract realities but not for concrete realities.

Dennett's final gambit is to protest that, even if the ontological argument is sound, the price philosophers like Plantinga must pay,

> for their access to purely logical proof is a remarkably bare and featureless intentional object. Even if a *Being greater than which nothing can be conceived* has to exist, as their arguments urge, it is a long haul from that specification to a Being that is merciful or just or loving—unless you make sure to define it that way from the outset, introducing anthropomorphism by a dodge that will not persuade the skeptics, needless to say.[42]

This paragraph is multiply confused. First, Dennett's claim that such a being would be a merely intentional object contradicts his apparent Platonism with respect to mathematical objects, for on that view they are not mere objects of thought like a centaur or unicorn but actually existing, mind-independent objects.[43] Second, the object proved to exist is neither bare nor featureless. Rather, it is maximally excellent in every possible world and therefore merciful, just, and loving, since these are all of them, moral perfections that must be possessed by a maximally excellent being. Third, there is no dodge at all in the argument. Rather, the property of maximal greatness is given a clear and explicit definition, as Dennett says, from the outset. There is nothing whatsoever philosophically unrespectable about asking whether such a property is possibly instantiated. Finally, whether the argument will persuade the skeptics is just irrelevant to whether the argument is a good one. I suspect that Dennett actually understates the problem here: the ontological argument will probably persuade few open-minded seekers, not to mention closed-minded skeptics. But, again, that only goes to show that the argument will probably not have much utility in evangelism, not that it is a bad argument.

I think that there are significant objections that can be raised to the ontological argument, which I have addressed elsewhere.[44] But with respect to Dennett's arguments, I think we can confidently say that these are not they.

In sum, Dennett's sketchy and casual treatment of the typical theistic arguments does not do justice to those arguments. Rather, his procedure betrays a lack of serious interest in those arguments, indicative of a mind already made up and eager to get on to other things.

4

Despair, Optimism, and Rebellion

Evan Fales

*"I will make all my goodness pass before you, and will proclaim
before you my name 'the* LORD*'; and I will be gracious to whom I
will be gracious, and will show mercy on whom I will show mercy.
But . . . you cannot see my face; for man shall not see me and
live."* —*Exod. 33:19-20, RSV*

I should say straight off that I'm not going to peer into the future of atheism. Prognostication's never been my calling; probably a good thing, since
the batting average of the prophets and sages hovers near zero, and I'm
not so naïve as to think I can do better. Instead, this paper is a meditation
on how life becomes meaningful for those who believe in God and an afterlife, and for those who do not.[1]

When I was a lad of thirteen, I had a sudden insight that solved for me
the puzzle of religious belief. The answer I had found to my question was:
fear of death. People accept religious teachings because it assuages their
fear of dying. I shared that insight with my friend Tom, who wrote a paper
advocating this idea for his English class. The teacher, a deeply religious
man, took offense and gave Tom an undeservedly bad grade.

I eventually abandoned necrophobia as the explanation of religious
belief, in part because I learned that there are a great many religions in
which there is no belief in an afterlife[2]—or at least not in any afterlife
worth writing home about.[3] For the millions of devout followers of these

97

religions, there is simply life—and they get on with it. These are thoroughly sane people who lead thoroughly sane, often satisfying lives. I mention them at the outset to point out that they represent an important alternative to the three attitudes mentioned in my title.

For the Western world, dominated as it has been by Christian ideas, matters are not so straightforward. Christianity takes some pride in historically having offered humankind the hope of a robust life after death. Christians have, in fact, offered a variety of conceptions of the afterlife, not just one. When they first came to hold such views, and how the notion evolved, are difficult to determine. This is not our present topic, but I shall have occasion to make brief mention of the question.

Because we human beings are able to think about our future, have long memories, and form deep bonds of affection with our comrades and family members, facing the fact of death is more difficult than for any other animal species. Nearly all of us fear death. But because our culture is permeated by a religiously grounded belief in an afterlife, loss of faith in God raises the question of death in a different and more anxious way than would be the case if religion had never offered the hope of eternal survival. It is this context that sharpens the connection, for Western believers and unbelievers, between the existence of God, the significance of death, and the very meaning of our lives. It is our religious history that has shaped the three responses to loss of faith mentioned in my title.[4]

I devote the body of this essay to examining these three responses. But first, it is necessary to say something about the problematic phrase, "the meaning of life." What is *it* supposed to mean? As a rough first attempt, we might say that a life is (or is not) meaningful if it is worth living. But worthwhile for, or to, whom? Is worth a matter of subjective appreciation, of being valued, by some person or persons? Or might the question of whether a life is worthwhile have an objective answer, quite apart from what anyone thinks about the matter?

There are innumerable Christians to whom the Christian story of salvation gives a defining sense of purpose and place in the cosmos. There are also innumerable Buddhists for whom the Buddhist understanding of life is equally central and self-defining. Much the same can be said, for populations of varying size, of Islam, Hinduism, Jainism, Taoism, secular humanism, communism, and literally hundreds of disparate religious traditions and cultures.

These are all large ideologies, each offering a grand vision in both theory and practice. Surely the gift of meaning can present itself in more humble guise. There are some who live for chess. For some, stamp collecting is a passion without which life would be a dull, miserable affair. Others are equally passionate about antique cars and—God help us—there are grown men whose lives are consumed by the challenge of computer games or by NASCAR races.

This last case will serve to remind us of the fact that, while any passion can give purpose and satisfaction to a life, not all passions are equal. We judge the worth of a way of pursuing one's life, not just in terms of the amount and intensity of the subjective sense of satisfaction it generates, but by other, nonsubjective standards as well. Some obsessions are unhealthy, even though a person might live and die in happy pursuit of them.

It is trivial, then, that a life might be made meaningful, in the strictly subjective sense, in any number of ways. The limits and boundaries that may constrain the range of such ways is a matter for empirical psychology, not for philosophy. Here I take it we are grappling rather with the question, Can some sense be attached to the notion that a life is or is not meaningful in some *objective* way or respect?[5] That a person's life is subjectively meaningful to him or her might, of course, be an important, possibly essential, all-things-considered component of objective worth. Conceivably, it is the *only* component. But this is by no means trivial; it would have to be shown. Here I shall assert, but not argue for, the view that subjective value—satisfaction, if you will—is indeed a component of the objective value of a life, but by no means the only component.

I am also going to assume, without argument, the ancient view that the best, most worthwhile kind of life involves pursuing the joint tasks of understanding oneself and of understanding one's place within the universe. One difference between stamp collecting and participation in a religious tradition or an ideological community such as, say, secular humanism, is that the latter, but not the former, involves by its very nature such reflective confrontation with the nature of human existence. Further, such traditions recognize, and struggle to help us find ways to come to terms with, those aspects of human existence that threaten to rob us of a sense of the ultimate rightness of things.

One might wonder whether there are features that all these life-affirming traditions have, more or less, in common. If there are such features, features that play a discernable role in the way those traditions provide a sense of fulfillment and worth to human lives, then perhaps they can teach us something general about the conditions human beings require to flourish and lead satisfying lives suffused with some higher—or anyway objective—sense of purpose. This, then, is an important larger question that wondering about the meaning of life can lead us to ask.

But there are also at least two other larger questions that should be distinguished from this one:

1. Does the very existence of human (or intelligent) life have significance, apart from what anybody might think about the matter?
2. Are there facts about the universe that obtain independently of what any human being knows or believes that can give purpose to or create meaning for human life?

I propose these larger questions as a partial explication of what might be meant by the suggestion that there are objective facts that give value to human life.

The questions need some explication. By "significance" in question 1 I mean: either as evidence for something that is intrinsically valuable, or as something that is itself instrumentally or intrinsically valuable. It is not clear to me whether, for example, a theist would want to allow that human life has intrinsic value, apart from the existence of God and God's valuing of human beings. Unbelievers, on the other hand—at least the optimists and rebels—can and typically do affirm the intrinsic value of human life. Theists will typically answer question 2 in the affirmative, for they think that the existence of God, and of certain features of the created order, provide such purposes—though the fulfillment of those purposes may require that humanity be informed of these facts. In fact, many theists go further: they assert that the existence of God, and of God's providence, are *necessary conditions* for the meaningfulness of human life.

In what follows, I shall be exploring answers to questions 1 and 2. I will begin by considering why a theist might believe that human life would be somehow meaningless, should there be no God or divine providence. Here it will be useful to distinguish between what I shall call temporal meaning and ultimate meaning. No theist will deny that life can offer a variety of satisfactions and fulfillments that supply part—a temporal or provisional part—of what it is to lead a fully worthwhile life. But the theist also believes, I think, that when the last and rarest stamp has been collected, when the dictatorship of the proletariat has been superseded by a classless utopia, there remains still a yawning gap between what we have achieved and the fulfillment of our true good, the good without which life cannot have ultimate meaning. Not only will life lack objectively a certain value, but our subjective nature will feel unfulfilled, empty, sadly lacking in something essential.

The most obvious thing that will be lacking, for most Christian theists at least, is eternal existence, or the assurance of an eternal existence, in the presence of God. The importance of this assurance, and of the conviction that it is provided by Scripture, was vividly brought home to me by Billy Warfel, who had been a high-school classmate of mine. I ran into Billy again in my seventeenth summer, at a local tent revival that I went to out of curiosity. Billy was the leader, it turned out, of the local Youth for Christ movement, and our discussion turned to Darwin. After I left that night, it occurred to me that I could prove species evolution if the Bible specified the dimensions of Noah's Ark. It did; and I made a quick calculation that showed the Ark to be not nearly capacious enough to hold all the living species of land animals. Returning the next evening, I put my case before Billy. Billy's response, which made an indelible impression on me, was to look me in the eye and to say, quietly: "I don't see any mistake in your argument. But if I were to accept that there are any errors in the Bible, my life would not be worth living at all."

Billy's sincerity was unmistakable. I let the matter drop. Other remarks he made indicated to me that it was the hope of personal salvation that stood uppermost in Billy's mind. But there is another concern that clearly moves many reflective Christians. It is the concern for justice. As the aphorism has it, the good die young. The good also often endure lives of enormous suffering, while the evil and the indifferent eat, drink, and make merry with ill-gotten gains. How can our deep passion for justice be reconciled with such enduring and pervasive inequities? An answer—I shall presently be examining its moral adequacy—is provided by the Christian story of salvation. (I say "the" Christian story. There are actually several Christian stories, but for the moment I shall simplify.) Setting aside myriad complications, the central thought is that the good receive a heavenly reward that amply recompenses their mortal suffering, while the evil receive appropriate punishment.

There is an intimate connection, I believe, between the thought that only in this way can justice be realized for human beings, and the thought that only if Christian soteriology, or some near neighbor, is true, can human life be objectively meaningful.[6] A necessary—though no doubt not sufficient—condition on a world, if it is to provide an arena in which the requirements of a meaningful human existence can be met, is that it is a just world. Why might this be so? I suggest—but will not argue for—two reasons. One is that justice is so fundamental to our conception of morality and of human well-being that a human existence in which the demands of justice are irredeemably unsatisfied appears to be a fundamentally defective, poor kind of existence. The other is that we think of justice as an *objective* demand, a demand that transcends the self-serving interests of partisans. Hence, we are satisfied with nothing less than that the universe be ordered in such a way that the principles of justice are woven into its very fabric. To believe that there is a God who sees to it that these principles are upheld is to believe that our deepest moral intuitions are upheld by, are in harmony with, the very foundations of the created order. Not only is the universe morally satisfactory; it is a universe in which we can feel welcome. The universe becomes a home to us. The appropriate emotion is joy.

A third conception of what it is for each of our lives—or the existence of humanity as a whole—to have objective meaning holds that meaning requires our existence to be not merely accidental: it requires that our existence fulfills some purposes that are not merely our own purposes. I shall not comment on this idea, except to note that I think it informs some Christian views of what makes life meaningful.

What, then, of the atheist who finds belief in God and in an afterlife to be intellectually unsustainable? An atheist might, I think, consider it hubris to regard life as meaningful only if we can enjoy the prospect of life eternal. An atheist may also plausibly regard it as conceit for us to imagine that our lives can have meaning only if we play some central or important part in the purposes of a master of the universe. But the atheist cannot so easily dismiss the concern for ultimate justice. If there is no just God, then there is no assurance that the manifold wrongs of this world will ultimately be set right, and indeed there is abundant evidence that many of them will not be. How are we to be reconciled to this fact?

An atheist who feels deeply the sting of injustice cannot be happily reconciled to the world; she cannot take whole-hearted joy in the world or feel fully at home in it. For her, the natural response to the problem of unrectified evil will be to feel alienated and forlorn. One response to a godless world is, therefore, what I shall call despair. It will involve a sense of loss, perhaps a longing desire for there to be, or to have been, a God.

I mean the notion of despair in this context to cover a variety of attitudes that mark understandable and defensible responses to a godless, often unjust world. We encounter the stolid, unflinching endurance of Sisyphus in Camus's essay, a determination that gives dignity even as it abandons hope. We might be reminded, too, of Bertrand Russell's grave observation:

> That man is the product of causes which had no prevision of the end they were achieving; that his origin, his growth, his hopes and fears, his loves and his beliefs, are but the outcome of accidental collocations of atoms; that no fire, no heroism, no intensity of thought and feeling, can preserve an individual life beyond the grave; that all the labours of the ages, all the devotion, all the inspiration, all the noonday brightness of human genius, are destined to extinction in the vast death of the solar system, and that the whole temple of Man's achievement must inevitably be buried beneath the debris of a universe in ruins—all these things, if not quite beyond dispute, are yet so nearly certain, that no philosophy which rejects them can hope to stand. Only within the scaffolding of these truths, only on the firm foundation of unyielding despair, can the soul's habitation henceforth be safely built.[7]

On the darker side, we find alienation and moral nihilism, as in Camus's *The Stranger*:

> It was as if that great rush of anger had washed me clean, emptied me of hope, and, gazing up at the dark sky spangled with its signs

and stars, for the first time, I laid my heart open to the benign indifference of the universe. To feel it so like myself, indeed, so brotherly, made me realize that I'd been happy, and that I was happy still.[8]

Happy: but bereft of hope. Bereft, too, and perhaps more frighteningly, of any connection to his fellow human beings, or to the possibility of a moral order.

On the other end of the spectrum, we find despair in a far more sympathetic guise—in, for example, the tragic figure of the heroic priest in Miguel de Unamuno's haunting tale, *Saint Emmanuel the Good, Martyr.*[9] (Indeed, as de Unamuno does not shrink from reminding us, what of Jesus himself: "My God, my God, why hast thou forsaken me?")

What all these figures share is the courage of their convictions and a firm, unyielding commitment to confronting the truth, as they understand it, with honesty. It is this that requires of us, whether we agree with their convictions or not, that we take them seriously. In various ways, each reflects the view that human existence is fundamentally tragic, because the universe is indifferent. Nevertheless, Sisyphus, Russell, and Emmanuel all affirm human dignity, so they are not moral nihilists.

A radically different attitude is possible—the hopeful attitude of the Enlightenment. Religion is not merely a fairy tale, but is allied with the forces of darkness and superstition. To free ourselves from the bondage of religious belief is to unchain the real potential of human reason, heretofore enslaved by theology, and to liberate the human potential to realize those goods that will most truly fulfill the natural and proper ends of humanity. Religion is not merely a hindrance to this great project, but a force that appeals to the most primitive, ignoble of human predilections, and, under the guise of faith, is a stake driven through the heart of reason. Once freed of this scourge, humanity can, with the aid of science and of good will, march forward toward a correct understanding of our universe and toward a moral social order.

This view—which I shall call optimism—commonly combines two attitudes. On the negative side, it commonly considers religious belief to be not only false and even irrational, but also to be morally harmful. On the positive side, it celebrates and reposes confidence in the ability of human reason, human moral instincts, and human affective capacities to achieve those human goods that confer upon our lives all the objective meaning that we can rationally want. There are many exemplars of this optimism. Here, tinged with caution, is a paradigm expression of this view, from the penultimate paragraph of James Frazer's magisterial *The Golden Bough*:

> We may illustrate the course which thought has hitherto run by likening it to a web woven of three different threads—the black thread of magic, the red thread of religion, and the white thread of science . . . carry your eye farther along the fabric and you will remark that, while the black and white chequer still runs through it, there rests on the middle portion of the web, where religion has entered most deeply into its texture, a dark crimson stain. . . . Will the great movement which for centuries has been slowly altering the complexion of thought be continued in the future? or will a reaction set in which may arrest progress and even undo much that has been done?[10]

For the moment, I want to discuss an aspect of the positive attitude of optimism. We shall in due course have to deal with the correlative negative thesis.

Optimism, often flying the banner of secular humanism, sees humanity as the master of its own fate. Often, it also sees humanity as the author of the moral law. This no doubt adds color to the charge, so often laid at humanism's feet, that it cannot explain or justify the objectivity of moral values. Now it is a mistake to think that morality is a matter of mere human invention or convention; but it is equally a mistake to think that morality can have no objective basis apart from the will of God.

That God plays no essential role in most objectivist theories of ethics is hardly news. The theory I favor is a form of naturalism. All complexities aside, there are certain moral truths that apply universally in virtue of certain universal facts about human beings: about our fundamental needs, desires, abilities, and natural ends. We are fundamentally social beings. Many of our personal ends can best be achieved, or can only be achieved, through cooperation with others. These facts, though some of them concern our mental states, are quite objective facts about human nature. They determine, in many respects, how it is rational for human beings to treat one another; and, because we are among other things rational beings, these reasons become reasons *for us*.[11]

The most substantial metaphysical claim that the ethical naturalist makes is, perhaps, the claim that there are objective teleological truths about human beings. That there *are* such truths is not, it seems to me, something that can seriously be disputed. Indeed, not only conscious beings have natural ends. There are, for example, conditions that are naturally good for or harmful to plants. Some theists—Alvin Plantinga, for example—have claimed that the naturalist cannot make good *sense* of the existence of such telic facts.[12] Well, I am not convinced that naturalists have yet made sufficient sense of them; but I consider it far from settled whether this is impossible. In fact—in part because all the evidence from evolutionary biology points in that direction—I put my money on the view that teleological facts about us have naturalistic explanations.

It is important to recognize the bearing of human origins upon the question of the metaphysical status of human ends. If it were true that human beings were designed by a supreme being to have by nature certain ends, then it would be true that, in giving us those ends, God would indirectly have determined the principles of action that properly guide human social behavior. However, it would remain the case that the basis of morality is to be found in facts about human nature. It is a genetic fallacy of sorts to suppose that objective moral truths cannot be justified except by appeal to a divine will, *even if* the ultimate cause of the relevant natural facts is such a will.

The optimistic atheist is not, then, bereft of intellectually reasonable ways of understanding the moral dimensions of human existence as placing objective constraints upon action while respecting—indeed promoting—the human good.[13] But what are the endeavors and rewards that contribute most fundamentally to the kind of meaningful existence an optimist can hope for? Here I suppose the answer is fairly evident. Devotion to family and friends, and to the well-being of all humanity, happy pursuit of one's calling, delight in the beauties of nature and art, commitment to moral ideals and courage in their defense: these are enough to fill a life with worthy goals and satisfactions. They certainly appear to be enough for many of the millions of people who, as I earlier noted, live their lives as nontheists.

Optimism is not without its discouragements. Perhaps the greatest of these, to my mind, derives from the evidence that our moral nature is not well adapted to the construction of equitable, peaceful social arrangements in the large-scale societies and communities of nations that our intellectual adaptations have produced. The theist can perhaps find reassurance that, however great the abundance of evil, God will set things right in the end. From an atheist's perspective, this assurance can actually prove dangerous, since it can, and often does, produce complacency, or worse.[14] Atheism, for its part, can induce a kind of fatalism instead of optimism.

Historically, optimism has often been associated with a confidence in the fundamental goodness of human beings. But because the evidence suggests quite clearly that human nature is a mixed bag, we are better served by realism combined with dedication to making the best of what nature has made us.[15] Because the atheist renounces belief in God and in an afterlife, he cannot look to God to restore the good, either in human history or outside it, in the hereafter. But that, in the optimist's view, makes life infinitely more precious, and the obligation to pursue the good while we can an infinitely deeper obligation.

I have said a few words about what the source for objective moral norms can be for the optimistic atheist. How do matters look on the other side—that is, for a theistic ethics? In particular, how do matters stand for theists who look to the Bible for definitive information on God's moral character and God's will respecting human ethical behavior?[16]

Here we must face a familiar, if painful, story. The God that Christians and Jews worship, the God of Abraham, Isaac, and Jacob, is understood to have inspired the canonical works that comprise the Hebrew Bible and the New Testament. We cannot set aside the manifold difficulties that attend the task of interpreting these ancient texts. As there is no possibility of doing justice to those issues here, I shall confine myself to the observation that many passages appear, at least, to contain straightforward assertions (whatever additional levels of meaning they may possess)—to report historical events, for example, or to convey the will of God. If they cannot be so read, then we must acknowledge that many, indeed probably most, earnestly seeking Christians and Jews have been seriously misled on matters of faith. Let us, then, proceed cautiously but straightforwardly.

It is not difficult to find in the books of the Hebrew Bible and New Testament passages that commend or prescribe praiseworthy, even heroic, moral ideals. Christians, in particular, are commanded, for example, not to pray in public (Matt. 6:1-6), to sell all their possessions and give the money to the poor (Matt. 6:19-34; Mark 10:17-31; Luke 12:33; *et passim*), to be longsuffering and patient (1 Cor. 13:4-7), and to love and benefit their enemies (Matt. 5:38-47)—injunctions that are, I fear, observed more often in the breach than in faithful adherence.[17]

This coin has, unfortunately, another side. For we are told that Yahweh is a severe god. Yahweh is a god who accepts child sacrifice (Judges 11), who personally sacrifices infants and adults alike upon the altar of the sins of their fathers and rulers (for example, 2 Sam. 12:13-24, 24:1-17), who hardens hearts with horrific consequences (Pharaoh's refusal to free the Israelites), who through Yahweh's prophet Moses commands the enslavement and forced concubinage of young virgins who have just witnessed the slaughter of their families at the hands of their captors (Num. 31:1-20).[18]

Confronted with this grim catalogue of crimes against humanity, how are we to respond? It's no good saying that many of these records are probably ahistorical. That may be; but it does not diminish the horror of the claims the stories make concerning God's character. Apologetics are really out of order here; better that people of faith should in silence cover their heads with ashes. The apologist otherwise runs the risk of losing his or her moral bearings altogether. More than one Christian has explained to me that, when God ordered the slaughter of even the children of the Amalekites (1 Sam. 15:3f.), it was because, though innocent, they would grow into sinful adults—a reasoning that echoes all too closely

the argument made by an opponent of the Wagner-Rogers bill, introduced during WWII, to provide temporary haven in the United States
for twenty thousand Jewish children from Europe: ". . . twenty thousand
children would soon grow into twenty thousand ugly adults." The bill was
defeated in Congress.

But some Christians take consolation in the thought that the God of
the New Testament is a kinder, gentler god. And, indeed, with a few exceptions (such as the murder of Ananias and Sapphira for withholding money
promised to the church and then lying about it), there are fewer special
acts of divine retribution that scandalize our moral sensibilities. There are,
to be sure, some injunctions that surprise and disturb, such as Jesus' strident demand that one hate one's family (Luke 14:25; Matt. 8:21, 10:34; *et
passim*).[19] More worrisome is the blanket condemnation of those who do
not accept the lordship of Jesus or the Holy Spirit, which consigns to eternal suffering a great mass of humankind (Matt. 12:30-32, 25:14-46; John
14:6). Beside this holocaust, the depredations inflicted by Israel upon its
neighbors pale in comparison, even if the goats are unerringly separated
from the sheep.[20]

These are, however familiar, criticisms that are perhaps too facile. It
would be interesting to pursue more deeply such questions as why Jesus
might have had such a deep animus toward family solidarity, but that would
take me too far afield. Instead, I want to raise another problem that lies at
the heart of Christian soteriology. For it is not easy to make moral sense of
the doctrine of vicarious atonement. The question is not merely whether
it is *only* through the voluntary death of Jesus on the cross that human
beings can be brought into a right relationship with God,[21] but whether
this sacrifice can have any salvific force *at all.* This is, moreover, a *moral*
question, as it is a question of restoring allegedly fallen human beings to a
condition morally proper for communion with God.

Our task is made more complex by the fact that Christians themselves
have been perplexed by the notion of vicarious atonement, and have been
unable to decide upon a single account of it. Some atonement theories,
for example, emphasize the doctrine of original sin, others do not. But let's
first consider that doctrine, which, I take it, is akin to doctrines of collective responsibility. Collective *guilt* is intelligible in a situation where human
beings act as a group, where the responsibility of individuals cannot effectively be identified or disentangled from that of others, and where individuals have voluntarily joined the group and accepted joint responsibility
for collective action. Collective *responsibility* for a group's action can sometimes intelligibly be assigned even to individuals who are not voluntarily
members of the group or partisans to its action, but it is hard to see how
moral guilt can properly be assigned to such individuals. Thus, I am unable
to make moral sense of the doctrine of original sin.

Some theories of atonement—for instance, substitution and sacrifice theories—have historically been propounded on the basis of legal theories. For example, substitution theories hold that Christ's sacrifice pays off an infinite debt that each of us owes to God by virtue of having disobeyed God. The debt is infinite, even for peccadillos, because the debt is proportional to the insult, which is proportional to the (infinite, in this case) difference in status of creature and Creator. Now to be sure, there may be a sense in which we owe God more respect than we owe our fellow creatures, but it is not easy to see in what sense we owe God *infinite* respect, or how disobedience insults the divine honor infinitely.

Indeed, this idea, defended most notably by St. Anselm, runs counter to a principle several times attested in the Bible (Deut. 10:17; Job 32:21, 34:19; Prov. 24:23; Matt. 22:16; *et passim*): that God "does not regard the position of humans." Though this phrasing is a bit odd, the meaning is clear: all are equal before God; it makes no difference whether one's station is high or low. That surely conflicts with Anselm's suggestion that the same offense is more grievous committed against a lord than against a peasant. But perhaps an offense committed against *God* is more grievous, because God's station is *infinitely higher* than the lord's. But that doesn't seem right: if station makes no difference when it comes to human persons, why should it for God? Indeed, insofar as a sin is an offense against God, it is a *victimless crime*; for mere humans cannot harm God.

Richard Swinburne is a contemporary defender of a sacrifice theory. Here I shall take note of just two features of Swinburne's defense of the theory. First, Swinburne suggests that the gravamen of the offenses each of us has committed against God is so serious that nothing less than (and possibly something more than) being hung on the cross would be our just desserts.[22] That seems frankly preposterous. No doubt the suffering of the cross would make a suitable punishment for a Hitler or a Stalin, but how many of us would consider justice done if our neighbor were to suffer such a fate?

My second objection concerns the economics of sacrifice. As Swinburne sees it, none of us has the resource—a pure unblemished life—to offer to God as a suitable sacrifice that can satisfy the penance and reparations we owe to God. There's nothing for it, then, if reparation is to be paid, but that God supply each of us with a worthy sacrifice to offer up to God: the sinless life of Jesus. To be sure, there's nothing stopping God from simply forgiving each of us our sins. Swinburne acknowledges this. What he does not recognize is that this is plainly what a good God *should* do. Not only would the terrible suffering of an innocent have been spared, not only would God's mercy have shone more brightly, but the business of offering us a sacrifice we then return to God would be unnecessary. Swinburne offers an analogy in explanation. A child breaks a window, and has no money with which to make restitution to the parent. But the parent steps in; the parent's solicitude for the child impels him or her to give the child the funds with which to satisfy the debt. It is hard to see this as other than a *charade*, a mock restitution that does not respect either the child or the significance of the offense. Very few parents, I am sure, would have recourse to such a handling of the situation. It is far more satisfactory to explain to a child the nature of what he or she has done, to invite remorse, and then to forgive.

It is even harder to see how a sacrifice, however high its value, can make God whole again with respect to our insult. After all, it is *our* moral orientation that God presumably cares about. Sacrifice theories do not respect the autonomy of agents. If my tree falls on your house in a storm, I can make restitution to you, and that's the end of it, precisely because there is no question of *the tree itself* having to be restored to a proper moral relationship with you. But we are not straying trees. I may be thankful that the burden of punishment has been lifted off my shoulders, but how can I be happy that someone else has—even voluntarily—unjustly suffered my just desserts?

Substitution theories have an even harder task of squaring atonement with our understanding of moral guilt. These theories, as I understand them, propose that Christ literally takes upon himself our sins, without thereby becoming sinful, and expiates them by suffering on the cross. But this is morally unintelligible. You can no more bear my guilt than you can author my acts. It is also morally repugnant that another should suffer, even voluntarily, to absolve me of wrongdoing. Moreover, it teaches us that we are morally helpless in the face of a depravity that our own efforts cannot control or master.[23] In addition, both substitution and sacrifice theories presuppose God's commandments to be so clearly and unambiguously published, and the divine nature to be so unimpeachable, that deviation is culpable. But this will not withstand examination.

Moral exemplar theories of atonement avoid some of the shortcomings of substitution and sacrifice theories, but they have moral difficulties of their own. Robin Collins and Marilyn Adams have proposed versions of this view that emphasize the role of Jesus' life and suffering death in enabling finite human beings to achieve union with God.[24] In Collins's case, God had to become manifest in a finite, yet perfectly loving, human being in order for us to be able to participate in the life of God. Adams believes that by suffering horrendous evil personally, in the Passion of Jesus, God is able to convey divine solidarity with us in a way that can make meaningful, in the end, humanity's own participation in horrendous evil.

I cannot do justice to these theories here, but I want to indicate why I find both of them baffling. Neither theory can show, to begin with, why it is *necessary* for salvation that God made the divine self manifest in the unique person of Jesus. After all, *any number* of stories might have the power to bring one or another of us close to God. Second, and more seriously, I do not see how these theories explain the necessity of the cross and the resurrection. The fact that someone is willing to die on my behalf is, certainly, a powerfully meaningful testimony to love—if I can make sense of how this death works on my behalf. Solidarity itself can give life meaning. But if I lose my hand in an accident, I do not wish that my best friend cut off his own hand in solidarity. The Dani tribespeople of Papua New Guinea practice chronic low-level warfare. When a man is killed, close female relatives amputate one of their fingers. Though I find a certain poignancy in this, I do not think it a good rule of thumb.

In moral exemplar theories, Jesus' life does not wash away the stain of sins past, but leads us toward reformation of our character. This is a congenial thought. It would carry greater weight were there evidence within Christendom of greater moral purity and courage than we find in the general run of humanity.[25] Because there is not, as nearly as I can judge, I think we should be skeptical that the example of Jesus' life has been as effective as might be hoped.

These are some of the reasons to doubt the moral acceptability of the notion of vicarious atonement. But what of the resurrection? Does it not hold out the promise of ultimate justice?[26] Supposing that Jesus' Passion could somehow pave the path to heaven for the faithful, will the moral balance of the universe have been fully preserved? I cannot see this. Even if hell could provide just punishment, and heaven abundant reward, how do those rewards wipe away injustice once done with divine acquiescence?

In Fyodor Dostoyevsky's *The Brothers Karamazov*, Ivan Karamazov tells the story of the serf boy who, before his mother's eyes, is torn to pieces by the master's hounds because he accidentally hurt one of them. Ivan insists that the little boy's mother dare not forgive the master on behalf of the boy. Can the boy, in heaven, forgive the master? Indeed he can; and let us suppose that restores community between boy and man. Can it, however, undo the injustice, make things as if it had not happened?[27].

Suppose a scientist has discovered a promising cure for some serious and widely occurring disease. To prove it out, he must perform an experiment upon a human subject. There is a substantial risk that, even if the experiment is successful, the subject will lose her hearing. The scientist can find no suitable volunteer; in desperation, he kidnaps someone and forcibly performs the experiment. It is successful, but the subject loses her hearing. To make it up to the subject, the scientist (who has a large grant), gives the subject her fondest wish: the chance to enjoy the rest of her life in comfort on Bermuda. The subject, in retrospect, regards the reward to have been worth the price. Shall we say that the scientist acted justly?

Consider Job. When Job calls upon the Lord to explain his suffering, God's response is startling. God blusters and swaggers, demeaning Job, deriding Job's paltry understanding, and magnifying God's own. What God does not do is to summon the moral courage to tell Job about the diabolical wager that is the real cause of his suffering. But, in the end, God restores to Job health, wealth, and children. And what of the children Job has lost? Is Job happy? I cannot improve upon Elie Wiesel:

> Therefore we know that in spite of or perhaps because of appearances, Job continued to interrogate God. By repenting sins he did not commit, by justifying a sorrow he did not deserve, he communicates to us that he did not believe in his own confessions; they were nothing but decoys. Job personified man's eternal quest for justice and truth—he did not choose resignation. Thus he did not suffer in vain; thanks to him, we know that it is given to man to transform divine injustice into human justice and compassion.[28]

One of the most profound differences in religious sensibility between Judaism and Christianity—if I may be permitted to speak in such general terms—is the way in which the relationship between human beings and God is conceived. Wiesel can write a play in which three *Purimspieler* put God on trial.[29] Marilyn Adams, in contrast, sounds a recurrent Christian note: "The metaphysical gap between God and creatures means that however mature adult human agency may seem in relation to other human beings, it never gets beyond (up to?) the infantile stage in relation to the Divine."[30] Is Adams suggesting, then, that, in the face of horrendous and inscrutable evils, in the face of a Bible that seems to mock our most fundamental moral convictions, in the face, above all, of our "infantile" inability to make moral sense of either, we are to remain in silent, indeed loving, submission to an incomprehensible deity?[31]

The infantilization of humankind in relation to God is one of the most disturbing features of Christian religious sensibility, especially in the context of moral judgment. It is asked of us to accept, or construct an apology for, moral horrors that Scripture attributes *to God*. In an essay on faith and reason, John Locke rightly observes that accepting as true revelation doctrines that contradict sense and reason would be to overthrow the very faculties that anchor belief in truth. Locke's point can be extended to doctrines that overthrow our deepest moral intuitions, as J. S. Mill pointed out.[32] Jesus tells us (Matt. 11:30) that his yoke is easy. But this yoke is not easy; indeed, I do not understand how it is possible to bear.[33]

For her part, the self-respecting unbeliever asks for nothing more—and nothing less—than the right and the responsibility to atone for her own failings, as best she can. Many of us, perhaps, have much to answer for. I certainly include myself. There is nothing for it but to make the best amends we can, and to resolve not to err again. We are not creatures so flawed that this is too much to expect from ourselves. It ill serves moral courage to so exaggerate our depravity and discount our capacity for self-correction as to make that task appear futile.

Those who essay to judge God face a thankless task. They are naturally accused of the sin of pride. When it is moral sanity that hangs in the balance, this is perhaps a sin one could be proud of. But it is not a matter of pride. It is a matter of defending human decency, at the price of revolt if necessary. Whether it is nobler to "return the ticket" to heaven, as Ivan does, to try with Oedipus to outwit the Fates, or, like defiant Captain Ahab, to take arms against a sea of troubles, I shall not judge; but what gives dignity to all of these is rebellion against a divine order both inhuman and inhumane.[34]

Rebellion requires belief that there be someone against whom to rebel. So it is not a cogent attitude for an atheist. But an atheist may still consider some of the attitudes of revolt to be appropriate, either as a way of expressing alienation from the indifference of the cosmos to human anguish, or as a counterpoint to religious belief, or conditionally, as the attitude that would be appropriate, if the God of Scripture were to exist.[35]

Whether unbelief yields an attitude of despair (or even resignation), of optimism, or of rebellion depends in part, as noted, upon whether one lacks belief that there is a god, or, believing that there is, lacks belief *in* that god. Many unbelievers, I am sure, find themselves drawn to more than one of these possibilities.[36] I myself feel strongly the tug of all three. But, if there *is* a God, and that God is the God of Abraham, Isaac, Jacob, and Jesus, then I affirm that there is one stance that is legitimate and justified. It is rebellion.

Some apologists tell us that God remains hidden from us so as not to coerce our worship. But God is not hiding out of solicitude for our freedom. We have not forgotten Job: therefore, we understand that God is hiding out of cowardice. God is in hiding because God has too much to hide. We do not seek burning bushes or a pillar of smoke. No: we wish to see God. Can God stand before us; can God see the face of suffering humanity—and live? *J'accuse.*

5

Getting Scientific about Religion

Hugh J. McCann

My aim in this essay is to assess the extent to which the knowledge claims made by religious believers are subject to appraisal by standards that, in one way or another, may be considered scientific. In what follows I will first discuss briefly why I think this is an important enterprise. I will then take up three different types of claims believers might make, and discuss whether and how they might be subject to scientific evaluation, and what kinds of results the evaluation might achieve. It will be seen that, depending on what kind of claim is being examined, both the appraisal and its outcome can vary greatly. What I will urge, however, is that there may in some areas be more hope for cooperation between scientific and religious outlooks than is often thought, and that where cooperation is less possible, there can at least be coexistence and mutual tolerance.

Two Ways of Getting Scientific

What does it mean to "get scientific about religion"? Actually, this expression can signify two entirely different types of endeavor. The first is that of treating the phenomenon of religion as itself an object of scientific scrutiny: to seek out its historical roots, to explore its manifestations in various cultural settings, above all to examine its social and psychological function, the influence it has on our lives, both individually and collectively.

Viewed in this light, religion is a social and cultural phenomenon much like any other. A good scientist will seek to explain how it got there and what keeps it in place, and to discern and evaluate the influences religions exert on their adherents and on the rest of society. The second type of "getting scientific" is quite different. In this activity, religion is treated as a source of knowledge claims—that is, assertions of what purports to be knowledge—and those claims are subjected to scientific scrutiny, with the aim of discerning their truth or falsity. Now, as we shall see, it is possible to develop different notions of what counts here as scientific scrutiny. But the basic idea should be clear. For if religion is a source of knowledge claims then that is something it has in common with science. And we may wish to know whether and to what extent the claims it makes can be evaluated scientifically, and whether those claims compete with assertions scientists might want to make.

To some this second enterprise will seem suspect at best. On the scientific side it may be thought hopeless to suppose that the claims of religion could ever withstand scientific scrutiny, so that the entire endeavor is a waste of time. And on the religious side some would deem it inappropriate even to subject the pronouncements of religion to this kind of appraisal. The teachings of religion, they would say, are intended for our spiritual betterment, which requires that those teachings be held as articles of faith, not knowledge.[1] Nevertheless, it is this second endeavor that I want to take up here. My reason for so doing is simply that I do not see how we can be scientific about religion in the first of our two senses if we do not also get scientific about it in the second.

To illustrate this point, we need only suppose that I decide to "get scientific" about science itself, but only in the first of our two senses. I might then portray science as an institution that arises out of the needs of humans to feed, clothe, and shelter themselves, to cure their ailments, to develop weapons so they will be safe from attack and empowered to destroy their enemies, and to possess the technical wherewithal to facilitate communication and make possible the various sorts of musical, dramatic, and other entertainments provided by the electronic media. Science has prospered, I might claim, only because of its success as a source of technology to serve these ends, and thereby to preserve social contentment. Science is, if not the opiate of the masses, at least their nanny, and it will survive only so long as it has no competition. But if by waving some magic wand we could provide independently for people's needs and wants—and perhaps also teach them to desire less—then, I might venture to predict, science would melt away like a South Texas snowfall, except of course insofar as it is able to infect other social institutions, such as our educational system.

Now I think any objective person must admit that this assessment misses an important point—indeed, the main point—about science.

Perhaps it is true that ordinary folk are interested in science mostly for what it can do for them. And certainly it is true that the scientific establishment would be far smaller, and its investigations proceed a lot more slowly, but for the technological developments to which they often give rise, and for which we are willing to pay. But even for ordinary folk, and certainly for its practitioners, science is something else: it is a source of knowledge. And it would be valued and pursued for that reason regardless of its technological power. To overlook this is to misread the social and cultural role of science, and to underestimate the forces that hold it in place. So if we want to develop a valid critical understanding of science, to "get scientific" about it, our examination simply has to include an evaluation of it as a source of knowledge claims.[2]

The same goes for religion. It, too, is treated by its practitioners, who vastly outnumber practitioners of science, as a source, or at least a unique repository, of knowledge claims. And it is as much valued for this as for other benefits, such as comfort in the face of life's anxieties, relief from our sense of worthlessness, or reassurance in the face of death. Indeed, without the purported knowledge that religion offers, it could not provide any other benefit. For it is precisely by enabling us to understand the universe and our destiny within it that religion promises to aid us in the business of living. Accordingly, any attempt to understand religion that fails to be scientific in our second sense as well as the first is apt seriously to misunderstand religion's social and cultural role, to underestimate its staying power. Only if the knowledge claims made by believers are subjected to serious appraisal—regardless of the appraisal's outcome—can religion be understood scientifically.

Natural Religion

What, then, can a scientific assessment of religious claims be expected to look like? In part, it would be a matter of assessing how well the claims believers are apt to make about the world square with what scientists are apt to say. But I do not think that is the place to begin, because such an approach is likely to focus immediately on the areas of greatest conflict—as illustrated by the recent argument over evolution versus creation. That kind of discussion is apt to become disputatious, if not hysterical, and hence to under-represent the extent to which science and religion are able to get along together. Rather, I think, the place to begin is with claims of what is sometimes called natural religion—that is, statements whose truth theologians say can be discerned independent of revelation, on the basis of ordinary experience. And I propose to consider as an example the foremost thesis of natural religion: that there is a God.

To say we can tell from our experience of the world that there is a God is, I suggest, to make a claim that is in spirit scientific, at least in this very broad sense: that it tells us that the thesis has empirical force, that the evidence of sensation matters to the truth or falsity of the claim. That this is so is the presumption underlying certain traditional arguments for the existence of God, namely, cosmological and teleological arguments, both of which point to facts of experience as justifying theistic belief. In my view, such arguments are best interpreted as inductive arguments that employ the method of hypothesis: that is, they offer the hypothesis that there is a personal creator as the best explanation for the existence and order of the world. And if we are willing to consider this kind of argument as at least broadly scientific, then it ought to be possible to evaluate the argument in a scientific spirit.

Now there are in general four ways in which an argument that employs the method of hypothesis can be attacked. The first is by questioning the principle of sufficient reason—that is, by suggesting that the phenomenon the hypothesis purports to explain has no explanation at all, that it is just a brute fact. In the present context, that would mean suggesting that the world just is, and that there is no explanation for its existence. I take it, however, that this sort of objection has no place in a scientifically motivated discussion. To my knowledge, no one has ever attacked Kepler's laws on the ground that the movements of the planets may have no explanation at all, or opposed Einstein's theory of special relativity on the basis that the Michelson-Morley experiment may simply have recorded a brute fact that has no accounting. And although in my career I have served as the outside member on a fair number of Ph.D. committees in the sciences, I have yet to see a doctoral candidate taken to task for overlooking the fact that perhaps the phenomena he or she was investigating simply don't have an explanation. There are two good reasons for this. First, the Principle of Sufficient Reason is not a premise in scientific argumentation, since it is not capable of independent confirmation. Second, whether a particular hypothesis explains a phenomenon does not depend on whether *some* hypothesis will work, but on whether *this* hypothesis offers a satisfying account of what is going on, an account that makes us feel we understand. I would urge that the hypothesis that there is a God should be viewed in the same way. Whether it explains the existence of the world depends not on whether we have independent assurance that there *is* an explanation, but on whether the hypothesis can be developed so as to offer a satisfying account of there being a universe, and of the features it has.

But there are more lines of attack to consider. A second tactic would be to argue that the hypothesis that there is a creator God is simply false, for while it may account for the existence of the world, it has other implications that are not borne out by experience. The familiar problem of evil is based on an objection of this kind, according to which the existence, or perhaps the amount, of evil in the world is not consistent with the world's having been created by a God, or at least a God of the kind ordinarily postulated by believers. The discussion that stems from this objection is both extensive and familiar. I shall pass over it here, however, since it is not all that relevant to the dialogue between science and religion. But our last two lines of attack are very relevant. First, it might be argued that although the hypothesis of a God offers some explanation for the existence of a universe, it does not offer a very good one, because it says very little about what sort of universe we should expect a personal God to create. Cosmological arguments seem especially disappointing in this regard; the mere existence of a contingent universe is all that they purport to explain. Teleological arguments are somewhat more satisfactory, since they lead us to expect an ordered world. And in their recent, "fine-tuning" formulation they stress specific points of mathematical refinement that are in themselves very impressive. Even so, however, the hypothesis of an intelligent designer does not enable us to *predict* these details, only to lay emphasis on them once they are disclosed.

We need to remember, moreover, that the mathematical elegance of the universe, or at least the part of it with which we are familiar, has been disclosed by the investigations of scientists, not theologians. This leads to the fourth type of attack that may be mounted against the hypothesis of a creator God. It may be argued that while this hypothesis does have some explanatory power as to the existence and order of the world, far better explanations are available, namely, explanations that treat the universe as evolving over time into the orderly whole of our present experience, in accordance with scientific law. Indeed, regardless of how he feels about religion, a proponent of science may very well want to dig in his heels on this point. Perhaps the approach to evaluating the God hypothesis I have described so far is fairly described as "scientific" in a very broad sense, inasmuch as it does emphasize the importance of evidence. But, our objector might continue, science in the proper sense, the sense manifested in the work of physicists, biologists, cognitive scientists, and so forth, has to be more narrowly defined. It is a matter of precise, often mathematical predictions that can be tested experimentally—which we have just admitted is not easily possible with the general claims of natural religion. But above all, science properly so-called is *natural* science: it seeks to explain natural phenomena in natural terms. The hypothesis of a creator does not do that. It speaks in supernatural terms, of a being whose activity transcends the natural order. Thus, the argument would run, this hypothesis has no place in the enterprise of seeking natural explanations, and it must for this reason be rejected by science proper. A proponent of science may argue, then, not only that the universe can be satisfactorily explained in natural terms, but that this is the only kind of explanation that has a right to be treated as truly scientific.

The conflict between science according to this narrow—and, I think most scientists would say, much more proper—definition and certain religious claims (some of them claims of natural religion and some not) has been at the bottom of a lot of recent controversy. And I must admit to having considerable sympathy for the position that science proper is and ought to be concerned with developing naturalistic explanations for things. Science as we know it evolved out of what was once called natural philosophy, as a discipline concerned with quantitative measurement of the empirically observable. It is not equipped to deal with claims about things not empirically observed, such as the actions of a creator. But there is a corresponding point on the other side: religion is of very little value at helping with the task that science performs so well, that of predicting and explaining in quantitative detail how things go in the world of sense experience. These things being the case, it looks as though both science and religion would prosper best if their respective practitioners could simply stay out of each other's hair. And I want to urge that when it comes to the hypothesis that a creator God is responsible for the existence of the universe, this is very easy to do. For the fortunate truth is that the phenomenon this hypothesis is supposed to explain—that is, the simple existence of the universe—though in one sense the preeminent natural phenomenon, is not a natural phenomenon at all, if by this we mean a phenomenon of the sort that science properly so-called aims to address.

Suppose for a moment that the universe had a temporal beginning, as the best evidence we have still indicates. If so, then the transition from there being nothing to there being something (assuming that idea even makes sense) is not a change in which any *thing* changed, since prior to the universe's appearance there was nothing at all. But that means there is no possibility of mathematical symmetry between the two states—nothing to quantify over, simply because there would be nothing to put on one side of the equal sign. Nor does it make sense to speak of a process, natural or otherwise, that would count as a process of the world's coming into existence. There is no natural process here, because there can be no transitional phase between having nothing and having something. Not only, then, is there nothing about the world's coming to exist to treat quantitatively; there is nothing even to describe, at least in naturalistic terms. Furthermore, essentially the same point would apply if, unexpectedly, the universe should turn out after all to have had a temporally infinite history. In that case, according to theists, the question of why there is something rather than nothing may still be raised, and once again there will be no mathematical symmetry nor any natural process pertinent to the issue, for the simple reason that natural processes have to begin with *something*, not nothing.

If this is correct, then the central claim of natural religion, the claim that there is a God, is one that can be examined in what I described above as a broadly scientific spirit, but not in the spirit of what I have called science proper. We can examine the claim that there is a God in terms of evidence, try to discern what kind of God this might be, and so forth. But we cannot treat these questions as matters for a science concerned strictly with the natural to investigate. There is not space to carry the discussion further here, but I think the same can be said for a lot of the claims of natural religion. If this is correct, then the claims of natural religion constitute a subject concerning which science and religion need not be in conflict, and may even turn out to be mutually informative.

Miracles

But the same is not true of a second kind of claim believers often make, and to which I now turn—namely, claims that speak of extraordinary events that, unlike God and the activity of creation, are very much a part of the world we inhabit. Some of these events come to us from Scripture: for instance, the parting of the Red Sea, or the numerous healings reported in the Gospels. But similar phenomena, healings in particular, are often reported in our own day as well. They are important to believers as demonstrating God's favor, and perhaps at times God's anger. But they can also serve other functions, such as to establish the credentials of someone who preaches a religious message. Let us, then, consider an example of such a claim. Imagine someone with an injury that x-ray diagnosis discloses to be a fractured fibula. Her leg is in a cast, and she is on crutches because it is too painful for her to walk. Being rather devout, she attends her usual church on Sunday where, as it happens, a healing service is held. Returning from the service, she claims that her injury is healed. "I felt the pain go away during the healing service," she says, "and now I can walk"—in proof of which she tosses her crutches aside and stumps around the room a bit. The next day she has the cast removed from her leg, and the injury never bothers her again.

Reports of cases like this are not at all unusual; if you watch the right television programs you will hear of them with a fair amount of frequency. But the events reported *are* unusual, in that they seem to deviate from the normal course of things. It is not unusual for fractured fibulas to heal; but in our example, the healing occurs too quickly. And such events, if real, present a challenge to what I have called science proper, in that they appear to defy natural explanation. Now, it is certainly possible that they are not real: a certain percentage of these cases are no doubt fraudulent in some way. But I think it would be foolish to suppose that they all are. Equally, it seems to me mistaken to suppose all such cases are instances of misdiagnosis, or of some other obvious factual error. So let us suppose that our example involves neither fraud nor factual error. How then should we react to it?

Some might claim that the answer is obvious, that what we have here is a miracle in the sense defined by Hume.[3] That definition requires two things: first, that there be a violation of scientific laws; and second, that this violation be a result of God having "intervened" in the course of nature. This account of our alleged healing seems to me, however, to be highly dubious for two reasons, one religious and the other scientific. The religious one pertains to the second of Hume's conditions. What does it mean to say that, on a given occasion, God intervenes in the course of nature? It appears to mean that on this occasion God plays a stronger hand than usual, that God is directly involved in what takes place rather than standing back from the course of events as God usually does. According to a lot of classical theology, however, this has to be mistaken. Aquinas, to cite just one, believed that God's activity as creator includes not just putting the world in place but sustaining it for its entire existence, so that God is as much responsible for the world surviving another second as God is for its being here at all. And if we think there can be no natural process that accounts for there being something rather than nothing, something like this has to be right.[4] But if it *is* right, then it is not possible for God to "intervene" in the course of events, because God is already as fully involved in the occurrence of everything that goes on as God could possibly be.

Where does this leave us, if we wish to claim what goes on in our example counts as a miracle? Of Hume's two conditions, all that remains is the requirement that what occurs involve a violation of scientific law. But now it is possible to mount an objection from the scientific side. How are we to know that such a thing has occurred? We do not know what all the scientific laws are, especially when it comes to human healing processes, which are notoriously dependent on the psychological state of patients and perhaps even those around them. There appears, therefore, to be plenty of room for the possibility that in religious settings there are principles at work that are not operative in ordinary circumstances, and which would permit the occurrence of extraordinary events without our feeling that the nature of things had been violated. Moreover, if we examine religious tradition we will find little that supports the Humean position on miracles. It is fair to suppose that neither the authors of Scripture nor the characters of whom they wrote had any conception whatever of a scientific law. Yet they had no difficulty identifying what they called "signs," for a sign was simply an event that was far enough out of the ordinary to indicate that, in the context in which it occurred, something of spiritual significance was going on. And much the same goes for contemporary observers. Perhaps some think they are defying science in claiming one or another event is a "miracle," but it is not obvious that this is so even the majority of the time.

It is also important in this context to consider what it means to say a scientific law has been broken. We are apt to think of scientific laws as pieces of (divine?) legislation, out there in some Platonic heaven, to which the world pays subservient obedience. But, of course, they are nothing of the kind. Scientific laws are propositions—or, if you do not believe in such things, then sentences. They exist in our heads and on the pages of our books, and nowhere else. And they rule nothing. Rather, they are descriptions we make of the way things are, of the nature of things. If this is kept in mind, I think it can be seen that there is something very strange about the claim that a scientific law has been violated. It amounts to claiming that the entities involved in the phenomenon in question have ceased having the nature they did and, momentarily at least, taken on a new one. Perhaps there is too much of the naturalist in my bones, but this feels unsatisfactory to me. Rather, I think we should see the nature of things as intrinsically such as to admit of exceptions to ordinary behavior when conditions warrant an exception. And I want to suggest that sometimes those conditions are partly spiritual in nature.

Of course, this idea would have to be found to work by systematic investigation—something of which, as far as I am able to gather, there is regrettably little in this field. Still, if the possibility I have outlined is correct, science and religion might be able to find considerable common ground on the subject of miracles. What I am suggesting is, however, a compromise, and the trouble with compromises is that they are apt to face objections from both sides. So what are the most obvious objections here? Well, on the scientific side the suggestion might be rejected out of hand, on the ground that it stretches the notion of a natural explanation too far. Returning to our example of healing, someone claiming to be a proponent of science might assert that we know from biomedical science how fractured bones heal, and we know that nothing of the kind described in this example can occur. The causes of healing have to be physiological, and neither prayer nor religious zeal has anything to do with physiology. So, the argument would run, either the case did not occur at all, or what did occur has a natural explanation, and that is that.

To this I can only reply that as far as I am able to tell, we simply do not know what this objection alleges we do. One need only look at statistics on life and health expectancy for religious and nonreligious people to see that in one way or another, religious zeal has a great deal to do with physiology.[5] Moreover, I am not claiming that in cases like the example I have given there occurs anything that is supernatural in some strict sense of the term. What I am talking about is simply what is sometimes called the power of prayer. That some such thing exists is indicated by the fact that hospitals are happy to have their patients prayed over, since it can do no harm and seems at least at times to speed the patient's recovery—though it must be admitted that reports of this are often pretty impressionistic. Suppose, however, that they are true, that prayer does sometimes help. And suppose also that when it does help, this is accomplished simply by raising the patient's morale. If so, and if by a "naturalistic" explanation you mean one that falls strictly under principles of physiology, then I submit that even for this phenomenon we do not yet have a naturalistic explanation. For in our present state of knowledge we are unable to say precisely how morale and physiology are related. Now, unquestionably there is some relation between the two—a relation which, once it is understood, ought to enable us to give an account of this phenomenon that most, at least, will consider "natural," no matter what it has to say about religious spirituality. And what I am suggesting is that this may be the tip of an iceberg, a part of a larger phenomenon, in which prayer and piety are able to have significant impact on biological and perhaps other natural events, in ways that we might come to see as an extension of what we currently think of as natural phenomena. It may turn out, of course, that this suggestion is mistaken—and if it is, then well and good. I would claim, however, that in our present state of knowledge, any attempt to rule it out a priori, as our present objection does, is very far from being scientific. Just the opposite; it abandons being scientific in both the senses I have described. It says, in effect, that anything there is to be learned about the subject of physical healing is in its general contours already known, and that any evidence to the contrary is to be ignored. I simply do not see how an objective person can take such a position.

But there is also an objection from the other side to consider. A religious believer might protest that the sort of picture I have presented weakens the notion of a miracle too much, and that unless the requirements of nature being overridden and of divine intervention are kept, miracles lose their theological force. Well, I am certainly ready to be proven wrong on this matter; I would urge, however, that there are reasons for thinking the concern which underlies this objection is largely groundless. We saw above that by sustaining the world in existence God is already directly involved in all that occurs, in which case it would be redundant to speak of God as "intervening." Moreover, it is not possible to take the example I have described as a genuine case of healing and at the same time claim nothing has been overridden. If a fractured fibula is healed in the space of a few moments, the normal healing propensities of bones have to have given way to something else. The difference is just that on the understanding I have suggested, the overriding is owing to the operation of other principles.

Second, it should be remembered that those principles, if they exist, have to do with human spirituality and its effects on the body. Scripturally, this is not at all out of order. In the New Testament, for example, Jesus repeatedly emphasizes the importance of faith to the accomplishment of the miraculous (for example, Matt. 9:22, 17:14-20). And when he is unable to work many signs in his hometown of Nazareth, the failure is imputed to his former neighbors' lack of faith, not to his own or his Father's reluctance (Mark 6:4-6).

It is not scripturally obvious, then, that a miracle requires that God be active in the world in ways God would ordinarily not be. Indeed, in some cases it is far from obvious even that the natural course of events need be overridden. The classic miracle of the Hebrew Scriptures is the parting of the Red Sea, which we are apt to imagine as Cecil B. DeMille portrays it, occurring over a few moments' time. But if we look at the scriptural account we get this:

> Then Moses stretched out his hand over the sea; and the LORD swept the sea back by a strong east wind all night, and turned the sea into dry land, so the waters were divided. And the sons of Israel went through the midst of the sea on the dry land, and the waters were like a wall to them on their right hand and on their left. (Exod. 14:21-22)

Now the description here of the waters being like a wall could be taken literally, but it may be just a figurative reference to the protection they provided. And once we take things that way it begins to look as if there isn't anything unnatural going on here at all. Perhaps, then, all this miracle required was a God who controls coincidences as God controls all else, and a prophet spiritually sensitive enough to show up at the right place at the right time. What makes us hesitant to accept such interpretations is, I think, a fear that if we do, we are giving up the idea that miracles are special manifestations of God's love or favor. But I see no reason to take things that way. If, as believers will often say, every sunrise is a sign of God's favor, then why aren't these events as well? And if they are as extraordinary as they often purport to be, then why should a believer not take them as special instances of God's work in the world?

Religious Experience

I have so far spoken of two kinds of knowledge claims that believers are likely to make: claims about the origin of the universe, and claims about particular events that are held to be wondrous or in some important way different from the ordinary course of nature. And I have argued that it may be possible to handle both types of claims in such a way that science and religion need not conflict. There is, however, a third class of religious knowledge claims about which I am far less certain—namely, claims based on what is usually called religious or mystical experience.

Religious experience is of many kinds and degrees, ranging from a sense of peace or comfort gotten in meditation to what are alleged to be confrontations with, or personal experiences of, God himself. There is no time for an assessment of all that could count, so let us simply take a fairly strong claim of this kind and examine it for a moment. Suppose someone tells us he has had an encounter with God. To simplify things a bit, let's make it someone who has read and agrees with what William James has to say about such experiences, so that he doesn't expect us to believe anything based on his testimony.[6] But for him, he says, the matter is settled: he knows that there is a God because he has learned it from direct experience. Is there a way to approach such claims in a scientific spirit?

In part, I think, the answer is yes, because those who make such statements are testifying to something they say they have observed. So we might try comparing the accounts of people who report such experiences, to see if the experiences they describe have a common content. Now even this project is likely to meet only with limited success, because the content of such experiences is notoriously difficult to describe (ineffable, says James), so that accounts of it vary immensely. But even if we became convinced that the content of such experiences was pretty uniform—and, what could prove a great deal harder, became convinced that the content is what we would expect if indeed the subject were in contact with the divine—what should we conclude? A believer may feel that the experiences are veridical, but a skeptic might think they are simply a common illusion to which religious people are in certain circumstances subject.

At present, I don't see how to resolve this issue in a way that is usefully scientific. It is, for example, no good treating claims of encounters with the divine as hypotheses. Those who have such experiences are not offering us the claim that there is a God as a hypothesis. They are not inferring that there is a God any more than a person looking at her hand infers that there is a hand before her. They are reporting what they allege to be their direct experience. What, then, are we to say? Should such reports be declared uniformly illusory? Surely not on the basis that ordinary empirical experience—experience with the usual five senses—has shown that so-called mystical experience cannot be veridical. Such a claim would be straightforwardly question-begging as to what kinds of experiences we may trust. Moreover, in my limited experience people who report such encounters are apt to tell you that if all the world of sensory experience is an illusion, yet what they experienced inwardly was real. So I see no way for science in the proper sense to address this issue, at least at present, and I don't think the broad sense of being "scientific" outlined earlier can make much progress either.

This failure is, I think, important because I believe that the broader range of religious experience constitutes the heart of the matter when it comes to explaining the phenomenon of religion. What holds religion in place is not arguments for the existence of God, concerning which, after all, debate can always be prolonged; nor is it external signs and wonders, with which few have any experience. It is not even the childlike tendency to believe parents and Sunday school teachers, or a Kantian sense of the sublime at contemplating the starry skies above or the moral law within— though I am sure these last two are important. Rather, it is the compelling nature of religious experience itself that holds things in place. This is not to say that every believer can report experiences of the sort related by a Meister Eckhart or a Teresa of Avila. But I think there is enough of the mystical in the lives of many believers—for example, in the born-again experience of many Christians—to make it the focal reality of religion for those who believe.

A skeptic might reject this, and certainly it can be argued that religious experience in general is an illusion: that believers first believe, and then experience the comforts of belief, and the delusions to which belief can give rise. And perhaps this is right to this extent: that some kind of prior belief or readiness to believe is necessary for religious experience to occur—though I don't know that even this is true. But one way or another, the testimony of people who report religious experiences suggests that they are compelling enough in their content and the way in which they occur that they breed conviction. I think that that conviction is in the end what holds religion and its institutions in place—so that to the extent it outreaches the scientifically empirical, it is simply another *kind* of phenomenon. We can, of course, ignore it if we wish; but in the end, I believe, it must be addressed, and I think it can only be addressed on its own ground.

6

The Twilight of Scientific Atheism

Responding to Thomas Nagel's Last Stand

J. P. Moreland

It is always interesting to follow trends in philosophy, and it is especially significant if one can discern historical patterns of ideas that run parallel in different branches of the discipline. Such patterns invite questions as to whether there is a common driving force underlying them, and if so, what that force is and why it has unfolded as it has.

I think just such a pattern has been unfolding for the last eighty years or so, and if this is correct, it raises some interesting possibilities.[1] Specifically, I think that insights into a specific pattern I will identify shortly allow us to focus our attention on a particular dialectical move whose prevalence and, more importantly, significance across philosophical disciplines thereby becomes apparent. In turn, it becomes clear that natural theologians have a greater duty to rebut or refute this move than may be noticed without locating it as part of that broader pattern and the paradigm crisis it signals.

But I am talking in abstractions. In what follows I shall identify the pattern in question, provide an examination of a dialectical move that is part of a particular incarnation of the pattern in a recent work published by Thomas Nagel, and respond to Nagel's employment of that move.[2]

Naturalism and Emergent Properties

In the first half of the twentieth century, emergent properties were defined epistemologically,[3] and naturalism developed from that definition.

Naturalism was defined in one of two ways. The first is empirically, in which we must eschew most, or at least a relevant range of emergent properties, specifically: normative properties in epistemology, aesthetics, and ethics, and various features of consciousness and the self, for instance, a Cartesian ego and various mental states. The second is ontologically in strict physicalist terms, in which the same result follows except that mind-independent secondary qualities may now be added to the list of forbidden entities. The list of eschewed entities is constituted by those whose appearance cannot be adequately explained by mechanical processes and combinatorial modes of explanation.

My purpose here is not to argue for the fact that each version of naturalism does, in fact, require rejection of the relevant emergent entities, though I believe that (or a somewhat weaker claim) to be the case. I merely note that the evidence for the ubiquitous acceptance of naturalism lies in the pervasive, naturalist pattern of treating such inexplicable entities so that they do not provide evidence against naturalism and, in turn, offer fodder for a theistic explanation.

To illustrate this pattern, consider treatments of consciousness and mental properties/events. In the first three decades of the twentieth century, experimental psychology (allegedly) finished making a clean break with philosophy, though during this period, the philosophical and, indeed, *scientific* conception of the ego and consciousness were clearly Cartesian.[4] Admittedly, during this time, the corrosive effects of empiricism were beginning to undermine belief in classic substances in favor of bundle theories, the result being that the Cartesian ego was beginning to go the way of the dodo. Still, consciousness was clearly conceived in Cartesian terms. But during the 1930s through the 1950s, empiricism morphed into that universal solvent, logical positivism, and the positivist infatuation with operational definitions gave rise to philosophical behaviorism and the analytic reduction of consciousness to body movements or their associated tendencies.

By the beginning of the 1960s, ontological naturalism replaced epistemically motivated positivist naturalism and, accordingly, type identity physicalism came to replace behaviorism as the appropriate naturalist account of consciousness.[5] Certain problems, for instance, multiple realization,[6] caused many to despair of type physicalism, and various attempts to repair it and a wild variety of physicalist versions of functionalism have been in a horse race ever since. And the eliminativists have seen the whole mess as so much wasted time, preferring to replace consciousness (or at least propositional attitudes) rather than trying to reduce it. All these naturalist strategies adopted some form or another of strict physicalism on the grounds that it was the required ontology in taking the naturalistic turn. Unfortunately, there was one small problem with all this: pains hurt and necessarily so. Setting aside thoughts, beliefs, and other propositional attitudes, phenomenal consciousness was a recalcitrant fact for all versions of strict physicalism. So, since around 1990, a growing number of naturalists have opted for some version of emergentism (at least) for qualia: John Searle, David Chalmers, Thomas Nagel, Colin McGinn, and most recently, Jaegwon Kim.[7]

Though I have neither the skill nor the space to justify my belief, I think that the same sort of pattern has occurred in other areas of philosophical investigation: secondary qualities, indexical facts—at least temporal and first-person ones—normative properties in aesthetics, ethics, and epistemology, action theory, and universals construed as abstract objects that can exist without being instantiated.[8]

Consider aesthetics and ethics.[9] Cognitivist realism in both areas was eliminated under positivist pressure and replaced by emotivism (late 1930s to 1940s) or prescriptivism (early 1950s to early 1960s). These moves were later replaced with various descriptivist versions of cognitivism (mid-1950s to late 1980s, though still held to the present). When these were found wanting (they left out the intrinsic normativity of aesthetic and ethical properties), at least some naturalists returned to cognitivist non-naturalist aesthetic and moral realism and made peace with them through different versions of emergentism.

Parallels with naturalized epistemology come readily to mind. In action theory, hard determinism was embraced as an important implication of naturalism, only to be replaced with different versions of compatibilism. And very recently, Timothy O'Connor has initiated what I predict is the beginning of a phase discernibly similar to the process of development in the other areas in which important features of agent causation—for instance, active power, an emergent individual suitably unified to be an enduring continuant—are cashed out in emergent terms that, allegedly, are consistent with a naturalist ontology.[10]

Finally, a similar pattern has occurred regarding universals construed as abstract objects that may exist uninstantiated.[11] Operating within empiricist constraints, in the 1960s naturalist Wilfred Sellars employed a linguistic strategy to eliminate Platonic universals in favor of certain word-tokens he invented. These word-tokens replaced allegedly abstract singular terms (such as "red") with concrete general terms (for example, his unique dot-quote treatment of "red things" as the term ·red-things·) that require quantification only over concrete particulars. Dissatisfied with purely linguistic treatments of properties, naturalists in the mid-1970s to late '80s (most importantly Keith Campbell) tried to restore properties to a naturalist ontology by treating them as abstract particulars and not universals. Around the same time, D. M. Armstrong claimed that a naturalist could quantify over universals as long as such universals (1) are not taken to exist uninstantiated and (2) are pulled back into space and time as multiply located entities. Dissatisfied with these solutions, many naturalists (for instance, Colin McGinn) claim that properties may be construed as abstract objects as long as the only properties that are instantiated are those that characterize straightforward physical facts. As long as abstract objects are well behaved from a naturalist perspective, a naturalist can just add them to her ontology.

I have two comments to make about this pervasive pattern. First, in my view, it was inevitable that philosophers would sooner or later reinstate the entities that went through various attempts to reduce or eliminate them, because the prepattern view of them is correct and the various reductive or eliminativist depictions are not plausible. Second, the return of these entities means that naturalism is taking on water as it adds to its ontology what I believe are naturalistically inexplicable *sui generis* after *sui generis* entities. I agree with naturalist Terence Horgan when he acknowledges, "in any metaphysical framework that deserves labels like 'materialism', 'naturalism', or 'physicalism', supervenient facts must be explainable rather than being *sui generis*."[12]

For present purposes, let's assume I am right about this second observation. I am entitled to this assumption because I am interested in analyzing naturalist strategies that acknowledge it. More specifically, I am interested in criticizing a naturalist pattern of treating such inexplicable entities so that they do not provide evidence against naturalism and, in turn, offer fodder for a theistic explanation. If this latter were allowed, then these recalcitrant entities could be taken as evidence for the existence of God.

Elsewhere, I have criticized such naturalist moves in various areas of philosophical investigation, and I shall limit my focus to an especially important naturalist account, namely, Thomas Nagel's treatment of objective reason.[13] Nagel's account is important not only for its ingenuity, but also because it is an essential component of a naturalist way out. If a naturalist is going to admit into his or her ontology an entity whose existence cannot be explained naturalistically, then he or she must adopt a dismissive strategy that in some way or other shows why it is no big deal that we do not have such an explanation. By minimizing the importance of the absence of such an explanation, the naturalist can block the negative impact of not having that explanation. And if the naturalist can also argue that for some reason or other we *cannot* have such an explanation, then the recalcitrant entity can be taken as a brute fact and avoid being fodder for a theistic argument.

Nagel's Dismissive Strategy

In contradistinction to what Nagel claims to be the self-refuting constructivist, relativist treatment of reason by postmodernists, Nagel takes reason to be absolutely authoritative, universal, objective, necessarily presupposed in all thinking, and such that "there is a natural sympathy between the deepest truths of nature and the deepest layers of the human mind."[14]

So characterized, reason raises a problem: ". . . there is a real problem about how such a thing as reason is possible. How is it possible that creatures like ourselves, supplied with the contingent capacities of a biological species whose very existence appears to be radically accidental, should have access to universally valid methods of objective thought?"[15] And Nagel claims that the main answers to the question are subjectivism, evolutionary naturalism, and theism.[16] Having set aside subjectivism on the grounds that, among other things, it is self-defeating,[17] Nagel seems to be stuck with evolutionary naturalism and theism.

To make matters worse, for various reasons that are not of major concern for present purposes, Nagel admits that it is virtually impossible,[18] even in principle,[19] for naturalism to provide an answer to this question. Briefly, he mentions three difficulties for any such naturalistic project. The first is hinted at above, namely, that the naturalist creation story is so radically contingent (for example, wind the clock back, play it again, and it is extremely unlikely that we would appear again) that it is unsuited to justify something that is universally and necessarily valid. Second, besides being contingent, those evolutionary processes are irrational, brute, non-teleological ones that reward organisms whose faculties serve the interests of reproductive advantage. And being a truth-gathering faculty is not particularly relevant to these processes. Thus, the evolutionary story not only fails to justify the rationality of our faculties, it actually provides a defeater for such rationality.[20] Finally, the nature of intentionality and the mental-world connection is both too odd to fit easily into a naturalist ontology and, in fact, it is too Platonistic, quasi-religious, or, indeed, theistic for a naturalist to embrace without a great deal of discomfort.[21]

As noted, Nagel acknowledges that there is an obvious theistic explanation for the existence and appearance of reason. The fundamental being, God, is himself rational, and God created us with cognitive capacities so that there would be a natural harmony between us and our noetic environment apt for gathering truth and gaining knowledge.[22]

By admitting the reality of an entity that cannot be reduced to or eliminated in favor of physical entities—reason and all that constitutes it—and by acknowledging the inadequacy, indeed, impossibility of naturalist attempts to justify its trustworthiness in human organisms or to explain its origin, Nagel provides the resources for a theistic argument for the existence of God. And he knows it. So Nagel must undermine the theistic alternative, and while he uses different arguments to do so (for example, theistic explanation is merely a placeholder for and not really an example of explanation),[23] the dismissive strategy is his trump card. This provides grounds for dismissing a theistic (and, if successful, any other) attempt to answer the question, and thereby greases the skids for taking the objectivity of our finite rational capacities as a brute fact.

What, exactly, is Nagel's version of the dismissive strategy? It is surprisingly simple: Nagel's solution as to how there could be such a thing as universal, normative, objective reason, along with a fundamental mind-world connection, is simply to dismiss the question by saying that it is self-defeating to seek a justification beyond reason for reason itself. All subjectivist attempts to criticize reason from the outside assume what they deny, and are self-defeating. Similarly, all attempts to use something more basic than reason to justify reason assume what they justify, and such attempts are either self-defeating or vacuous.[24] Rather, reason is its own authority and its validity is universal, so reason is its own justification. To seek further justification for it evidences a serious confusion. Any attempt to explain or justify reason will have to use reason and, thus, it will be pointless. So a naturalistic or theistic attempt at such a justification is attempting what is neither needed nor can be done. Reason just is and that's the end of the story. One must trust his or her cognitively relevant faculties themselves, believing in what reason tells him or her in virtue of the content of the arguments reason delivers. In this way, reason is self-justifying.

Defeaters for Nagel's Way Out

There is nothing wrong with a dismissive strategy per se. Given two rivals, sometimes one will consider a phenomenon basic and not in need of a solution, empirical or otherwise. It may, therefore, disallow questions about how or why that phenomenon occurs and, thus, can hardly be faulted for not providing such an account. As Nicholas Rescher has pointed out:

> One way in which a body of knowledge S can deal with a question is, of course, by *answering* it. Yet another, importantly different, way in which S can deal with a question is by disallowing it. S *disallows* [Q] when there is some presupposition of Q that S does not countenance: given S, we are simply not in a position to raise Q.[25]

Unfortunately, Nagel's specific version of a dismissive strategy is a complete failure. To show this, we need to look at two things: a set of important distinctions Nagel fails to make and an application of these distinctions to Nagel's strategy. First, let's look at some distinctions.

Self-refuting statements (sentences, propositions) exhibit at least three characteristics.[26] First, they are indicative assertions that refer to a group of entities we may call "a domain of discourse." Second, they express conditions of acceptability (truth/falsehood, epistemic justification, real/ nonexistent) that each member in the domain fails to satisfy. Third, the statement itself is a member of the domain.

With this in mind, two distinctions are important. The first is between a first-order statement of a domain and a second-order statement about that domain. Sometimes a statement about a domain is not a member of the domain. For example, the statement, "there are no moral absolutes," is a statement about the domain of moral rules and it is not itself a moral rule, so it is not a statement of, but merely one about, moral rules. Again, if one asserts in German that there are no English statements, then the assertion is not self-refuting because it is not itself a member of its domain of discourse. If the assertion were made in English, then it would be self-refuting. If the second-order statement is not within the first-order domain of discourse, this is sufficient for the statement to be self-referentially consistent.

In the context of self-refutation, another distinction gets at pretty much the same thing, namely, the difference between use and mention. You may use something (language, English, a specific word such as "red," reason, one's own existence, truth) without mentioning it. When that occurs, then we have another case in which the item being used is not a member of the domain of discourse. Only in this case, the surface appearance seems to imply that the item is, in fact, a member of the domain, and by showing that this is not the case, the use/mention distinction has solved a number of philosophical problems.

For example, it used to be argued that the characterization of a universal (for instance, redness) as an entity that all concrete particulars in the relevant natural class (for example, the class of red things) have in common is circular. The argument went this way: (1) What do all members of the class of red things have in common? Answer: Redness. (2) What is redness? Answer: What all members of the class of red things have in common. The argument allegedly showed that this definition of a universal is circular. The solution involved claiming that redness is mentioned in the answer to (1) and used in the answer to (2). The result is this: The term *redness* is the name for what (is ostensibly) defined by the class of red things, and the entity it names is what all those members have in common, namely, the property of redness.[27]

Applied to our discussion of self-refutation, we may say that a second-order claim about a domain uses a particular statement. And if a second-order claim is also a member of the first-order domain of mentioned entities (for example, statements) then the statement is used to mention itself precisely because it is itself a member of the domain of mentioned entities.

In sum, in the relevant contexts and domains, a second-order claim is used to mention the members of a first-order domain. If the second-order claim is not a member of that domain, then it is used and not mentioned. If it is, it is used to mention itself, and it is also self-refuting if it fails to satisfy its own standards of acceptability.

Is it sufficient for a statement to be self-refuting that it be within its domain of discourse? The answer is no. The statement, "All sentences of English are less than fifteen words long," is not self-refuting. Is it sufficient for a statement to be self-refuting that it be within its domain of discourse in which each member fails to satisfy the appropriate conditions of acceptability? The answer is pretty clearly yes, but this admission is not enough to justify Nagel's dismissive strategy, as he seems to assume. *The reason is that we can index to a possible world the relevant referring term in the used second-order statement to prevent that statement from being mentioned.* Consider a possible world w in which there are no English sentences longer than three words. This may be because no one speaks English in that world or because they are just short-winded. Now consider the statement: (3) No English sentences-in-w are longer than three words. We have used (3) to talk about a domain of discourse that includes all and only English sentences-in-w. In this case, (3) is used but not mentioned; (3) is not in the domain of discourse; (3) remains a second-order statement about a domain in which it fails to appear as a member; and (3) is not self-refuting.

Unfortunately, sometimes Nagel fails to distinguish the second-order question when asked in the context of skepticism and subjectivism: (1) "Is reason objective?" from the second-order question(s): (2a) "Could reason have failed to be objective?" or (2b) "How could there be such a thing as objective reason?"[28] On other occasions, he seems to think that because his dismissive strategy works with the first question, it may be applied with equal success to the second question(s). Thus, he says regarding it,

> . . . some things can't be explained because they have to enter into every explanation. The question 'How can human beings add?' is not like the question 'How can electronic calculators add?' In ascribing that capacity to a person, I interpret what he does in terms of my own capacity. And since I can't get outside of *it*, how can I hope to get outside of and explain the corresponding thing in anyone else? . . . Perhaps there is something wrong with the hope of arriving at a complete understanding of the world that includes an understanding of ourselves as beings within it possessing the capacity for that very understanding. I think something of this kind must be true. There are inevitably going to be limits on the closure achievable by turning our procedures of understanding on themselves.[29]

What shall we say in response to Nagel? As a starter, note that (1) ("Is reason objective?") uses reason to mention itself, that is, it is about all cases of reason, including itself. Prima facie, Nagel's dismissive solution works for the first-question case because reason is both used and mentioned. But his strategy does not work for the second question(s) (2a) and (2b) because they implicitly contain indexing and, thus, use reason but don't mention it, that is, they use reason to describe a situation in which reason is not objective or fails to obtain. It is easy to conceive of possible worlds in which there is not such a thing as objective reason. Thus, "Could reason have failed to be objective?" becomes "Is there a possible world w in which there is no objective reason?" Or "Given that there are possible worlds in which reason is not objective and ones in which it is, the existence of objective reason is a contingent fact and we may ask why there is such a thing as objective reason in the actual world."

But, you may wonder, how could reason itself fail to be objective? As Nagel points out, the fundamental principles of reason—the laws of logic—are necessary such that there is no possible world in which they are not valid. The answer depends on what one means by "reason." If "reason" means the truth of the fundamental laws of logic, for instance, noncontradiction, *modus ponens,* then the second-order question(s) is, indeed, pointless, as Nagel points out, whether the modal term is understood as ontological or epistemic.

But if "reason" is understood to refer to contingent aspects of a wider notion of reason or to the faculties of specific organisms in some possible world, then the second-order question(s) is perfectly appropriate. After all, we can easily think of worlds in which, say, induction fails, sensory faculties do not represent the external world accurately, or the "universal and necessary" principles of objective reason are not exemplified. In such cases, we are using reason (in our second-order question[s]) but not mentioning it (in the envisioned possible world). We are using reason to ask: Could there be some possible world w in which the relevant features of reason are not exemplified by entities in w?

It is this second notion of reason that Nagel must rule out if his dismissive strategy is to be successful, but it is pretty obvious that it cannot be so ruled out. At the very least, Nagel has provided no reasons for thinking that w is not a possible world, and I think it is obvious that it is. But the matter does not need to be left there. There are two analogous areas of philosophical discourse that further illustrate the inadequacy of Nagel's strategy.

First, with respect to the question, "Why should I be moral?" there is a distinction between interpreting the question as a first-order one from within the moral point of view (in which case the "should" is a moral "should," the question is pointless, and may be answered only by the vacuous response, "Because it is morally right to act and think morally rightly") versus a second-order one from outside the moral point of view ("How could there be such a thing as the moral point of view? Why is it rational to accept the moral point of view?"). Admittedly, when one asks the second-order moral question, one is no longer operating from within morality, but when one asks the second-order rational question, one is still operating within rationality. Still, the indexing strategy mentioned above provides the appropriate analogy for the dispute about "Why should I be moral?" As we have seen, understood according to the indexing strategy, the question, "How could there be such a thing as a rational point of view?" is an intelligible question that cannot be dismissed.

The design argument provides a second analogous area of philosophical debate. Advocates of the design argument sometimes cite as evidence for a Designer the occurrence of various factors necessary for the existence of life (for example, universal fine-tuning factors such as the various cosmic constants, local fine-tuning factors such as the properties of water, and so on). Critics from Hume to the present have responded in this way: We should not be surprised by these data. If the world had been one in which intelligent life could not have arisen, then we should not be here to discuss the matter. The factors are necessary for people to be around to puzzle over them and, thus, we should not be surprised at their occurrence. It is self-defeating to seek an explanation for why the factors conducive for our existence obtained. If they hadn't, we wouldn't be here to debate the topic. It's hardly surprising that we showed up in a world with the factors required for our existence as opposed to showing up in a world without those factors!

This response is analogous to Nagel's defense of reason. To see what is wrong with it, let us suppose that an advocate of the design argument cites a number of factors, a through g, that are part of the world and are necessary preconditions for the emergence of life. Hume and his followers interpret the design argument as follows: As we have already seen, theists are supposedly saying, "Isn't it amazing that the factors necessary for life preceded us instead of some other factors that make life preceding us impossible!" In other words, theists are comparing these two different world courses: World Course #1: a through g obtain and human beings appear; World Course #2: alternate factors (say h through n) obtain and human beings appear. Note that worlds 1 and 2 differ only in the factors that obtain in them, but the presence of human beings is held constant. Now this is indeed a bad argument, because, again, it is hard to see how humans could emerge in any world other than one in which the factors necessary for their emergence are actualized!

But this is not the correct interpretation of the design argument. Advocates of the design argument are offering the following comparison: World Course #1: a through g obtain and human beings appear; World Course #2: alternate factors (say h through n) obtain and no human life appears. Advocates of the design argument are claiming that the emergence of any life, including human life, was incredibly unlikely and required the actualization of a delicately balanced set of preconditions, and the realization of these preconditions requires explanation provided by the existence of a Designer. Even the atheist J. L. Mackie saw the flaw in Hume's criticism:

> There is only one actual universe, with a unique set of basic materials and physical constants, and it is therefore surprising that the elements of this unique set-up are just right for life when they might easily have been wrong. This is not made less surprising by the fact that if it had not been so, no one would have been here to be surprised. We can properly envisage and consider alternative possibilities which do not include our being there to experience them.[30]

Broad Theistic Implications of Nagel's Failed Strategy

Nagel confuses parallel cases of these two interpretations of the design argument by dismissing questions about rationality as though they were like the first interpretation. But according to the (correct) indexing approach, questions about rationality are like the second interpretation, and Nagel's "solution" not only fails to address this question, but by acknowledging the availability of a theistic solution and the inadequacy of a naturalistic solution, it actually provides grounds that strengthen the force of the theistic alternative. Put differently, by admitting the uneliminable, irreducible existence of objective reason, and by acknowledging the existence of a theistic solution along with the inadequacy of a naturalistic one, Nagel puts too much weight on his dismissive strategy as a way of avoiding theism. Given the failure of that strategy, Nagel has actually clarified and inadvertently provided support for the theistic option.

But there's more. So far I have shown that the indexed questions are not in the slightest affected by Nagel's dismissive approach. And these questions are among the ones Nagel himself mentions and about which he worries. Moreover, as Alvin Plantinga has shown and as Nagel acknowledges, naturalistic evolutionary answers to the second-order question indexed to naturalistic evolutionary worlds actually provide defeaters for rationality in those worlds for which theism would provide a defeater defeater.[31] Given that the actual world is a rational world, we then have evidence for theism and against naturalism. At the very least, we have an argument for the fact that it is irrational to accept evolutionary naturalism.

Plantinga's argument has been the subject of much debate, and I do not want to enter that dialogue here. My purpose is to draw out an implication for Nagel's first question from my refutation of his dismissive strategy. Nagel takes himself to apply successfully his strategy to the first question, and then to apply it to the second question(s). I plan to go the other way. By showing his strategy fails for the second question(s), I believe I have grounds for undercutting his strategy regarding the first question.

Plantinga wisely focuses his argument on a hypothetical population of creatures for which we have grounds for doubting or should be agnostic about the reliability of their cognitive faculties.[32] In this way, he follows what I am calling an indexing strategy. Plantinga uses a thought experiment involving a widget factory. A person who sees several red widgets on the assembly line would have a defeater for the belief that they are red if the shop superintendent told her that they are being irradiated by a variety of red lights. They may still be red, but she is no longer rational in believing they are red on the basis of the way they appear to her. If the shop vice-president later tells her that the shop superintendent is an unreliable person, she now has a defeater defeater and may properly be agnostic about the widgets. It is easy to conceive of cases in which this second defeater was later defeated, the third was defeated later still, and so on.

Continuing with the indexing strategy, naturalistic evolution provides a defeater for taking the rational faculties of creatures in such a world w to be reliable. But what if we apply the problem to us in the actual world? Does Nagel's dismissive strategy block such a move? I don't think so. Clearly, if I myself were in the widget factory, I would go through various epistemic situations as defeaters, defeater defeaters, and so forth came my way. In such a case, it would not be rational for me to trust my senses. But what about reason itself, especially as it is employed at the level of abstract thought characteristic of Nagel and those who disagree with him? Can reason be used to undercut reason?

By getting a beachhead established regarding the second question(s), I believe we can use reason to undercut reason as it is used and mentioned in question (1). In such a context, in which we grant the legitimacy of problems with rationality surfaced by question(s) (2) and subsequently ask about (1), we have what Plantinga calls a pragmatically circular situation involving a skeptical dialectical loop.[33] The naturalistic evolutionist uses reason to argue for this view, but he then comes to have a defeater for the reliability of his rational faculties (in Nagel's terms, the objectivity of our reasoning). This provides him with a defeater of naturalistic evolution. But given that this defeater for naturalistic evolution relies on his reasoning and beliefs, he has a defeater for this defeater of naturalistic evolution. He now has no defeater for believing both that his rational faculties are reliable and that naturalistic evolution is true. But he is now in his original position, namely, that of believing naturalistic evolution, which provides a defeater for the reliability of his rational faculties. Plantinga concludes: "So goes the paralyzing dialectic. After a few trips around this loop, we may be excused for throwing up our hands in despair, or disgust, and joining Hume in a game of backgammon."[34]

I do not need this stronger claim (namely, that my rebuttal of Nagel's dismissive strategy with respect to question(s) [2] provides a defeater for an affirmative answer to question [1]) for my main task in this chapter to be a success. That task was to defeat Nagel's dismissive strategy regarding question(s) (2). I have not attempted to evaluate all of Nagel's case against a theistic explanation for human rationality. I have simply tried to surface and respond to Nagel's dismissive strategy, a strategy that, in the nature of the case, must bear a lot of weight in Nagel's project.

Such dialectic moves are on the increase and it is important for theists to take note of them and show where appropriate exactly why they fail. I have attempted to do that regarding Nagel's discussion of reason. By refusing to accept reductive or other naturalized treatments of reason and rationality, and by admitting both that naturalism is incapable by itself of explaining the existence of reason and that many argue that theism does provide the best explanation, the dismissive strategy is called upon to carry more dialectical weight than it can bear.

And while I have not been able to argue for it here, I believe the same point applies to the other atheistic naturalist dismissive strategies referred to earlier in this chapter. If I am correct about this, then the future of intellectual atheism (if such there be) is not bright. It must return to the failed reductive or eliminative strategy, a strategy that requires one to deny some fairly obvious facts about the world, or must try to dismiss theistic attempts to employ these facts—facts that in principle are incapable of naturalistic explanation—as part of a cumulative case for the existence of God. In this latter case, it must dismiss what seems to many of us to be a fairly obvious explanation of these facts. I, for one, would not like to be on the horns of that dilemma.[35]

7

God, Naturalism, and the Foundations of Morality

Paul Copan

French Catholic philosopher Jacques Maritain helped draft the United Nations Declaration of Human Rights (1948), which recognizes "the inherent dignity" and "the equal and inalienable rights of all members of the human family." Further, it affirms: "All human beings are born free and equal in dignity and rights. They are endowed with reason and conscience and should act towards one another in a spirit of brotherhood." What is missing, though, is any foundation or basis for human dignity and rights. In light of the philosophical discussion behind the drafting of the Declaration, Maritain wrote: "We agree on these rights, providing we are not asked why. With the 'why,' the dispute begins."[1]

The dispute about morality involves a host of questions about whether objective/universal moral values exist and whether humans have dignity and rights—and if so, what their source is. Are moral values emergent properties, supervening upon natural processes and social configurations, or are beliefs about moral values an adaptation hard-wired into human beings who, like other organisms, fight, feed, flee, and reproduce? Does God offer any metaphysical foundation for moral values and human dignity, or can a Platonic, Aristotelian, categorical imperative (Kantian), or Ideal Observer ethic adequately account for them?

This essay argues, *first*, that objective moral values are an inescapable, properly basic bedrock. Moral subjectivism is inadequate to account for our fundamental intuitions, including ones about evil. *Second*, certain naturalistic moral realists commonly confuse the *order of knowing* with the *order of being*. Since all humans are God's image-bearers, it isn't surprising that they are capable of recognizing or knowing the same sorts of moral values—whether theists or not. The metaphysical question is the more fundamental: How did there come to *be* morally responsible persons in the absence of God and as products of valueless processes? I would maintain that a moral universe is far less likely—indeed extremely difficult to come by—if God does not exist. Naturalism provides a poor context for objective moral values, duties, and human dignity.

Third, in various ways, naturalism undermines objective ethics despite attempts to root it in science. *Fourth*, a naturalistic evolutionary account of morality fails to engage our deepest moral intuitions about right and wrong, and it leaves us skeptical about whether we can have confidence about fundamental epistemic and moral convictions. Any confidence would borrow metaphysical capital from a worldview like theism, as humans have been made in the image of a faithful, truthful, and rational Being. *Finally*, despite the claims of naturalistic moral realists, any appeals to Plato's Euthyphro dilemma fail to render God superfluous in accounting for the source of objective moral values.

A moral universe and human dignity are best explained in the context of a morally excellent, worship-worthy Being as their metaphysical foundation, as opposed to nontheistic alternatives,[2] and naturalism in particular.[3] If objective moral values and human dignity and rights are a reality (and there is very good reason to think they are), then it is extremely likely that some intrinsically valuable Being and Creator exists.

The Proper Basicality of Moral Values

We are wise to assume that our senses, our powers of reasoning, and our most fundamental moral instincts are not systematically deceiving us. We should—and typically do—take for granted their adequate function. Indeed, even the most radical skeptic assumes this as he confidently draws his skeptical conclusions. He appropriates various logical laws to prove his point and, no doubt believing those claiming to have knowledge to be in error, presumes that others ought to share his inferences. Whatever epistemological blunders humans may make, they are not sufficient to justify a deep skepticism. Yes, humans may misperceive or make logical missteps. However, such mistakes hardly call into question the general reliability of our sense or reasoning powers; indeed, they presuppose it. The ability to detect error presumes an awareness of truth.

Likewise, despite flawed moral judgments, there still are certain moral truths that we can't *not* know—unless we suppress our conscience or engage in self-deception.[4] We possess an in-built "yuck factor"—basic moral intuitions about the wrongness of torturing babies for fun, of raping, murdering, or abusing children. We can also recognize the virtue of kindness or selflessness, the obligation to treat others as we would want to be treated, and the moral difference between Mother Teresa and Josef Stalin. Those not recognizing such truths as properly basic are simply wrong and morally dysfunctional. We need no social contract or established methodology to recognize the rights of all humans before the law as well as the wrongness of racism or ethnocentricism. For instance, blacks had value before any civil rights legislation in the United States or South Africa. We can agree with Nicholas Rescher, who observes that if members of a particular tribe think that sacrificing firstborn children is acceptable, "then their grasp on the conception of morality is somewhere between inadequate and nonexistent."[5]

Morality isn't a superficial feature of our world. Atheist David O. Brink asserts, "Our commitment to the *objectivity of ethics* is a deep one."[6] Kai Nielsen deems such a moral awareness to be "bedrock":

> It is more reasonable to believe such elemental things [as wife-beating and child abuse] to be evil than to believe any skeptical theory that tells us we cannot know or reasonably believe any of these things to be evil. . . . I firmly believe that this is bedrock and right and that anyone who does not believe it cannot have probed deeply enough into the grounds of his moral beliefs.[7]

That is, basic moral principles are *discovered*, not *invented*, and persons with a decently functioning conscience can get a lot of moral things right. As C. S. Lewis has pointed out, law codes across civilizations and throughout history (Egyptian, Babylonian, Greek, Native American, and so on) reveal a continual resurfacing of the same basic moral standards—do not murder, break promises, take another's property, or defraud.[8] Despite our faulty moral judgments, we would be wrong to abandon the quest for goodness or become moral skeptics: "we cannot always or even usually be totally mistaken about goodness," Robert Adams affirms.[9]

Such an affirmation of human dignity, rights,[10] and duties is something we would readily expect if God exists—but *not* if humans have emerged from valueless, mindless processes (more below). The Jewish-Christian Scriptures assume that humans are morally responsible agents who can generally know what is good and that we ought to do it. The prophet Amos delivers severe divine warnings to surrounding Gentile nations for their atrocities and crimes against humanity—ripping open pregnant women, breaking treaties, acting treacherously, stifling compassion. The underlying assumption is that these nations—even without God's special revelation—should have known better (Amos 1–2). The same perspective is expressed more explicitly by Paul, who speaks of Gentiles without the Law of Moses who still have a law—a conscience—"written in their hearts" (Rom. 2:14-15).

Philosopher Thomas Reid argued that basic moral principles such as, "treat another as you desire to be treated," are simply commonsensical— obvious to those who have not ignored their conscience. He claimed he did not know by what reasoning—demonstrative or probable—he could convince the epistemic or moral skeptic:

> The sceptic asks me, Why do you believe the existence of the exter-
> nal object which you perceive? This belief, sir, is none of my manu-
> facture; it came from the mint of Nature; it bears her image and
> superscription; and, if it is not right, the fault is not mine. I ever
> took it upon trust, and without suspicion.[11]

According to Reid, morality begins with certain axioms or first prin- ciples, which are self-evident to the properly functioning human being. To reject God's law written on our hearts (the conscience with its fundamental inclinations) is to act unnaturally.[12] Being God's image-bearer, the atheist can recognize the same moral truths as the theist because this "faculty [is] given him by God." If God had not bestowed this faculty upon humans, none of us would be "a moral and accountable being."[13] Although basic moral principles—to be kind, selfless, and compassionate; to avoid tortur- ing for fun, raping, or taking innocent human life—are accessible and knowable to morally sensitive human beings, some improperly function- ing individuals may be self-deceived or hard-hearted sophists.

Thus, we should reasonably believe what is apparent or obvious to us unless there are overriding reasons to dismiss it (the credulity principle)— a belief that applies to our *sense* perception, our *reasoning* faculty, and our *moral* intuitions/perceptions. In general, we take for granted the inno- cence of these capacities until they are proven guilty. We should accept their testimony *unless* we have strong reasons to doubt them. Indeed, the common argument from evil launched against belief in God still takes for granted a fundamental standard of goodness or a design-plan, which is difficult to account for if God does not exist and the material universe is the sum total of reality.

Robert Audi offers a description of how such moral intuitions func- tion. They are (1) *noninferential* or *directly apprehended*; (2) *firm* (they must be believed as propositions); (3) *comprehensible* (intuitions are formed in the light of an adequate understanding of their propositional objects); and (4) *pretheoretical* (not dependent on theories nor themselves theo- retical hypotheses). Such moral knowledge emerges not from reflection on abstract principles but from reflecting on particular moral cases. And however strong, these prima facie intuitions are *not* thereby indefeasible. That is, they may be adjusted or refined in light of other considerations or overriding circumstances. For instance, keeping a promise may be overridden by circumstances preventing me from keeping it, but I still have a duty to explain to my friend why I could not keep the promise.[14]

Consider Daniel Dennett's declaration that, given our evolution, ethical decision-making "holds out scant hope of our ever discovering a formula or an algorithm for doing right." Rather than despairing, he advocates using our "mind-tools" to "design and redesign ourselves" as we continually search for better solutions to the sorts of moral challenges we face.[15] This point is well taken, and the pursuit of universal moral agreement is not going to be achievable. However, the discerning moral realist will take into account circumstances, motives, and conflicting moral duties—not to mention the importance of moral dialogue and the moral lessons learned from history and moral reforms. We can reject a simplistic "algorithm" approach while acknowledging genuine moral duties and the importance of virtuous character. So we can still live wisely and morally despite moral puzzles and challenges.[16] The existence of "gray areas" doesn't mean that we cannot readily recognize basic objective moral values. We must begin with the clear and move to the unclear, not vice versa—and proceed as wisely as we can. Dr. Samuel Johnson reminds us: the fact that there is such a thing as twilight does not mean that we cannot distinguish between day and night.[17]

Knowing versus Being, Metaphysical Contexts, and Choosing the Better Alternative

Knowing versus Being

Certain atheists may question how God's nonexistence would adversely affect the goodness of compassion, mercy, justice, and other virtues. Richard Dawkins—despite his moral subjectivism—maintains that we do not need a God nor must we believe God is constantly policing us in order to be good. In fact, if belief in God would suddenly vanish from the world, people wouldn't become "callous and selfish hedonists, with no kindness, no charity, no generosity."[18]

Likewise, Daniel Dennett (a moral realist) challenges the notion that goodness is opposed to scientific materialism: "There is *no reason at all* why a disbelief in the immateriality or immortality of the soul should make a person less caring, less moral, less committed to the well-being of everybody on Earth than somebody who believes in 'the spirit.'" He adds that a "good scientific materialist" can be concerned about "whether there is plenty of justice, love, joy, beauty, political freedom, and yes, even religious freedom" as the "deeply spiritual."[19] And he quite rightly observes that those calling themselves spiritual can be "cruel, arrogant, self-centered, and utterly unconcerned about the moral problems of the world."[20]

According to naturalistic moral realists, one can *both* affirm objective moral values (for example, that kindness is a virtue) *and* deny the existence of God—with perfect consistency. David O. Brink insists that "the objectivity of ethics is not hostage to the truth of theism."[21] William Rowe, another atheist, asserts that morality (or logic or mathematics) has the same objective status for atheist and theist alike: "the claim that God is needed for morality to be objective is absurd."[22] Christians will give the same reasons as atheists about, say, the immorality of rape (for example, "rape violates the victim's rights and undermines societal cohesion"). No need to appeal to God's existence![23]

However, theists can readily admit that nonbelievers can *know* moral truths. But *knowing* (epistemology) must be distinguished from *being* (ontology), the latter being the more fundamental. *Epistemologically*, the atheist is right: because *all* humans have been made in God's image (Gen. 1:26-27, 9:3; James 3:9)[24] and are thus intrinsically valuable (endowed with dignity, conscience, rights, duties, and the basic capacity to recognize right and wrong), it is no surprise that nontheists of all stripes know the same sorts of moral truths as believers. *Ontologically*, however, a nontheistic metaphysic (that is, the *actual ground* or *basis* that makes moral knowledge possible) is inadequate: Why think impersonal/physical, valueless processes will produce valuable, rights-bearing persons?[25]

Theism has the metaphysical wherewithal to account for such values: there is an intimate connection between (*a*) a good God and Creator (the metaphysical foundation) and (*b*) human dignity/rights, and general moral obligations. God is the necessarily good Source of all finite goods.[26] So anyone can *know* that humans have rights and dignity and obligations. But, more crucially, how did they come to *be* that way—particularly if they are the result of valueless, cause-and-effect physical processes from the big bang until now? Theism offers the requisite foundations.

The Metaphysical Context

The more plausible metaphysical context for grounding human rights and dignity is this: we have been *created* with a *moral constitution* by a supremely valuable being, and we are "hard-wired" to function properly by living moral, deeply relational lives. So if humans have intrinsic, rather than instrumental (or no) value, the deeper, more natural context offering a smoother transition is a personal, supremely valuable God as the source of goodness and creator of morally responsible agents. The naturalist's context of a series of impersonal, valueless causes and effects producing valuable beings is shocking—an utterly incongruous outcome given the context.

Various naturalist moral realists have claimed that moral properties or objective moral values somehow emerge or supervene upon a sufficiently neurologically complex organism[27]—or once certain complex social configurations arise (what Richard Boyd calls "homeostatic property clusters").[28] For instance, the racial injustice of apartheid would supervene upon certain (natural) social, legal, and economic conditions.[29]

Despite such claims, problems regarding the emergence of dignity and duties remain. If intrinsic value does not exist from the outset, its emergence from nonvaluable processes is difficult to explain. It doesn't matter how many nonpersonal and nonvaluable components we happen to stack up: from valuelessness, valuelessness comes.

Brink suggests a parallel to support his naturalistic moral realism— namely, the supervenience of the *mental* upon a complex *physical* brain and nervous system: "Assuming materialism is true, mental states supervene on physical states, yet few think that mental states are metaphysically queer."[30] Such optimism is exceedingly unwarranted, though, as many naturalists themselves admit. For instance, Ned Block acknowledges that we have "no conception"—"zilch"—that enables us to explain subjective experience or to *begin* to account for conscious life: "Researchers are *stumped.*"[31] Jaegwon Kim wonders how "a series of physical events, little particles jostling against one another, electric current rushing to and fro" could blossom into "conscious experience": "Why should *any* experience emerge when these neurons fire?"[32] Consciousness *is* metaphysically queer given naturalism! Colin McGinn avers that the emergence of consciousness "strikes us as miraculous, eerie, even faintly comic."[33] So Brink's confidence is ill placed. By contrast, the theist has no such challenges if a supremely self-aware Being exists—from consciousness, consciousness comes.

The same applies to moral values. Instead of a supervenience model, theists can plausibly argue that a *personal* Creator, who makes human *persons* in the Creator's image, serves as the ontological basis for the existence of objective moral values, moral obligation, human dignity, and rights. Consider: (1) Without the existence of a personal God, there would be no persons at all. (Indeed, God is the sufficient reason for why anything exists at all; for if the universe came into existence a finite time ago, as physicist Paul Davies suggests, the only options appear to be that it was simply uncaused—a metaphysical impossibility—or that something outside the universe caused its existence.)[34] And (2) if no persons would exist, then no moral properties would be instantiated or realized in our world.

Without this personal God and Creator of other persons, it is extraordinarily difficult to account for the instantiation of moral properties. Moral values—the instantiation of moral properties—and personhood are inter-twined: moral properties are instantiated through personhood, which is ontologically rooted in God's personhood.

Now various nontheistic moral realists—not to mention some the-ists[35]—maintain that statements such as "Murder is wrong" would hold true even if God does not exist. They are simply brute facts and necessary truths. In reply, we could offer the following responses:

1. *Simplicity:* If naturalistic moral realists assume (*a*) a preexistent (Platonic) moral realm of brute facts and the eventual evolution of (*b*) valuable human beings corresponding to it, we have two utterly unconnected moral realities. Theism, however, offers a ready and far simpler connection: humans have been made in the image of a good God—the source of objective moral values.

2. *Asymmetrical Necessity:* Even if "Murder is wrong" is a necessary truth, it, first, need not be analytic (compare "Water is H_2O"), and, second, a necessary truth may require some kind of explanation (for example, "Water is necessarily H_2O" still requires' an explana-tion for water's existence and structure).[36] In the case of morality, we are still left wondering how value and obligation came to be thrust upon a valueless context of unguided matter in motion to have a context for the truth of "Murder is wrong." Third, certain necessary truths are logically prior to or more metaphysically basic than others, which may derive from or be entailed by them.[37] Like-wise, the necessity of moral truths does not diminish their need for grounding in the character of a personal God. God, who necessar-ily exists in all possible worlds, is the source of all necessary moral (and logical) truths that stand in asymmetrical relation to God's necessity. God's existence and nature are explanatorily prior to any necessary truths, whether moral or logical.[38]

3. *Cosmic Coincidence (or Arbitrariness):* If moral facts are just brute givens and necessarily true, there is left unexplained a huge cosmic coin-cidence between the existence of these *moral facts* and the eventual emergence of *morally responsible agents* who are obligated to them. That this moral realm appears to be *anticipating* our emergence is a staggering cosmic concurrence that begs an explanation. The naturalistic moral realist may prefer another scenario, however: she may simply argue that certain a priori truths emerge based on the make-up of naturalistically evolved human beings. Dennett appeals to the parallel of certain "a priori" and "timeless" truths about the game of chess; *once* the game is devised, certain fixed truths pertain to it.[39] In response, not only does such a perspective actually imply belief in essentialism (that humans have a fixed *nature*)—something

Dennett and his ilk repudiate. But we are also left with the *arbitrariness* problem: humans could have evolved differently (see below) and thus could have developed different—even opposing—moral "truths" appropriate to them.

4. *Accounting for Human Value:* The naturalist's position still offers no good reason to think that valuable, morally responsible human beings should emerge from valueless processes. Theism offers a far more plausible context for human value.

Deciding between Naturalism and Theism

Let us try to bring a few of these strands together. In deciding which hypothesis—naturalism or theism—presents the most plausible context for objective moral values and human dignity, we should consider at least three guidelines for preferring one over the other: Which is the more natural, the more unifying, and the more basic?

1. *We should prefer the theory that affords the more natural (that is, less ad hoc) transition from the overall theory to the entity in question.* Theism offers a more suitable context for objective moral values, which flow readily from a wise, supremely valuable Being to that Being's valuable image-bearers. Naturalism affords no such smooth transition from a context of undirected valueless processes to objective moral values and human dignity.

2. *We should prefer a worldview that is a kind of grand unifying factor for a wide range of features.* Better explanations are unified and interconnected rather than fragmented and unrelated. The existence of objective moral values and human dignity are only part of the bigger picture that is better explained by God's existence.

How then do we best account for the existence of valuable, morally responsible, self-aware, reasoning, truth-seeking, living human beings who inhabit a finely tuned, beautiful universe that came to exist a finite time ago? Is this best explained naturalistically—namely, the result of disparate valueless, mindless, lifeless physical processes in a universe that came into existence from nothing? Or is the better unifying explanation a supremely valuable, supremely aware, logical, truthful, powerful, intelligent, beautiful Being? This Being serves as a natural unifier and thus the superior explanation and grounding to the naturalistic alternative of a remarkable string of highly contingent features.[40] (As Dennett writes, "just the tiniest amount" of change in the universe's variables would mean life could not have emerged: "we almost didn't make it!")[41] As philosopher of science Del Ratzsch observes, "When a value is produced by a long, tricky, precarious process, when it is generated and preserved by some breathtaking complexity, when it is realized against all odds, then intent—even design—suddenly becomes a live and reasonable question."[42]

3. *We should prefer a hypothesis/worldview whose relevant features are deeper or more basic than those in alternative worldviews.* Any hypothesis will have an explanatory stopping point. The question is: Which hypothesis most adequately furnishes the deepest ontological foundations or more ultimate explanations for its relevant features? For example, is the "miraculous, eerie, even faintly comic"[43] phenomenon of consciousness or the staggering breadth and variety of beauty a mere surd, or is there some deeper, more basic explanation to account for its existence? What if we can go a *step further* to account for it?

We could say the same about human dignity and rights or reason. Naturalism's metaphysic seems inadequate to offer a deep account for such features in our world.[44] A deeper, more stable explanation is available through theism, which "offers suggestions for answers to a wide range of otherwise intractable questions."[45] George Mavrodes rightly observes that moral values and obligations cannot be deep in a world of matter, energy, natural laws, and chance.[46] By contrast, a world created by God has goodness and purpose deeply embedded within it.

Theism has a distinct advantage over gradualistic naturalistic accounts of morality as Dennett, Martin, or Brink might espouse. (We should add that theism need not be viewed as inherently incompatible with an evolutionary process, which God could have initiated; as we note below, Darwin himself believed that God was responsible for getting the evolutionary ball rolling.) Theism offers the more "natural" moral context to move us seamlessly from value to value instead of naturalism's attempt move from valuelessness to value.

The Inadequacy of Various Naturalistic Moral Systems

We should mention the red herring of naturalistic philosophers, who appeal to various objectivistic ethical systems that purportedly can safely overcome the any essential God-morality connection. Again, such confidence is poorly placed.

Consider Aristotle's eudaimonistic virtue ethic. Despite his rich ethical discussion and even his mention of God, critical gaps and shortcomings remain: (*a*) the questionable notion of *intellectual* activity (as opposed to loving relationships) as central to our natural human task (*ergon*) and fulfilling our goal (*telos*); (*b*) the radical evil embedded in human nature that inclines us to self-centeredness and profound evil—what comes "naturally" may often undermine human flourishing; and (*c*) the inability to account for human value and rights. Despite Aristotle's valuable insights, his system is both incomplete and fraught with significant problems.[47]

Neither can naturalists take comfort in Kant's categorical imperative and kingdom of ends. First, the often-misunderstood Kant actually posits

God, freedom, and immortality in order to make sense of morality; his is not a secular ethical system but one that requires God's existence.[48] Second, the more fundamental question for those who take a secularized Kantian position is, "Why should humans be treated as ends rather than means? Why think they should have value given their valueless origins?" Indeed, Kant's system *presupposes* and *posits* human dignity and personal responsibility; naturalism lacks the necessary metaphysical resources to account for them.

Despite the naturalistic appeal of a Rawlsian neocontractarianism with its wide reflective equilibrium[49] or an Ideal Observer theory (a "good" is what an ideal observer would approve under ideal conditions),[50] such theories are long on epistemology but short on ontology: they specify how to *recognize* moral duties and virtues, but equally fail to provide a decent metaphysical account of human dignity and rights or make sense of moral obligation given naturalism's metaphysic. They lack ontological completeness.

Naturalistic Evolutionary Ethics

Though a moral realist, Daniel Dennett maintains that the human fixation on human rights is a misguided, though fortuitous, "rule worship" that contributes to human well-being and social cohesion. The presumption of "natural and imprescriptible rights" is nothing more than (good and useful) "nonsense upon stilts," to use Jeremy Bentham's dismissive phrase.[51]

According to Michael Ruse, a moral subjectivist, we merely *think* morality is objective, but Ruse informs us that isn't so.[52] We believe the *illusion* of moral realism and moral obligation; without this strong impulse, Ruse declares, we would disregard or disobey morality. "If you think about it, you will see that the very essence of an ethical claim, like 'Love little children,' is that, whatever its truth status may be, we think it binding upon us *because we think it has an objective status.*"[53] This is a *corporate illusion* that has been "fobbed off on us by our genes to get us to cooperate."[54]

Despite the arguments of naturalistic moral realists, their naturalistically rooted ethic presents two problems: we are faced with the apparent arbitrariness of our moral beliefs, and we appear to be justified in our skepticism or agnosticism concerning moral living. Note also that my argument would be opposed only to *naturalistic* evolution, not evolution per se. In his *Origin of Species*, Darwin himself is not writing as an intellectually fulfilled atheist![55] Besides affirming that God impressed laws upon nature and breathed life into creation, Darwin uses the word "creation" over 100 times and (in the *Origin's* inscription) approvingly cites Francis Bacon's acknowledgment of both the "book of God's word" (special revelation) and "book of God's works" (divine revelation in nature). Even if naturalists can furnish (1) a complete gradualistic biological account of evolutionary development and (2) an account of ever-increasing moral awareness in human minds, this need not conflict with God as Creator or the source of objective moral values, Daniel Dennett notwithstanding. As we have argued, value from value is more "natural" than value from valuelessness.

Arbitrary Morality?

Given naturalism, it appears that humans could have evolved differently and inherited rather contrary moral beliefs ("rules") for the "chess game" of survival. Whatever those rules, they would still direct us toward surviving and reproducing. Ruse (with E. O. Wilson) gives an example: instead of evolving from "savannah-dwelling primates," we, like termites, could have evolved needing "to dwell in darkness, eat each other's faeces, and cannibalise the dead." If the latter were the case, we would "extol such acts as beautiful and moral" and "find it morally disgusting to live in the open air, dispose of body waste and bury the dead."[56] So our awareness of morality ("a sense of right and wrong and a feeling of obligation to be thus governed") is of "biological worth," serves as "an aid to survival," and "has no being beyond this."[57] Though rare in human societies, Eskimos permit infanticide in the face of scant resources for the sake of survival. And what of suttee (widow burning), honor killings, or female circumcision? Or should we think of Larry Arnhart's serial monogamy as "natural"— as opposed to lifelong monogamy, which frustrates natural, promiscuous desires in males?[58] Should such practices be prohibited or condemned? It is hard to see how Ruse could protest.

Take another example: *A Natural History of Rape*[59] (coauthored by a biologist and an anthropologist) maintains that rape can be explained biologically: when a male cannot find a mate, his subconscious drive to reproduce his own species pushes him to force himself upon a female. Such acts happen in the animal kingdom (for example, male mallards or scorpion flies). Now the authors do not advocate rape; in fact, they claim that rapists are not excused for their (mis)behavior. To say that rape is good because it is biologically advantageous ("natural") is to commit the naturalistic fallacy (moving from *is* to *ought*).

However, if the rape impulse happens to be embedded into human nature from antiquity and if it confers biological advantage, how can the authors suggest that this behavior *ought* to be ended? Is this not committing the naturalistic fallacy as well? Indeed, the authors' resistance to rape, despite its "naturalness," suggests objective moral values not rooted in nature.

An ethic rooted in nature appears to leave us with arbitrary morality. Theism, on the other hand, *begins* with value; so bridging the is-ought gulf is a nonissue.

Skepticism about Ethics

An ethic rooted in naturalistic evolution ends up being subjectivistic and ultimately reduces to relativism. Ethics is simply illusory, as Ruse argues (and, as Dennett notes, naturalistic evolution doesn't leave room for genuine natural rights). So Westerners may find abhorrent practices such as female circumcision or a widow's self-immolation on the funeral pyre of her husband (outlawed in India under the British Raj). But why presuppose moral duties or human dignity and rights? On what metaphysical basis should one oppose such practices? If ethical beliefs are simply hardwired into us for our fitness and survival, we have no reason to think these beliefs are *true*; they simply *are*. If, as Francis Crick argues, human identity ("you") is simply "the behavior of a vast assembly of nerve cells and their associated molecules,"[60] then such a perspective is only accidentally correct. After all, this belief itself is the result of "the behavior of a vast assembly of nerve cells and their associated molecules"!

Whether the naturalist holds a realistic or nonrealistic view of morality, one can legitimately ask: *Can we even trust our minds if we are nothing more than the products of naturalistic evolution trying to fight, feed, flee, and reproduce?*[61] Darwin himself was deeply troubled by this:

> With me the horrid doubt always arises whether the convictions of man's mind, which has been developed from the mind of the lower animals, are of any value or at all trustworthy. Would any one trust in the convictions of a monkey's mind, if there are any convictions in such a mind?[62]

Regarding ethics, Darwin claimed: "Thus at last man comes to feel, through acquired and perhaps inherited habit, that it is best for him to obey his more persistent impulses."[63] The evolutionary process, however, is interested in fitness and survival, not in true belief. The problem with naturalistic evolution is that not only is *objective morality* undermined; so is *rational thought*. Our beliefs—moral or epistemic—may help us *survive*, but we can have no confidence that they are *true*.[64]

So we *may believe* that we have intrinsic value and moral duties and that our free actions make a difference, and these beliefs *could well help* us survive as a species; but they may be *completely false*. If we are blindly hard-wired by nature to accept certain beliefs because of their survival-enhancing value, then we would not have access to the *truth-status* of these beliefs. They may aid our survival, but how could we know whether they are true or false?

Along these lines, Elliott Sober rejects two chief arguments used to argue that ethics must be subjective—the naturalistic (is-ought) fallacy and the genetic fallacy ("ethical beliefs can't be true if they're the product of evolution").[65] However, all of this seems beside the point if naturalism is true. We *still* can't be confident about which—if any—of our beliefs are true. If they are true, it is by accident rather than through some epistemic virtue. *And* we are still left wondering how a valueless universe should produce objective moral values and rights-bearing moral beings to appreciate them. At best Sober's analysis leaves us agnostic as to the existence of objective moral values.

So, the fact that we do not proceed as (global) skeptics about reason or sense perception or fundamental moral beliefs suggests borrowing from a worldview like theism (in that we have been made in the image of a truthful God). And, again, if one takes the skeptical route, one still relies on the very cognitive faculties whose unreliability is the conclusion of one's skeptical argument.[66] One assumes a trustworthy reasoning process to arrive, ironically, at the conclusion that reasoning cannot be trusted.

The fact that humans can be interested in truth seeking, not merely survival, flies in the face of naturalistic Darwinism. Commenting on the notion of our "increated" orientation toward truth, Richard Rorty calls this as "un-Darwinian" as the notion of humans having "a built-in moral compass" or conscience.[67] Thus, it appears that a naturalistic evolutionary process cannot sufficiently explain—or explain away—certain bedrock moral beliefs or our quest for truth. And if we claim that such basic beliefs should be questioned in the name of our impulse to survive and reproduce, then this skeptical conclusion is itself the result of those same impulses.

Naturalism does not inspire confidence in our belief-forming mechanisms. Indeed, naturalism has the potential to undermine our conviction that rationality and objective moral values exist. If our *beliefs*—moral or epistemic—are survival-enhancing by-products of Darwinistic evolution, why think that we actually *have* dignity, rights, and obligations—or that we are thinking rationally? A theistic worldview, on the other hand, does inspire confidence that we can *know* moral (and rational) truths—even if they do not contribute one whit to our survival.

Naturalism's Undermining of Ethics

Despite its appeal to "science," naturalism's materialist ontology not only fails to produce moral values, but positively undermines them. This becomes apparent as we examine the properties of matter, the nature of scientific description, and the notable representation of naturalists who deny objective goodness (even if they may prefer it). Further, naturalism has embedded within it a number of features that could readily undercut moral motivation.

Moral Values Defy Physical Description

Naturalists seem increasingly to take their worldview to involve a strict materialism. As Kai Nielsen puts it, "[Naturalism] is the view that anything that exists is ultimately composed of physical components."[68] However, material or physical properties such as extension, color, shape, or size are far different from moral values, which are not blue, ten centimeters long, or rough to the touch. No physics textbook will include "moral value" in its attempted description of matter. Michael Martin claims that there is "no a priori reason why objective moral values could not be constituted by matter."[69] But there is. There is a *background* or *contextual* problem for the naturalist who believes in objective moral values: How do we move from a universe that originates from no prior matter into a universe of valueless matter and energy, eventually arriving at moral values, including human rights, human dignity, and moral obligation? It is hard to see how the naturalist could bridge this chasm. Matter just does not have moral properties, let alone mental ones.

Goodness Is Scientifically Superfluous

Some naturalistic moral realists believe that recent developments in the philosophy of science—together with "naturalistic" developments in epistemology and philosophy of language—can help in the articulation and defense of moral realism: "moral realism can be shown to be a more attractive and plausible position if recent developments in realist philosophy of science are brought to bear in its defense."[70] Other naturalists are not so sanguine about naturalism's ability to pull goodness out of the ontological hat. Thomas Nagel puts it candidly: "There is no room for agency in a world of neural impulses, chemical reactions, and bone and muscle movements." Given naturalism, it is hard not to conclude that we're "helpless" and "not responsible" for our actions.[71] Zoologist Richard Dawkins admits, "Science has no methods for deciding what is ethical."[72] Harvard's Marc Hauser, who believes that we come evolutionarily equipped with an "innate moral grammar," claims much the same thing—that science is about making *descriptions*, not moral prescriptions.[73] Though not a naturalist, Derk Pereboom nicely summarizes naturalism's perspective on moral responsibility: "our best scientific theories indeed have the consequence that we are not morally responsible for our actions. . . . [We are] more like machines than we ordinarily suppose."[74]

Contrary to what naturalistic moral realists claim, "scientific explanation" seems to call for rejecting the existence of objective moral values rather than bloating their ontology. A methodologically naturalistic science would require stripping off: Why insert objective moral values (*ought*) when bare scientific descriptions (*is*) seem to be all that is required? Why not use *non*moral terms and explanations of certain events that naturalistic moral realists typically take as morally weighted? Why not eliminate objective morality in the name of simplicity?

Naturalistic moral realists claim that moral facts help explain certain actions performed by individuals—for example, "Hitler killed millions of Jews because he was morally depraved." But are such moral facts explanatorily *necessary*? Perhaps a "strictly scientific" response should simply stop with a nonmoral description: Hitler, being bitter and angry, held many false beliefs about the Jews (for example, that they were responsible for Germany's defeat in WWI). Hitler sought to destroy the Jews as a way of releasing his hostilities.[75] While moral facts may be *relevant*, they are not necessary to *explain* Hitler's behavior. Thus, in the spirit of Ockham's razor, why multiply entities or explanations unnecessarily? Why can't natural, descriptive facts do the explanatory work? The scientific account suggests that moral facts are dispensable.[76]

It is difficult to see why the naturalist must resort to moral explanations when parsimony suggests another course—the descriptive one. If we are going the route of "facts" and "science," then why get side-tracked by the prescriptive? The is-ought problem still seems difficult for the naturalist to overcome.

Naturalists Themselves Confess . . .

Science's metaphysical failure to account for goodness is further reinforced by a large portion of naturalists who admit that natural processes without God cannot bring us to moral responsibility and goodness: these don't square well with naturalism. We have already cited Nagel, Dawkins, and Hauser. In addition, Bertrand Russell believed that "the whole subject of ethics arises from the pressure of the community on the individual."[77] E. O. Wilson locates moral feeling in "the hypothalamus and the limbic system"; it is a "device of survival in social organisms."[78] Jonathan Glover considers morality a "human creation" and calls on humans to "re-create ethics."[79]

If humans are simply more developed animals, why think there are moral duties to which they must subscribe—or that they are even morally responsible? John Searle admits that we have an intuition of freedom (that "we could have done something else"), but he rejects libertarian freedom because of his commitment to the "scientific" approach to reality. Otherwise, we would have to postulate a self that could potentially disrupt the "causal order of nature."[80]

Given such a perspective, no wonder Simon Blackburn confesses that he cannot adequately answer the relativist's challenge: "Nature has no concern for good or bad, right or wrong. . . . We cannot get behind ethics." Questions of moral knowledge and moral progress can only be answered "from within our own moral perspective." Blackburn prefers "dignity" to "humiliation."[81] If, however, we have been created in the image of a good, supremely valuable, and free being and have been endowed with moral value and "certain unalienable rights," then the theist is able to offer a much more plausible context for affirming human dignity, rights, and responsibility than the naturalist who wants to be a realist but doesn't quite know how. Atheist J. L. Mackie had it right when he affirmed that objective goodness, given naturalism, is "odd" and "unlikely"; if it exists, it must be rooted in "an all-powerful god."[82] He opted for the idea that human beings "invent" right and wrong.[83]

Naturalism May Undercut Moral Motivation

The popular writer Michael Shermer affirms that our remote ancestors have genetically passed on to us our sense of moral obligation within, and this is (epigenetically) reinforced by group pressure. Ultimately, to ask, "Why should we be moral?" is like asking, "Why should we be hungry or horny?"[84] C. S. Lewis noted that given such conditions, moral impulses are no more true (or false) "than a vomit or a yawn."[85] Thinking "I ought" is on the same level of "I itch." Indeed, "my impulse to serve posterity is just the same sort of thing as my fondness for cheese" or preferring mild or bitter beer.[86] Naturalism's inability to get beyond descriptions of human behavior and psychology does not inspire confidence for grounding moral obligation. At best, one should remain agnostic about it—which doesn't do much to encourage the pursuit of virtue.

Furthermore, if, as can be argued, humans could have evolved a different set of moral beliefs that might nevertheless enhance survival (for example, rape as biologically beneficial), then this, too, takes the wind out of the sails of moral motivation. If we are simply animals, why refrain from raping or practicing infanticide[87] when this is "natural" or "widespread" in nature? It seems that those who vehemently resist such practices are smuggling in metaphysical capital from another worldview that clearly demarcates valuable, responsible moral agents from environment-bound, instinct-guided animals.

The Euthyphro Problem

In a *Calvin and Hobbes* cartoon strip,[88] the mischievous imp Calvin is pondering the lyrics of "Santa Claus Is Coming to Town": ". . . He knows if you've been bad or good; so be good, for goodness's sake!" Calvin reports his musings to Hobbes, his striped sidekick and co-conspirator. "This Santa Claus stuff bothers me . . . especially the judge and jury bit." Why, Calvin wonders, does Santa carry such moral authority? "Who appointed Santa? How do we know he's impartial? What criteria does he use for determining bad or good?"

Along these lines, Socrates, in Plato's *Euthyphro* dialogue (10a), once asked: "Is what is holy holy because the gods approve it, or do they approve it because it is holy?" Various philosophers of religion have followed up on this question to show that no necessary connection exists between God and objective morality. They present the dilemma in (roughly) this way: either God's commands are *arbitrary* (something is good *because* God commands it—and God could have commanded "You *shall* murder/commit adultery")—or there must be some *autonomous moral standard* (which God consults in order to command). Robin Le Poidevin maintains that "we can, apparently, only make sense of these doctrines [that God is good and wills us to do what is good] if we think of goodness as being defined independently of God."[89] Steven Pinker, who believes that our evolutionary hard-wiring fully accounts for our moral beliefs and sense of moral obligation, claims that Plato made quick work of the idea that God is "in charge of morality" since God's dictates would be "divine whims."[90]

Such claims, though, are misguided. Why think our alternatives are reduced to these two—(a) a moral standard that exists completely independently of God (which God must apparently consult when issuing commands) or (b) divine arbitrariness or capriciousness?

Although divine commands may serve as a partial guide to living rightly (for example, God's civil laws to theocratic Israel),[91] God's good character with accompanying "divine motivations"[92] is the more ultimate and underlying reality; God's moral nature is more fundamental to God's worship-worthiness than God's commands—a point nontheistic philosophers seem to ignore.[93] Even divine command theorist Robert Adams points out, "It matters what God's attributes are. . . . It makes a difference if you think of commands as coming from someone who completely understands both us and our situation. It matters not only that God is loving but also that he is just."[94] Elsewhere Adams speaks of God's commands springing from a good design and purpose; such commands are conducive to human flourishing: "It matters to the plausibility of a divine command theory, for example, that we do not believe that God demands cruelty."[95]

Indeed, the ultimate resolution to this Euthyphro dilemma is that *God's good character* or *nature* sufficiently grounds objective morality. So we do not need to look elsewhere for such a standard. We have been made in the divine image; without it we would neither be moral beings (let alone exist) nor have the capacity to recognize objective moral values. The ultimate solution to the Euthyphro dilemma shifts the grounding of morality from the *commands of God* to something more basic—that is, the *nature* or *character* of God. Thus, we human beings (who have been made to resemble God in certain ways) have the capacity to recognize this, and thus God's commands—far from being arbitrary—are in accordance with that nature and also with how we have been designed. We would not *know* goodness without God's granting us a moral *constitution*. We have rights, dignity, freedom, and responsibility because God has designed us this way. And we can grant Pinker's assumption that fundamental moral convictions that prohibit torturing babies for fun or raping are hard-wired into us evolutionarily while rejecting the notion that this hard-wiring grounds human morality. Such hard-wiring is quite compatible with God's existence, but it runs into trouble if morality is strictly natural, as we noted above.

As an aside, God's designs for us are for our good and well-being, not our harm (Deut. 6:24; 10:13). Contrary to the skeptic's caricatures of God as a divine police officer or cosmic killjoy, God issues commands that are rooted in God's good nature and are in line with the maximal function and flourishing of human beings. Indeed, these commands spring from the love and self-giving nature of God, who is *pro nobis* (for us).

Furthermore, in light of (1) our ability to recognize basic moral values and ideals, as well as (2) our moral failures to live up to these ideals, this "moral gap" suggests the need for (3) divine grace to enable us to live as we ought. So, rather than Kant's "ought implies can," we failing humans may still cast ourselves upon God's mercy and grace; that is, "ought implies can—*with* divine assistance."[96]

There are other points to ponder. What if the naturalistic (or nontheistic) moral realist pushes the Euthyphro dilemma further? What if she calls God's character itself into question? Is the very *character* of God good because it happens to be God's, or is God's character good because it conforms to some external standard of goodness? I briefly respond below.

- If the naturalistic (or nontheistic) moral realist is correct about there needing to be some moral standard external to God, then she herself cannot escape a similar dilemma, *mutatis mutandis*: Are these moral values good simply because they are good, or is there an independent standard of goodness to which *they* conform? Her argument offers her no actual advantage over theism. And if two entities are sufficient to establish a relation (here, God's good character and moral values), inserting yet a third entity—some moral standard independent of God to assess the connection between them—becomes superfluous. The skeptic's demand is unwarranted.
- The naturalist's query is pointless in this regard also: we must eventually arrive at some self-sufficient and self-explanatory stopping point beyond which the discussion cannot go. Why is this

"independent moral standard" any less arbitrary a stopping point than God's nature?

- God, who is essentially perfect, does not have obligations to some external moral standard; God simply acts, and it is good. God naturally does what is good. God does not fulfill moral obligations but simply expresses the goodness of the divine nature. As H. O. Mounce suggests, "God cannot hold anything good unless he *already* values it. But then his valuing cannot *depend* on its being good."[97]
- The idea that God could be evil or command evil is utterly contrary to the very definition of God (who is intrinsically morally excellent, maximally great, and worthy of worship); if we are really talking about "God," then this God cannot be some evil creator of the universe.
- The acceptance of objective values assumes a kind of ultimate goal or design plan for human beings. This would make little sense given naturalism (since we are the products of mindless, unguided processes), but it makes much sense given theism, which presumes a design plan or ideal standard for human beings.
- Even if there were some moral standard independent of God, it still would fail to account for how humans, given their valueless, unguided, materialistic origins came to be morally valuable, rights-bearing, morally responsible beings. There seems to be no reason to think that the Euthyphro dilemma poses a serious threat to a theistically rooted ethic.[98]

For all their huffing and puffing, naturalistic moral realists are mistaken about the "threat" that the Euthyphro dilemma poses for God's being the ground of objective moral values.

Conclusion

Unlike the UN Universal Declaration of Human Rights, which takes human rights and moral obligations for granted, another historic document—the Declaration of Independence—presents the essential grounding for "certain unalienable" human rights and dignity. These are rooted in "our Creator," a personal Being who has uniquely made human beings. Without God, it seems exceedingly difficult to account for objective moral values, obligations, human rights, and human dignity.

John Rist has observed that there is "widely admitted to be a crisis in contemporary Western debate about ethical foundations."[99] It seems that taking seriously a personal God and Creator, who is the infinite Good and source of all finite goods—including human dignity—would go a long way in providing the needed metaphysical foundation for human rights and objective moral values. Apart from such a move, it seems that the crisis may become only more pronounced.

Maritain argued that God and objective morality cannot plausibly be separated since God, the Creator of valuable, morally responsible human beings, is the very source of value. Ethical systems—and official documents regarding human rights—that ignore this foundation will necessarily be incomplete. To close with Jacques Maritain:

> The truths which I have just recalled were not discovered and for-mulated by moral philosophy. They spring from a higher source. They correspond, nevertheless, to an aspiration (a trans-natural aspiration) so deeply rooted in man that many philosophers have undergone its attraction, and have tried to transpose it into purely rational terms, an attempt which, lacking the indispensable data, could only be disappointing.[100]

If objective moral values exist, we have good reason for believing in God. Of course, a successful moral argument does not reveal that the God of Abraham, Isaac, Jacob, and Jesus exists—a full-blown and robust theism. The moral argument, however, can be supplemented with other successful theistic arguments and with God's specific revelation in Jesus of Nazareth. That said, the moral argument does point us to a supreme personal moral Being who is worthy of worship, who has made us with dignity and worth, to whom we are personally accountable, and who may reasonably be called "God."

The God Hypothesis in the Future of Atheism

Ted Peters

While studying philosophy as an undergraduate, I took a shirt cardboard and with a felt pen made a sign to hang on the wall of my dormitory room. The top half read: "God is Dead!"—Nietzsche. The bottom read: "Nietzsche is dead!"—God. The obituary of God just might be premature, I thought.

The atheism of my college days at Michigan State University is now effete. This was the atheism of Nietzsche's disciples in the Third Reich, Freudian projection, the empty transcendence of Heideggerian and existentialist philosophy, along with Soviet Marxism and Chinese Maoism. Atheism as a curiosity spread among intellectuals, offering spice and malice to university life in Europe and America. Atheism as an ideology was forcedly spread internationally by marching Soviet and Chinese armies; and domestically it was spread by arrests and executions of Christian bishops or Buddhist monks. With the fall of the Berlin Wall combined with the rise of capitalism in China, and with the taint of Nazism that grew into a dark spot on the reputation of Martin Heidegger, much of the atheism of my youth has dried up like spilled ketchup on a soiled napkin. It is still visible, but its taste is long gone.

What we see today is a spicy new breed of aggressive atheists. Like evangelicals, these atheists are out to convert religious persons to atheistic beliefs, and to convert our culture to a secular and scientific way of life. Rather than announce the death of God, these evangelical atheists encourage the death of religion. The problem, as these atheists perceive it, is found in our belief in the existence of God. Even worse, belief in God teaches large human populations to think irrationally and to engage in violence. If we could eliminate irrational belief in an unseen and nonexistent God, then the amount of violence in our world would immediately shrink to manageable levels. There is a moral urgency to the atheist gospel of the early twenty-first century.

Three planks make up the platform of the evangelical atheists. First, the god that people believe in does not exist; therefore, religious belief is irrational. Second, belief in this nonexistent god constitutes religion, and religion incites violence. Third, science is rational and peaceful. Science is rational because the physical world it studies actually exists; and, in addition, the scientific method is self-correcting in contrast with religious dogma, which is rigid and resistant to modification. This absolute status of dogmatic beliefs within religion prompts violence against outsiders, against those who fail to hold the same rigid beliefs. In sum, science saves. If we turn to science and abandon our religious ways, our society will become increasingly rational and peaceful. This is the gospel of the New Atheism.[1]

In what follows I will explicate the core assertions in the program of the evangelical atheists. We will see that the existence of God appears as a scientific hypothesis, a hypothesis that allegedly can be invalidated by appeal to scientific evidence. We will also see just how vehement the New Atheists are in laying the responsibility for the violence in today's world on the doorsteps of churches and temples and especially mosques.

Then I will select one aspect of the atheist argument for special attention, namely, the idea that we can confirm or disconfirm a so-called God hypothesis. I will attempt to show that both science and theology share a hypothetical structure. The reason that Richard Dawkins cannot validate his God hypothesis is that he looks for evidence strictly within the domain of the natural world we have inherited from our evolutionary past. This is not where God can easily be found, even though God is certainly not absent.

God is transcendent to nature, not restricted to the domain of evidence Dawkins examines. Now, here is a subtle but decisive point: the kind of evidence important to a Christian theologian has to do not with God's existence, but with the divine character. Just any ol' god will not do for a Christian. What is decisive to Christian consciousness is that God is gracious. The God of grace has promised to transform nature, as well as history. What is revealed in the Gospel of Jesus Christ is God's promise of a new creation, a transformed world. Affirming this promise takes the form of anticipatory or proleptic thinking for the theologian. It is open to God's eschatological confirmation. In fact, Christian theology relies upon God's future fulfillment for its present truth. While we await the fulfillment of

God's promise, our knowledge of the God of grace remains provisional, unproven. In this very modest and limited way, theologians and genuine scientists share in hypothetical thinking.

What Kind of God Does Not Exist?

Just what kind of god do evangelical atheists repudiate belief in?[2] For the most part, they disbelieve in the God of classical theism, especially the divinized old man with a beard. Sam Harris contends that "the biblical God is a fiction, like Zeus and the thousands of other dead gods whom most sane human beings now ignore."[3] The divine being rejected by Michael Schermer, publisher of *Skeptic* magazine, is a bit more sublime than Harris's bearded Zeus. Schermer disbelieves in God when "*understood to be all powerful, all knowing, and all good; who created out of nothing the universe and everything in it with the exception of Himself; who is uncreated and eternal, a noncorporeal spirit who created, loves, and can grant eternal life to humans.*"[4]

Science educator Richard Dawkins, similarly, says he is rejecting every divine figure, including Yahweh, Jesus, Allah, Baal, Zeus, or Wotan. He is attacking all of them at once. All belief in such divinities can be swept up into a single "God hypothesis," which Dawkins claims he can falsify scientifically. "I shall define the God Hypothesis more defensibly: *there exists a super-human, supernatural intelligence who deliberately designed and created the universe and everything in it, including us.*"[5] He falsifies the hypothesis by declaring that the existence of God, "though not technically disprovable, is very improbable indeed."[6]

Like Dawkins, physics professor Victor Stenger subjects the monotheistic God of Judaism, Christianity, and Islam to scientific analysis. He hypothesizes that if such a God did in fact exist, then this God would have the attributes that would affect material phenomena and thereby provide objective evidence for this existence within the natural universe. His scientific analysis makes the assumption that is generally the case for science, namely, methodological naturalism, according to which the scientist "seeks natural accounts of all phenomena."[7] After providing his sometimes insightful refutations for such claims as the fine-tuning of the universe, creationism, intelligent design, and traditional arguments against atheism, Stenger draws a "definitive" conclusion, namely, that "the hypothesis of God is not confirmed by the data. Indeed that hypothesis is strongly contradicted by the data."[8] Therefore, God does not exist.

What shall we do now without God? As a substitute for this nonexistent divine intelligence, Dawkins advocates "an alternative view: *any creative intelligence, of sufficient complexity to design anything, comes into existence only as the end product of an extended process of gradual evolution.*"[9] Note carefully the logic here. If God would exist, it would take the form of an eschatological existence, not a primordial existence. "If (which I don't believe for a moment) our universe was designed, and *a fortiori* if the designer reads our thoughts and hands out omniscient advice, forgiveness and redemption, the designer himself must be the end product of some kind of cumulative escalator or crane, perhaps a version of Darwinism in another universe."[10]

It appears that Dawkins here rejects a divine creator of the past; but perhaps he'll welcome one in the future. Could this be what he is saying? Even with this slim opening toward the coming into existence of a future intelligence, Dawkins closes the door on divinity. No God existed at the beginning, at the origin of the universe or at the origin of life; and no God now guides the evolutionary process of speciation. Natural selection does. What was once simple has created something complex: natural selection has produced an intelligent designer, us. We *Homo sapiens* are the most intelligent beings in nature's earthly history to date. And we might expect even higher intelligence to develop in the future. The evolutionary development of the human race is what Dawkins believes in; and he assumes that belief in evolution requires disbelief in God. What Dawkins in effect has done is substitute natural selection for divine providence; and he has substituted the revelatory power of Darwin's theory for Scripture.

Before we move on to the atheist explanation and critique of religion, let us pause for a moment to note just what Dawkins and Stenger have done here. They have placed the question of God's existence into a scientific hypothesis. Then they claimed to have examined the relevant empirical evidence. On this basis, Dawkins claims that this evidence renders the God hypothesis "very improbable." Evidently his measurement is so precise that he can place this hypothesis between possible and impossible, right into the improbable category. Stenger, in contrast, does not need a refined measure of probability, because his disconfirmation is "definitive."

What might be surprising to persons of religious sensibility is the assumption made here, namely, that the existence of God can be formulated as a scientific hypothesis. This implies, of course, that the scientific method pursuing the kind of empirical evidence assumed in methodological naturalism is capable of proving or disproving God's existence. This is curious, because scientific method looks indefatigably for natural explanations of natural phenomena. Science does not look for supranatural or spiritual or any other transcendent reality. Because God is not just one finite or physical cause among others in the closed causal nexus of the natural world, it seems odd that one would make God's existence an explicitly scientific question. This would be like going duck hunting with a fishing pole. Everyone would understand with a smirk if such a hunter returned home with no game.

What counts as science in the method of Dawkins and Stenger is the assumption that all causation belongs to a single plane of activity, to a single closed causal nexus. Christian theologians have long distinguished between primary and secondary causation, the former attributed to God and the latter to natural processes. A recent Vatican study, *Communion and Stewardship*, makes this point clearly. "In the Catholic perspective, neo-Darwinians who adduce random genetic variation and natural selection as evidence that the process of evolution is absolutely unguided are straying beyond what can be demonstrated by science. Divine causality can be active in a process that is *both* contingent and guided. Any evolutionary mechanism that is contingent can only be contingent because God made it so."[11]

Be this as it may, to approach the question of God's existence as a hypothesis prompts a certain level of intrigue. This is worth addressing theologically. To the role of hypothesis in science and theology we will return a little later in this chapter.

Can Religion Be Explained if No God Exists?

Two explanations for the origin of religion are touted by the New Atheism, one psychological and the other biological. According to the psychological explanation, religion is the failed attempt by the human psyche to shield us from the fear of death. The bleak nothingness of the grave shocks us into creating an intellectual system of denial. Belief in a nonexistent god who will take us to heaven in the afterlife is the specific form this denial takes. "Atheism rejects the existence of God as fiction devised by men desperate to keep on living in spite of the inevitability of death," writes Michel Onfray.[12]

The biological explanation involves Charles Darwin's theory of evolution. So comprehensive is evolutionary theory that it can encompass religion, says Daniel Dennett. Evolution can explain religion in terms of the adaptation of the human species to its environment. In all other species, terms such as "survival" and "adaptation" refer to making babies—that is, the species that survives fills its environment with its own population. But, of course, the human race does not measure its evolutionary triumph in terms of baby making. Rather, humanity's contribution to the history of life on our planet is the evolution of ideas, especially religious ideas. "We are the only species on the planet that has ever existed than can decide that an idea is more important than having more grandchildren than your neighbor," says Dennett in his contribution to this book.[13]

Now, traditionally, we have asked theologians to explain religion. Theologians typically explain religion by appeal to their understanding of God, which is itself a religious understanding. But, because religion is irrational and science is rational, Dennett believes that science can provide a better explanation of religious behavior than theologians can. From an atheist's point of view, theologians no longer earn an honest living.

Dennett contrasts narrow-minded religion with open-minded science. He celebrates the ability of science to correct itself by admitting new evidence and altering its theories. Religion is dubbed irrational, because religion is unable to do this. "But where are the examples of religious orthodoxy being simply abandoned in the face of irresistible evidence? Again and again in science, yesterday's heresies have become new orthodoxies. No religion exhibits that pattern in its history."[14] Here is the conclusion reached by the evangelical atheists: intelligent people think rationally, rely upon science, and deny the existence of God.

What Is Wrong with Religion?

Wired writer Gary Wolf announces: "the New Atheists . . . condemn not just belief in God but respect for belief in God." He goes on. "Religion is not only wrong, it's evil." Religion is evil because it incites violence. To fight for peace, we need to replace religious belief with a more rational way of handling affairs. "A band of intellectual brothers is mounting a crusade against belief in God."[15] The New Atheists are crusading for nonbelief.

There are "four irreducible objections to religious faith," says Christopher Hitchens, namely, "that it wholly misrepresents the origins of man and the cosmos, that because of this original error it manages to combine the maximum of servility with the maximum of solipsism, that it is both the result and cause of dangerous sexual repression, and that it is ultimately grounded on wish-thinking."[16] Hitchens assumes that "the attitude of religion to science is always necessarily problematic and very often necessarily hostile."[17] Although Hitchens might hope that we would simply evolve ourselves right up and out of religion into an epoch of scientific reason, he finds himself unable to be optimistic. "Religious faith is, precisely *because* we are still-evolving creatures, ineradicable."[18] Hitchens's complaint is that religion poisons everything in the human way of life. Even if we cannot rid ourselves of religion, Hitchens can dream of a society without it.

The chief complaint among atheists is that religion sponsors violence. Michel Onfray lets loose with the big cannons. Referring to Christianity, Judaism, and Islam, he writes: "the religion of the one God . . . seeks to promote self-hatred to the detriment of the body, to discredit the intelligence, to despise the flesh, and to prize everything that stands in the way of a gratified subjectivity. Launched against others, it foments contempt, wickedness, the forms of intolerance that produce racism, xenophobia, colonialism, wars, social injustice. A glance at history is enough to confirm the misery and the rivers of blood shed in the name of the one God."[19] In order to build a bridge across the rivers of shed religious blood, Onfray calls us into a form of battle between religion and anti-religion: "we must fight for a post-Christian secularism, that is to say atheistic, militant, and radically opposed to" the three monotheisms.[20]

Similarly, Sam Harris complains that "religious faith remains a perpetual source of human conflict."[21] In order to bring global peace, we need to stamp out religion. The religions Harris particularly wants to eliminate are Islam, Christianity, and Judaism. These irrational and violence-prone holdovers from a premodern era must be dispensed with. "All reasonable men and women have a common enemy. . . . Our enemy is nothing other than faith itself."[22]

Harris has a hit list, and Islam sits on the top of it. We ought not to think it is only the "extremists" who are a danger to society, warns Harris. Islam at its core is violent. "The idea that Islam is a 'peaceful religion hijacked by extremists' is a fantasy . . . because most Muslims are *utterly deranged by their religious faith*."[23] Harris places the blame for global violence on the worship taking place inside churches, synagogues, and especially mosques.

The evidence Harris rallies for his brief against Islam is found in the Qur'an itself. Thought to be literally the word of God, this book teaches devout Muslims to commit themselves to holy war against all non-Muslims. Harris cites one dangerous passage after another, such as, "The only true faith in God's sight is Islam. . . . He that denies God's revelations should know that swift is God's reckoning" (Qur'an 3:19). The Qur'an and its concept of *jihad* or holy war are essential not just for suicide bombers, but for all devout Muslims. "On almost every page," writes Harris, "the Koran instructs observant Muslims to despise nonbelievers. On almost every page, it prepares the ground for religious conflict. . . . Islam, more than any other religion human beings have devised, has all the makings of a thoroughgoing cult of death."[24] According to Harris, this cult of death gets additional energy from teaching young men that, if they become suicide bombers, they will go straight to paradise, avoid the judgment, and receive a reward of seventy virgins for their pleasure. What can we expect from a religious teaching such as this? "The only future devout Muslims can envisage—*as Muslims*—is one in which all infidels have been converted to Islam, subjugated, or killed."[25]

Islam is a cult of death, Harris says. As such, Islam poses a threat to the Western way of life. Now, just what should Western civilization do to defend itself? First, we should teach rationality. We should teach our children to think critically, to evaluate religious claims on the basis of evidence. Once we have examined religious beliefs, they will be seen to be unfounded. Science will replace faith. We will emerge from our outmoded faith into the freedom of a truly liberal society. If teaching reason is less than adequate, however, then we should move toward a second form of self-defense, a military defense.

To Harris we might ask the question: Will this gradual conversion from irrational religion to rational atheism move fast enough to prevent inundation by the Islamic menace? Can we pass through the transition before Muslims get their hands on nuclear or biological weapons? Perhaps not. Might preemptive self-defense be called for? Yes, says Harris. This threat might even call for a nuclear first strike. "The only thing likely to ensure our survival may be a nuclear first strike of our own. Needless to say, this would be an unthinkable crime—as it would kill tens of millions of innocent civilians in a single day—but it may be the only course of action available to us, given what Islamists believe."[26] Harris is giving expression to Western anxiety, to fear; and this leads him to propose his own form of atheist jihad against Islam. "The West must either win the argument or win the war. All else will be bondage."[27] Harris is ready to fight for peace. In the name of rationality, tolerance, and peace, Harris proposes nuclear obliteration of a religion that sponsors the violence he wants to rid us of.

What Dawkins recommends is more modest, although he too advocates tolerance without respect for religion. Dawkins makes certain that he is not singling out only extremist religion; he opposes even mainline religion. "I do everything in my power to warn people against faith itself, not just against so-called 'extremist' faith. The teachings of 'moderate' religion, though not extremist in themselves, are an open invitation to extremism."[28] Dawkins continues: "Suicide bombers do what they do because they really believe what they were taught in their religious schools; that duty to God exceeds all other priorities, and that martyrdom in his service will be rewarded in the gardens of Paradise."[29] The very tolerance shown by moderates imputes respect to religious fundamentalists and extremists who do not deserve that respect. For Dawkins and Harris, evidently only an extremist form of atheism can combat both mainline and extremist forms of religion.

Now, just who is calling the kettle black? It certainly looks like the critics of religion are as absolutistic or even fanatical as the religious nuts they seek to obliterate. Alister McGrath connects evangelical atheism with fundamentalism, especially with reference to Dawkins. "It is a form of absolute dichotomist thinking that is typical of fundamentalisms, whether religious or antireligious. Where some divide the world into the saved and the damned, Dawkins divides it into those who follow the ways of rationalism and superstition."[30]

Are Atheists as Peaceful as They Claim?

As we have seen, the new breed of atheists accuses religion for its role in violence. The hint is that if atheists would take charge, we could eliminate violence and live in peace. The morality among atheists is higher than that among religious practitioners, we are led to believe.

Now, let us press this claim, and subject it to review. Let us look at war and genocide in the twentieth century and ask: How have atheists contributed? Here is one description:

> The most horrible genocidal atrocities of the past century and, indeed, in recorded history, Hitler's Holocaust in Central Europe, Stalin's purge of non-Communists in the former Soviet Union and Eastern Bloc, and the Khmer Rouge's killing fields in Cambodia (which currently holds the record for the largest number of human casualties) were all perpetrated in the name of atheistic ideologies that made no provisions for an afterlife and were sometimes directed at eliminating those who believed in an afterlife. What more compelling evidence could there be that it is misguided to point the finger of blame for this or other humanly perpetrated atrocities at religion per se or at the belief in some form of life after death?[31]

Our evangelical atheists have confronted this criticism before. Harris, for example, tries to dismiss such damning evidence because these genocides were perpetrated not by true rationalists but by rationalists contaminated by ideology. Stalin and Mao were victims of Marxist ideology. And Nazism was not genuine atheism either, because it fed off Christian anti-Semitism. "Nazis were agents of religion."[32] Even if atheists perpetrated genocide, we can still say atheism is scientific and good while religion is unscientific and bad.

The response of Dawkins is similar. Dawkins claims Stalin's atrocities were due not to his atheism but to his Marxism; and Hitler was probably a Catholic influenced by Martin Luther's anti-Semitism that relied upon the theory of eugenics. Curious.

> Stalin was an atheist and Hitler probably wasn't but even if he was, the bottom line of the Stalin/Hitler debating point is very simple. Individual atheists may do evil things but they don't do evil things in the name of atheism. Stalin and Hitler did extremely evil things, in the name of, respectively, dogmatic and doctrinaire Marxism, and an insane and unscientific eugenics theory tinged with sub-Wagnerian ravings. Religious wars really are fought in the name of religion, and they have been horribly frequent in history.[33]

Even though atheists are responsible for genocide on a horrendous scale, the Marxist and Nazi perpetrators belong to the equivalent of a different sect or denomination of atheism, not the scientific kind of atheism Dawkins and Harris espouse. In short, a specifically scientific, rational, critical form of atheism would not, once in power, engage in genocide; rather, it would eliminate the atrocities of both religion and the unorthodox forms of historical atheism. This seems to be the position advocated here by the new evangelical atheists.

Dawkins's attempt to exonerate atheism by extricating science from Nazi genocide does not persuade Marilynne Robinson. Even though anti-Semitism certainly predated the rise of Darwinism, during the second decade of the twentieth century it was at such low ebb that it had virtually no active influence on German society. It bordered on the forgotten. What happened then was that Hitler adopted Darwinian eugenics into his program of racial hygiene; and within the eugenic theory he redefined the "Jew" in genetic or racial rather than religious terms. Hitler produced a scientized racism. The winds of the *Zeitgeist* then began to blow in the direction of genocide. It was science, not religion, that propelled Nazi Germany toward the Holocaust, says Robinson.

> To Dawkins's objection that Nazi science was not authentic science I would reply, first, that neither Nazis nor Germans had any monopoly on these theories, which were influential throughout the Western world, and second, that the research on human subjects carried out by those holding such assumptions was good enough science to appear in medical texts for fully half a century. This is not to single out science as exceptionally inclined to do harm, though its capacity for doing harm is by now unequaled. It is only to note that science, too, is implicated in this bleak human proclivity, and is one major instrument of it.[34]

In short, to identify atheism with pure science in order to distance it from the Nazi atrocities fails in its attempt to persuade us that a scientized atheism would usher in human virtue and world peace.

What Response Does the Atheist Challenge Elicit from Christian Theology?

The evangelical atheists are posing quite a challenge to Christian belief. I think this challenge warrants a pause and a re-asking of the question: Just how do we know what we think we know about God? Is the existence of God a hypothesis that is open to confirmation or disconfirmation?

Christian knowledge is based upon revelation. This revelation is of two types, natural revelation and special revelation. To what extent does the atheist challenge affect what we know from these two sources? To this matter I now turn. I will briefly treat four subtopics dealing with our knowledge of God: general revelation, special revelation, the theology of the cross, and the hypothetical character of Christian claims.

What Does Natural Revelation Tell Us about God?

Romans 1:20 reads: "Ever since the creation of the world his eternal power and divine nature, invisible though they are, have been understood and seen through the things he has made. So they are without excuse."[35] The apostle Paul asserts that the invisible God who created this world can be perceived by observing and reflecting on the things of this world. Knowledge of God is available for those who are willing to allow this knowledge to enter their minds. Yet, we human observers can resist. We can turn off this awareness. We can deny our speculations about a creator and acknowledge that only what is created exists. The presence of God within the world of nature is ambiguous—that is, we can interpret what we learn either as giving evidence of God or not. Those who perceive but refuse to see are described by the apostle as "without excuse."

Perhaps we should pause here for a moment. Objective evidence of the creator God's presence can be seen within our created world; yet, this evidence is not in itself completely persuasive. If we are so motivated, we can interpret it away. Perhaps we can borrow an element from Jesus' parables. Some listeners hear the point, while others miss it. In Mark 4:9 Jesus says, "Let anyone with ears to hear, listen!" Perhaps when it comes to natural revelation, we need the eyes of faith to see it as revelation. This would suggest that rather than a *natural theology*, we are working with a *theology of nature*.

But we are getting ahead of ourselves. What we are talking about here is natural revelation, sometimes described as general revelation. It is awareness of the invisible divine reality that is generally or universally available to all people of all times and all places. General revelation can be shared by Christian and non-Christian believers, by all those with eyes of faith who can see the fingerprints of the creator God. Psalm 8:3 reads: "When I look at your heavens, the work of your fingers, the moon and the stars that you have established. . . ." The golden-tongued St. John Chrysostom speaks for the Christian tradition both East and West when he says, "with respect to the heavens . . . the Scythian and Barbarian, and Indian, and Egyptian, and every man that walks upon the earth shall hear this voice; for not by means of the ears, but through the sight, it reaches our understanding."[36] When we perceive the intricacies and beauty of our natural world, from within us we can sense the rising up of questions: Who made all this? What is its source? What is its future? Such questions can be asked by people in any region or climate. These questions bring to the surface an inner intuition of the divine.

> All things bright and beautiful,
>   All creatures great and small,
> All things wise and wonderful,
>   The Lord God made them all.
>
> Each little flower that opens,
>   Each little bird that sings,
> He made their glowing colours,
>   He made their tiny wings . . .
>
> He gave us eyes to see them,
>   And lips that we might tell
> How great is God Almighty,
>   Who has made all things well.
> (Cecil Frances Alexander, 1818–1895)

When Christendom was pregnant and giving birth to what we now know as modern science, many of the empirical researchers as well as the learned theologians worked with the concept of the *two books*. One book is the Bible. The other book is the natural world. What scientists such as Galileo and Newton learned from studying the natural world, they say, complements what we learn from the Scriptures. Nature teaches us about God as creator, while the Bible teaches us about God the redeemer (as well as God the creator). In his *Advancement of Learning*, Francis Bacon contends that "Our Saviour lays before us two volumes to study, if we will be secured from error: first, the scriptures, revealing the will of God; and then the creatures expressing his power . . . due to a mediation of the omnipotency of God, which is chiefly signed and engraven upon his works."[37] Similarly, the *Belgic Confession* of the Dutch Reformed Church describes nature as an open book for scientific reading: "We know him [God] by two means: First, by the creation, preservation, and government of the universe, since that universe is before our eyes like a beautiful book. . . . Second, he makes himself known to us more openly by his holy and divine Word."[38] In the Christian library we find two revelatory books: the Bible and the book of nature.

> I raised my eyes aloft, and I beheld
> The scattered chapters of the Universe
> Gathered and bound into a single book
> By the austere and tender hand of God.
> (Dante Alighieri, 1265–1321)

Just what is happening with our New Atheists? Are they reading the book of nature rightly? Why do they miss seeing the divine fingers that have placed the sun and the moon and the stars in our heavens? In the case of Richard Dawkins, he deliberately turns the existence of God into a scientific hypothesis—that is, he looks for an explanation of God claims in the same domain in which he looks for claims about the natural world. Then, he concludes that it is very improbable that God exists. Dawkins's appeal to empirical evidence fails to prove the existence of the kind of god he is looking for. What this indicates is that the manner in which Dawkins gathers evidence does not permit the revelation of a transcendent reality. It is possible to look at our world but not see God. It is possible to read the book of nature and attribute what is written there to itself, a book without an author. This is what Dawkins has done.

With regard to natural revelation, we have just noted that this revelation is ambiguous. Scientific viewers can look at the created world and either recognize or not recognize evidence of its creator. The scientific method is neutral on the God question, because it looks solely for natural explanations of natural phenomena.

What Does Special Revelation Tell Us about God?

Special revelation comes to us courtesy of the Bible. The term "special revelation" can refer to the Bible itself or, more frequently in our own era, to the Gospel of Jesus Christ to which the Bible gives witness. Jesus Christ is the Word of God incarnate, and the Bible is a collection of human words that present to us the divine Word. To identify special revelation with the words of the Bible is characteristic of orthodox or fundamentalist Christianity, while identifying special revelation with the person of Jesus Christ reported by the Bible is more characteristic of neo-orthodox and liberal Christianity. In both cases, the Bible provides the printed book that, along with the book of nature, provides us with knowledge of God.

Perhaps the chief attribute of the God revealed in the Scriptures is grace. God is gracious. God creates out of love for the world; and God redeems out of this same love. The ancient Hebrews experienced God's gracious love—called *chesed* or "mercy" in the Old Testament—in the form of liberating power during the exodus. Deuteronomy 4:34, 37 states: "by a mighty hand and an outstretched arm. . . . He brought you out of Egypt with his own presence, by his great power." While the Hebrews were slaves in the land of Egypt, God rescued them and escorted them to the land of promise. God transformed a group of slaves into a people, the people of God. This exodus was an unpredictable and unmerited act on the part of God, an act of divine grace.

In the New Testament, this same divine grace is responsible for the incarnation, life, death, and resurrection of Jesus Christ. John 3:16 declares:

"For God so loved the world that he gave his only Son, so that everyone who believes in him may not perish but may have eternal life." By raising Jesus Christ from the dead on the first Easter, God issues to the human race a promise that more resurrections are to come. We too will rise as the Messiah did. First Corinthians 15:20 proclaims: "But in fact Christ has been raised from the dead, the first fruits of those who have died." Our resurrection will occur at the advent of the new creation, the full establishment of the kingdom of God. Just as the Nazarene rose to new life on the first Easter, all of the present creation will rise into the consummate new creation. For us now to have faith in God's promise is to live daily in anticipation of this future fulfillment. In 2 Corinthians 5:17 we read: "So if anyone is in Christ, there is a new creation: everything old has passed away; see, everything has become new!" In faith, we today can at least fragmentarily embody ahead of time what God has promised for our future healing, renewal, and transformation. This is the message of redemption revealed to us in the printed book, the Bible.

I suggest we think of the Bible as the criterial source and formal norm for theological reflection. The material norm—the truth that the Christian faith proclaims—is the Gospel of Jesus Christ. How do we learn about this gospel? From the Bible. The Bible is the primary source for this revelation. We have nowhere to go other than the Bible to gain trustworthy knowledge of Jesus Christ and the gospel message. Therefore, the Scriptures become the judge that measures our own explications of the faith. This is why I refer to the Bible as the *criterial source* and the *formal norm*.[39] Or, more simply, the Bible is where we go for special revelation.

Christian believers will readily rely upon the Scriptures, both Old and New Testaments, as special revelation. Non-Christians might not. Islam has its own holy book, the Qur'an. Muslims claim the text of the Qur'an was dictated by God to his chosen prophet, Muhammad. We have competing authorities here. One nullifies the other, so it seems at least. We could not rationally adopt both the Bible and the Qur'an as the criterial source, let alone as the material norm for our Christian faith's reflection.

Does this place the Bible right along with the book of nature into an ambiguous situation—that is, can we read the book of nature along with the Bible and still retain the option to either believe or disbelieve? Yes, this seems to be the case. We cannot escape the freedom placed upon our subjectivity, the freedom to believe or disbelieve any religious or anti-religious claim.[40] Nature and Scripture may be sources for knowing God, but we are still free to misread or deny what is revealed. Genuine textual authority is not imposed from above, say our hermeneutical philosophers; rather, a text can be dubbed authoritative only when large numbers of persons voluntarily find guidance in it. What this means is that appeal to special revelation or proof-texting is not likely to be persuasive to an atheist for whom Scripture is not authoritative.

What Does the "Theology of the Cross" Tell Us about God?

What Christians believe about God would become even less persuasive to an atheist if we were to engage the *theology of the cross*. With this label, we refer to the paradox within special revelation, namely, God is revealed in, with, and under what is not divine. Specifically, the event of the cross reveals God in a most unexpected and mysterious way. In the cross we see tragedy, defeat, suffering, and death. Yet, to the eyes of faith, the God of meaning, victory, salvation, and resurrection is present. In, with, and under the weakness of the cross, the power of God is present. In, with, and under the degradation of Jesus, the glory of God is present.

The theology of the cross comes to us from the Reformation, especially the work of Martin Luther. The Reformer writes, "The manifest and visible things of God are placed in opposition to the invisible, namely, his human nature, weakness, foolishness. . . . It does [a theologian] no good to recognize God in his glory and majesty, unless he recognizes him in the humility and shame of the cross. . . . 'Truly, thou art a God who hidest thyself' (Isa. 45:15)."[41] The heart of God along with God's willingness to share the sufferings of the world God so loves come to articulation in the event of the cross.

Now, much could be said about this rich insight. However, I would like to draw just one implication, namely, any attempt to confirm the atheist's God hypothesis in a so-called scientific manner could never admit this kind of evidence found in the cross.

The event of the cross toward which the Scriptures aim our eyes is an event of revelation. Yet, this mode of revelation cannot in any way be placed in the same categories of knowledge with which a scientist might work. To study the natural world scientifically is to examine our world with microscopes and telescopes and other measuring devices; and then the scientist cautiously reports what is confirmable knowledge. The paradoxical and mysterious dimension of the cross event simply cannot be turned into subject matter for empirical research. It should come as no surprise to a theologian of the cross that Dawkins and Stenger are unable to verify their God hypothesis based upon what they construe as empirical evidence.

Christians who place their faith in the God of grace revealed in, with, and under the cross of Jesus Christ are unaffected by such a God hypothesis. This is the case for two reasons. First, the God Dawkins or Stenger is testing for is not exactly the same God revealed in the cross. Oh yes, we are talking about the omnipotent God of theism who is responsible for the creation of the world, to be sure. Yet, what Christian faith discerns in the cross is that God is gracious; and this cannot be discerned when asking about the creative power behind natural phenomena. Second, the two pathways to knowledge are not consonant. To set out to confirm or disconfirm a scientific hypothesis is to look for relevant evidence that supports or challenges the hypothesis. All such evidence is evaluated positively. Revelation through the cross, in contrast, provides negative knowledge, or at least paradoxical knowledge. We see weakness, but power is revealed. We see defeat, but victory is revealed. We see sin, but forgiveness is revealed. We see disgrace, but grace is revealed. The truth or falsity of this Christian claim cannot be adjudicated by an appeal to scientific research. That Dawkins and Stenger do not even raise the question of God's graciousness to the level of a hypothesis is no surprise, to be sure; but it signifies that they do not address what is at the heart of Christian belief in God.

Can We Treat the Christian Claim Regarding God as a Hypothesis?

We have just noted three things. First, even though the God of creation is revealed in the world of nature, this revelation is ambiguous. Scientific viewers can look at the created world and either recognize or not recognize evidence of its creator. The scientific method is neutral on the God question, because it looks solely for natural explanations of natural phenomena. Second, appeal to special revelation in the form of scriptural testimony to God's redemptive work is less than fully persuasive. Scripture is authoritative only for those who in faith cede authority to it. An atheist simply denies this authority and goes his or her own way. Third, learning through the theology of the cross that the God of creation is also a God of grace diverts the eyes of faith even further away from scientific method. Paradox and mystery of this type do not count as evidence for a scientific hypothesis.

Where does this leave us? Might there be any way in which we could consider the question of God as a hypothesis? Yes, there are two ways or paths: wagering and anticipating. The first way—the way of the wager—is to consider the existence of God as a hypothetical reality that not only explains our universe but also provides a map for us to follow in holy living. What has been nicknamed "Pascal's wager" might provide an example. In his *Pensées* of 1670, Blaise Pascal contended that the hypothesis of God's existence could not be conclusively decided by science or metaphysics. The issue could be settled only by an existential or practical decision to live as if Christian claims about God are true. If one wagers that God exists and it becomes confirmed, then one gains an infinite blessing. If it is disconfirmed, one suffers only a finite loss. What is distinctive about this wager is the move from rational reflection to a practical or existential decision.

American philosopher Charles Sanders Peirce refined somewhat the interaction between hypothetical reflection and pragmatic living. Peirce tendered a version of the God hypothesis as a natural direction that human thought takes. He described speculative thinking with the term *musement.*

"Enter your skiff of Musement, push off into the lake of thought, and leave the breath of heaven to swell your sail. With your eyes open, awake to what is about or within you, and open conversation with yourself."[42] Peirce's skiff pushes off into the sea of musement about the comprehensive source and ground of the universe to which we belong; and he considers all things "in the light of the hypothesis of God's Reality." The person who considers the God hypothesis and "pursues that line of reflection in scientific singleness of heart, will come to be stirred to the depths of his nature by the beauty of the idea and by its august practicality, even to the point of earnestly loving and adoring his strictly hypothetical God, and to that of desiring above all things to shape the whole conduct of life and all the springs of action into conformity with that hypothesis."[43] To live the life of faith will over time confirm—existentially confirm—the God hypothesis.

The second path the God hypothesis can follow is that of anticipation. Christian faith is attached to Christian hope; and this hope takes its bearing from what God has planned for our future. Until God's future becomes actual, we place our faith in what is invisible and our hope in what is promised. The structure of faith and hope together prompts in the mind of the theologian something similar to a hypothesis. A hypothesis is a proposition set forth as an explanation that is subject to evidence-gathering and reasoning to see whether it might be true or false. A hypothesis is a provisional judgment that is subject to future confirmation or disconfirmation. Because the Christian claim includes the eschatological vision of the kingdom of God, it is inescapably hypothetical until God's kingdom becomes actualized. Because God's raising of Jesus on Easter has become for us a promise of the coming new creation, our claim regarding God's redemption remains provisional until this divine promise is fulfilled.

The hope of the apostle Paul is oriented toward the eschatological actualization of God's promise for full revelation. What Paul knows now in part will be replaced with the fullness of knowledge. What Paul knows now is dim; but in the future he will be blessed with the bright light of truth. First Corinthians 13:12 declares: "For now we see in a mirror, dimly, but then we will see face to face. Now I know only in part; then I will know fully, even as I have been fully known."

The contrast between what Paul knows now in part with the fullness of eschatological knowledge could have a double meaning. It could refer subjectively to Paul's current fragmentary knowledge compared to a more comprehensive revelation yet to come. Or, objectively, Paul could be anticipating a future awareness of God's presence that imbues all things; he could be anticipating that all things in creation will finally realize their total dependence upon God for their explanation. Without God, the individual things of our universe cannot be understood realistically. All creatures can be fully understood only when perceived in their proper place as God's creatures. The whole of reality can be understood only in light of the God who creates and recreates. Here is how Wolfhart Pannenberg presents it: "*The reality of God is always present only to subjective anticipations of the totality of reality . . . which means that they are subject to confirmation or refutation by subsequent experience.* Anticipation therefore always involves hypothesis."[44] For the Christian to think eschatologically is to think hypothetically about the whole of reality in relation to the one God, the God who raised Jesus from the dead and who promises fulfillment in the new creation.

Anticipating the fulfillment of the divine promise given us by God in Jesus' Easter resurrection, we can look forward to resolving the paradox of the theology of the cross. Once God has confirmed the divine promise for a new creation, then the meaning of Jesus' crucifixion will find its rightful place and cease to be the mystery that it is for us now. Only in light of our trust in the future does the cross count as empirical evidence for the graciousness of our redeeming God.

We can refine this hypothetical structure of Christian hope by appeal to the work of Robert John Russell. Russell contends that the Easter resurrection of Jesus is the first instance of a new law of nature—that is, what happened to Jesus when God raised him will happen to the rest of God's beloved creatures at the advent of the eschatological new creation. Or, to put it another way, the laws of nature upon which today's scientists rely apply comprehensively to past and present phenomena in nature. What understandably goes unobserved by today's scientists is the prospect that the laws of nature tomorrow might be different. Today, dead people remain dead. Tomorrow, the dead shall rise.

This future resurrection will not be a miracle—that is, only a miracle. Rather, it will be more than a miracle; it will be the way the transformed natural world works. "Within the context of the coming new creation the Resurrection of Jesus will be the first instance of a general, regular phenomenon, the general resurrection from the dead and life everlasting. It might better be termed 'the first instance of a new law of the new creation' (FINLONC)."[45] This is God's promise to us. When we try to explain our world in terms of this promise, our explanation takes a hypothetical form.

This element makes the theological enterprise look a bit different from what is widely assumed. The very use of the word *dogma* in common parlance suggests that religious beliefs are tenaciously held in the face of countervailing evidence, that theologians are rigid and atavistic. Dennett, cited above, assumes "religious orthodoxy" cannot abandon any of its claims and renew itself, even though science can. It certainly must be admitted that at points in the Christian tradition dogmatic rigidity has exerted intellectual tyranny. Yet, by placing a magnifying glass over the theological method of reflecting on the implications of Christian faith and hope, we can see the inescapable hypothetical structure at work. Unless and until God fulfills this divine promise, we can see only in a mirror dimly.

In sum, we can find hypotheses in both science and theology. Hypothetical structures can be found in both types of thinking. With this observation we can consider theology to be scientific, in at least a limited sense. The test of both depends on the future confirmation of a hypothesis. With these considerations in mind, we should expect that the attempt by Dawkins or Stenger or others to confirm the God hypothesis through scientific research would fail—at least if they are looking for the kind of God in whom Christians place their hope. Given evidence drawn from the present laws of nature, the God who promises a new creation would seem invisible. Only when the scientist looks at the whole of nature in light of its past and future might the question of God arise; and even then it could not be answered apodictically on this side of God's eschatological consummation.

Conclusion

Spokespersons for the new breed of aggressive atheists assume they have a patent on scientific knowing, and that scientific methods for knowing this world can be applied satisfactorily to the question of God's existence. When they hypothesize that God exists and then examine the evidence, they find they can invalidate the hypothesis. God does not exist, they conclude.

The kind of divine figure who ends up without existence here is either the bearded old man, Zeus, or the invisible creator god of classical theism. The graciousness of God that is decisive for the Christian is revealed in the mysterious paradox of the cross and the promise of the resurrection. Neither the cross nor the resurrection is subject to scientific assessment, at least in the science we are currently used to. The cross cannot be scientifically interpreted because its truths about God are revealed under their opposites in the human Jesus; this is paradoxical. Nor can the resurrection be scientifically interpreted if science restricts itself to looking for explanations based upon the laws of nature that obtain for the past and present. The truth of the Christian claim for a coming new creation is subject to divine confirmation in the future. It is now available to Christian hope in only a provisional and anticipatory form. Until we see God face to face, we will see God only dimly.

It has not been my task in this chapter to defend the world's religions from the criticisms leveled by the atheists. Some criticisms regarding the role of religious leaders in inciting violence should be taken seriously, despite the unwillingness of our atheist colleagues to acknowledge responsibility for the atrocities of their twentieth-century predecessors. Rather, my task has been to show how the formulation of the God hypothesis within the rubric of science is not equipped to evaluate what is so important to

Christians, namely, that what is revealed in the cross and resurrection of Jesus Christ is that the God of our creation and redemption is a God of grace. To live daily with faith in the God of grace leads to a gracious form of living—a loving form of living—that is neither irrational nor violent in its intention.

Notes

Preface

1. Alister McGrath, *The Twilight of Atheism: The Rise and Fall of Disbelief in the Modern World* (New York: Doubleday, 2004).

Introduction

1. Pippa Norris and Ronald Inglehart, *Sacred and Secular: Religion and Politics Worldwide* (Cambridge: Cambridge University Press, 2004), 25.

2. Phil Zuckerman, "Contemporary Numbers and Patterns," in *The Cambridge Companion to Atheism*, ed. Michael Martin (Cambridge: Cambridge University Press, 2007), 57–59.

3. Ibid., 59.

4. Jan N. Bremmer, "Atheism in Antiquity," in *The Cambridge Companion to Atheism*, 12.

5. Anselm, *Proslogion*, II-III, in *Anselm of Canterbury: The Major Works*, ed. Brian Davies and G. R. Evans (New York: Oxford University Press, 1998), 87–88.

6. Thomas was especially concerned to respond to thinkers such as John Damascene, who maintained that knowledge of God's existence is innate. See Frederick Copleston, *A History of Philosophy*, Mediaeval Philosophy (Garden City, N.Y.: Image, 1962), 2:55–56.

7. For a fuller discussion of this see Linda Trinkhaus Zagzebski, *Philosophy of Religion: An Historical Introduction* (Malden, Mass.: Blackwell, 2007), chap. 2.

8. Gavin Hyman, "Atheism in Modern History," in *The Cambridge Companion to Atheism*, 27–28.

9. Michael Buckley, *Denying and Disclosing God: The Ambiguous Progress of Modern Atheism* (New Haven: Yale University Press, 2004), 42.

10. Gary Wolf, "The Church of the Non-Believers," http://www.wired.com/wired/archive/14.11/atheism_pr.html, accessed 16 February 2008.

11. What exactly makes for "good science," or even "science," is a philosophical question, specifically a question that is addressed by philosophy of science. It is not a question that science can answer. It is also a question to which widely divergent answers have been given. Simply put, there is no widespread agreement on the matter.

12. Richard Dawkins, review of *Blueprints: Solving the Mystery of Evolution* by Maitland A. Edey and Donald C. Johanson, *New York Times Review of Books* (9 April 1989), 35. To put this oft-quoted sentence from Dawkins in context, he is referring here to "the fact" of evolution rather than Darwin's theory of natural selection. By

"fact," I take it that he means evidence of evolution such as fossils, vestigial organs, and so on, rather than the mechanism in which he and others believe so strongly in via inference.

13. Daniel Dennett, "Shame on Rea," http://ase.tufts.edu/cogstud/papers/rearesponse.htm, accessed 5 March 2008.

14. Wolf, "The Church of the Non-Believers."

15. Richard Dawkins, *The Blind Watchmaker: Why the Evidence of Evolution Reveals a Universe Without Design* (New York: W. W. Norton, 1996), 6.

16. Richard Dawkins, *The Selfish Gene* (New York: Oxford University Press, 1989), 1.

17. Daniel C. Dennett, *Darwin's Dangerous Idea: Evolution and the Meanings of Life* (New York: Simon & Schuster, 1995), 63.

18. One often hears that those who reject Darwinism are opposed to science. That the battle is over Darwinism, not science, is made clear simply by observing that not only are many conservative Christians scientists and physicians, but that conservative Christian dollars fund hospitals and medical research. Whether or not conservative Christians are exercising good scientific judgment is another issue, but clearly the broad-brush charge that those who reject Darwinism are unscientific is simplistic.

19. Dennett, *Darwin's Dangerous Idea*, 18.

20. Stephen Jay Gould, "Impeaching a Self-Appointed Judge: Book Review of *Darwin on Trial* by Phillip E. Johnson," *Scientific American* 267, no. 1 (July 1992): 119.

21. I am indebted to John Lennox for this analogy. See John C. Lennox, *God's Undertaker: Has Science Buried God?* (Oxford: Lion, 2007), 44.

22. Dinesh D'Souza, *What's So Great About Christianity?* (Washington, D.C.: Regnery, 2007), 67–79.

23. Friedrich Nietzsche, *The Will to Power*, trans. Walter Kaufmann and R. J. Hollingdale (New York: Vintage, 1968), 401. For those reading the original language or working with different translations, the section quoted is found in aphorism 765, "Redemption for all guilt."

24. Keith Ward, *Is Religion Dangerous?* (Oxford: Lion, 2006), 179–80.

25. Alister McGrath, *The Twilight of Atheism: The Rise and Fall of Disbelief in the Modern World* (New York: Doubleday, 2004), 1–169, esp. 21–47.

26. Patricia Smith Churchland, "Epistemology in the Age of Neuroscience," *Journal of Philosophy* 84 (October 1987): 548–49. Italics in original.

27. Richard Rorty, "Untruth and Consequences," *The New Republic* (31 July 1995), 32–36.

28. Alvin Plantinga, *Warrant and Proper Function* (New York: Oxford University Press, 1993), 216–37. For a thorough discussion of this argument, involving both theists and nontheists, see James Beilby, *Naturalism Defeated: Essays on Plantinga's Evolutionary Argument Against Naturalism* (Ithaca: Cornell University Press, 2002).

29. Richard Dawkins and Steven Pinker, "Is Science Killing the Soul?" http://www.edge.org/3rd_culture/dawkins_pinker/debate_p4.html, accessed 5 March 2008.

30. A partial list of books by Dennett addressing these and other topics includes *Brainstorms* (Cambridge, Mass.: MIT Press, 1978); *Consciousness Explained* (Boston:

Little, Brown, 1991); *Kinds of Minds: Towards an Understanding of Consciousness* (New York: Basic, 1996); *Brainchildren: Essays on Designing Minds* (Cambridge, Mass.: MIT Press, 1998); and *Sweet Dreams: Philosophical Obstacles to a Science of Consciousness* (Cambridge, Mass.: MIT Press, 2005).

31. John R. Searle, *The Rediscovery of Mind* (Cambridge, Mass.: MIT Press, 1992), 9.

32. The center's advisory board is made up of Susan Blackmore, Paul Bloom, Paul Brocks, Daniel Dennett, Sheldon Drobny, Owen Flanagan, Ursula Goodenough, Joseph Hilbe, Nicholas Humphrey, Brian Leiter, Thomas Metzinger, Tamler Sommers, and John Symons. See http://www.centerfornaturalism.org/index.htm, accessed 10 March 2008.

33. http://www.naturalism.org/tenetsof.htm, accessed 10 March 2008.

34. For Dennett's contributions, see *Elbow Room: The Varieties of Free Will Worth Wanting* (New York: Oxford University Press, 1985); *The Intentional Stance* (Cambridge, Mass.: MIT Press, 1987); *Freedom Evolves* (New York: Viking, 2003).

35. Dawkins, *The Selfish Gene*, 11.

36. For a useful brief survey of the various perspectives on memes as well as a useful bibliography on the subject, see Susan Blackmore, "Meme," in *Encyclopedia of Evolution* (New York: Oxford University Press, 2002), 2:713–16.

37. Ibid., 2:716.

38. Ibid., 2:716.

39. Daniel Dennett, "The New Replicators," in *Encyclopedia of Evolution*, 1:E83–92.

40. Blackmore, "Meme," 2:716.

41. Ibid., 2:716.

Chapter 1

1. Dr. Charles Kelley, president of New Orleans Baptist Theological Seminary, welcomed the audience prior to the dialogue and explained that a hallmark of Baptist theology is the conviction that all individuals are free to believe according to the dictates of conscience, and no human authority, whether civil or ecclesial, has any right to coerce belief. Baptists believe in persuasion, not coercion, and the freedom of all persons to believe as they will before God.

2. TED stands for "Technology, Entertainment, Design." It is an annual conference that brings together leading thinkers in various fields to network and discuss new ideas. TED is devoted to giving millions of knowledge-seekers around the globe direct access to the world's greatest thinkers and teachers. http://www.ted.com/index.php/pages/view/id/5, accessed 27 May 2008.

3. Paul B. MacCready, "Future of Technology: A New Perspective: Part One: An Ambivalent Luddite at a Technological Feast," http://www.designfax.net/archives/0899/899trl_2.asp, accessed 27 May 2008.

4. Phil Zuckerman, "Atheism: Contemporary Numbers and Patterns," in *The Cambridge Companion to Atheism*, ed. Michael Martin (New York: Cambridge University Press, 2007), 47–65.

5. Laurie Goodstein, "Evangelicals Fear the Loss of Their Teenagers," *New York Times*, 6 October 2006.

6. Gregory S. Paul, "Cross-National Correlations of Quantifiable Societal Health with Popular Religiosity and Secularism in the Prosperous Democracies: A First Look," *Journal of Religion and Society* 7 (2005).

7. Rick Warren, *The Purpose-Driven Life: What on Earth Am I Here For?* (Grand Rapids: Zondervan, 2002), 77.

8. Ibid., 80.

9. You can view it online at http://www.ted.com/index.php/talks/view/id/94, accessed 27 May 2008.

10. Hugh S. Pyper, "The Selfish Text: The Bible and Memetics," in *Biblical Studies/Cultural Studies: The Third Sheffield Colloquium*, ed. J. Cheryl Exum and Stephen D. Moore (Sheffield: Sheffield Academic, 1998), 70.

11. Michael Shermer, *How We Believe: Science, Skepticism, and the Search for God* (New York: Freeman, 2000), 16–31.

12. Daniel Dennett, *Breaking the Spell: Religion as a Natural Phenomenon* (New York: Viking, 2006), 9.

13. The final two years (optional) of British secondary education, usually taken in preparation for university study.

14. See Stephen Shennan, *Genes, Memes and Human History: Darwinian Archaeology and Cultural Evolution* (London: Thames & Hudson, 2002).

15. Maurice Bloch, "A Well-Disposed Social Anthropologist's Problem with Memes," in *Darwinizing Culture: The Status of Memetics as a Science*, ed. Robert Aunger (Oxford: Oxford University Press, 2000), 189–203.

16. Simon Conway Morris, *Life's Solution: Inevitable Humans in a Lonely Universe* (Cambridge: Cambridge University Press, 2003), 324.

17. Dennett, *Breaking the Spell*, 344.

18. Alan Costall, "The 'Meme' Meme," *Cultural Dynamics* 4 (1991): 321–35.

19. Richard Dawkins, *A Devil's Chaplain* (London: Weidenfield & Nicholson, 2003), 124.

20. Peter B. Medawar, *The Limits of Science* (Oxford: Oxford University Press, 1985), 66.

21. Ibid.

22. Dawkins, *A Devil's Chaplain*, 34.

23. See Ernan McMullin, *The Inference That Makes Science* (Milwaukee: Marquette University Press, 1992); Stathos Psillos, "Simply the Best: A Case for Abduction," in *Computational Logic: Logic Programming and Beyond*, ed. Robert Kowalski, Antonis C. Kakas, and Fariba Sadri (Berlin: Springer, 2002), 605–25.

24. C. S. Lewis, "Is Theology Poetry?" in *Essay Collection and Other Short Pieces* (London: HarperCollins, 2000), 21.

25. Robert Boyd and Peter Richerson, *Culture and the Evolutionary Process* (Chicago: University of Chicago Press, 1985).

Chapter 2

1. Michael Martin, *Atheism: A Philosophical Justification* (Philadelphia: Temple University Press, 1990).

2. See Bruno LaTour and Steve Woolgar, *Laboratory Life: The Construction of Scientific Facts*, 2d ed. (Princeton: Princeton University Press, 1986).

3. Alister McGrath, *The Twilight of Atheism: The Rise and Fall of Disbelief in the Modern World* (New York: Doubleday, 2004), 60–67.

4. Ibid., 234.

5. Ibid., 232–33.

6. David Hume, *The Natural History of Religion*, in *David Hume: Writings on Religion*, ed. Antony Flew (La Salle, Ill.: Open Court, 1992), 146–47.

7. McGrath, *The Twilight of Atheism*, 235.

8. Roger Scruton, "The Philosopher on Dover Beach," *The Times Literary Supplement*, 23 May 1986, 565.

9. McGrath, *The Twilight of Atheism*, 179–83.

10. Ibid., 179.

11. Ibid.

12. Ibid., 182–83.

13. Ibid., 180.

14. Alister McGrath, "Has Science Eliminated God? Richard Dawkins and the Meaning of Life," 2. http://www.st-edmunds.cam.ac.uk/cis/mcgrath/pdf/mcgrath_lecture.pdf, accessed 10 January 2008.

15. David Hume, *Dialogues Concerning Natural Religion*, ed. Richard H. Popkin (Indianapolis: Hackett, 1986), 15.

16. Richard Dawkins, *The Blind Watchmaker* (New York: Norton, 1986).

17. McGrath, "Has Science Eliminated God?" 4.

18. Ibid.

19. Mark Isaak, *The Counter-Creationism Handbook* (Berkeley: University of California Press, 2007), 113–28.

20. Michael J. Behe, *Darwin's Black Box: The Biochemical Challenge to Evolution* (New York: Free Press, 1996); William A. Dembski, *The Design Inference. Eliminating Chance through Small Probabilities* (New York: Cambridge University Press, 1998).

21. For rebuttals of intelligent design, see Kenneth R. Miller, *Finding Darwin's God: A Scientist's Search for Common Ground Between God and Evolution* (New York: Cliff Street, 1999); Robert T. Pennock, *Tower of Babel: The Evidence against the New Creationism* (Cambridge, Mass.: MIT Press, 1999); Robert T. Pennock, ed., *Intelligent Design Creationism and Its Critics: Philosophical, Theological, and Scientific Perspectives* (Cambridge, Mass.: MIT Press, 2001); Niles Eldredge, *The Triumph of Evolution and the Failure of Creationism* (New York: W. H. Freeman, 2000); Niall Shanks, *God, the Devil, and Darwin: A Critique of Intelligent Design Theory* (Oxford: Oxford University Press, 2004); Matt Young and Taner Edis, *Why Intelligent Design Fails: A Scientific Critique of the New Creationism* (New Brunswick, N.J.: Rutgers University Press, 2004);

Mark Perakh, *Unintelligent Design* (Amherst, N.Y.: Prometheus, 2004); P. Kitcher, *Living with Darwin: Evolution, Design, and the Future of Faith* (Oxford: Oxford University Press, 2007); and Isaak, *The Counter-Creationism Handbook*; and, of course, many entries in the online talk.origins archive (see http://www.talkorigins.org/).

22. Daniel Dennett, *Darwin's Dangerous Idea: Evolution and the Meanings of Life* (New York: Simon & Schuster, 1995).

23. McGrath, "Has Science Eliminated God?" 6.

24. Ibid., 12.

25. For example, see John C. Whitcomb and Henry M. Morris, *The Genesis Flood: The Biblical Record and Its Scientific Implications* (Grand Rapids: Baker, 1961); Duane T. Gish, *Dinosaurs by Design* (Colorado Springs: Creation-Life, 1992).

26. McGrath, "Has Science Eliminated God?" 14–16.

27. Quoted in James Carroll, *Constantine's Sword: The Church and the Jews— A History* (New York: Mariner, 2002), 213.

28. Quoted in ibid., 368.

29. John Beversluis, *C. S. Lewis and the Search for Rational Religion*, 2d ed. (Amherst, N.Y.: Prometheus, 2007).

30. McGrath, *The Twilight of Atheism*, 189–92.

31. Tomás de Torquemada (1420–1498) was the Grand Inquisitor of Spain for many years, leaving to posterity an image of extraordinary fanaticism and implacability.

Chapter 3

1. Quentin Smith, "The Metaphilosophy of Naturalism," *Philo* 4, no. 2 (2001): 3–4. A sign of the times: *Philo* itself, unable to succeed as a secular organ, has now become a journal for general philosophy of religion.

2. "Modernizing the Case for God," *Time* (7 April 1980), 65–66.

3. What about the existence of the fact itself? A fact may be taken to be a true proposition. Propositions exist necessarily, if they exist at all. What is contingent about them is their truth value. So the proposition exists by a necessity of its own nature, while its truth value may or may not have an explanation.

4. Richard Taylor, *Metaphysics*, 4th ed., Foundations of Philosophy (Englewood Cliffs, N.J.: Prentice-Hall, 1991), 100–101.

5. Crispin Wright and Bob Hale, "Nominalism and the Contingency of Abstract Objects," *Journal of Philosophy* 89 (1992): 128. Wright and Hale's principal target is Hartry Field's claim that mathematical objects exist contingently and inexplicably.

6. Daniel Dennett, *Darwin's Dangerous Idea: Evolution and the Meanings of Life* (New York: Simon & Schuster, 1995), 181. Note well that the question need not be stated contrastively; one could simply ask why anything at all exists.

7. Moreover, the *kalam* cosmological argument complements the Leibnizian argument by giving reason to think that the universe does not exist necessarily. An essential property of a metaphysically necessary and ultimate being is that it

be eternal, that is to say, without beginning or end. If the universe is not eternal, then it could not be a metaphysically necessary being. But it is precisely the aim of the *kalam* cosmological argument to show that the universe is not eternal but had a beginning. It would follow that the universe must therefore be contingent in its existence. Not only so; the *kalam* argument shows the universe to be contingent in a very special way: it came into existence out of nothing. The atheist who would answer Leibniz by holding that the existence of the universe is a brute fact, an exception to the Principle of Sufficient Reason, is thus thrust into the very awkward position of maintaining not merely that the universe exists eternally without explanation, but rather that for no reason at all it magically popped into being out of nothing, a position that might make theism look like a welcome alternative.

8. One thinks of the famous case of the indigent man who darned his silk stockings with wool until he finally had a pair of wool stockings! They were clearly not identical to the original stockings. It might be said that had the man darned his socks with silk, then the ultimate outcome would have been the same pair of stockings despite their having none of the matter of the original pair. Less controversially, I remain identical over time despite a complete exchange of the material constituents of my body for new constituents. Analogously, universes could be identical across possible worlds even though they are composed of wholly different collections of quarks. The disanalogy, however, is that difference across possible worlds is no kind of change at all; there is no enduring subject that undergoes intrinsic change from one state to another. So it is more like the case of comparing pairs of stockings or human bodies that have no connection with each other.

The claim here becomes even more obvious when we reflect that it seems broadly logically possible that the fundamental building blocks of nature could have been substances quite different from quarks and so characterized by different laws of nature. Even if the laws of nature are taken to be broadly logically necessary, rather than necessary in some weaker sense called nomological necessity, it is possible that different laws of nature could have held because substances endowed with different dispositions and capacities than quarks could have existed. To think that in such a case it is the same universe in view would be like thinking that a particular pane of glass, for instance, could retain its identity if it had been made of steel.

9. Bede Rundle, *Why there is Something rather than Nothing* (New York: Oxford University Press, 2004).

10. Alexander Pruss, critical notice of Bede Rundle, *Why there is Something rather than Nothing, Philosophia Christi* 7 (2005): 210.

11. Daniel Dennett, *Breaking the Spell: Religion as a Natural Phenomenon* (New York: Viking, 2006), 242.

12. Ibid., 244. In a note he adds, "Descartes had raised the question of whether God had created the truths of mathematics. His follower Nicolas de Malebranche (1638–1715) firmly expressed the view that they needed no inception, being as eternal as anything could be." Presumably, Dennett means to say that they, being eternal, needed no *cause*; that is, being eternal, they had no inception and so needed no creating cause. Cf. the same claim verbatim in *Darwin's Dangerous Idea*, 184–85.

13. Quentin Smith, "The Uncaused Beginning of the Universe," in William Lane Craig and Quentin Smith, *Theism, Atheism, and Big Bang Cosmology* (Oxford: Clarendon Press, 1993), 120.

14. Arthur Eddington, *The Expanding Universe* (New York: Macmillan, 1933), 124.

15. Ibid., 178.

16. Stephen Hawking and Roger Penrose, *The Nature of Space and Time*, The Isaac Newton Institute Series of Lectures (Princeton: Princeton University Press, 1996), 20.

17. Alex Vilenkin, *Many Worlds in One: The Search for Other Universes* (New York: Hill and Wang, 2006), 176.

18. Dennett, *Breaking the Spell*, 244.

19. Ibid., 242.

20. See figure 17.1, Vilenkin, *Many Worlds in One*, 180.

21. See Peter Lipton, *Inference to the Best Explanation* (London: Routledge, 1991).

22. William A. Dembski, *The Design Inference: Eliminating Chance through Small Probabilities* (Cambridge: Cambridge University Press, 1998).

23. Robin Collins, *The Well-Tempered Universe* (forthcoming).

24. S. W. Hawking, "Cosmology from the Top Down," paper presented at the Davis Cosmic Inflation Meeting, UC Davis, 29 May 2003.

25. Dennett, *Darwin's Dangerous Idea*, 177.

26. T. Rothman and G. F. R. Ellis, "Smolin's Natural Selection Hypothesis," *Quarterly Journal of the Royal Astronomical Society* 34 (1993): 201–12.

27. Vilenkin, *Many Worlds in One*, 112.

28. Ibid., 214.

29. Ibid., 61.

30. Roger Penrose, *The Road to Reality: A Complete Guide to the Laws of the Universe* (New York: Knopf, 2004), 762–65.

31. For literature see Don N. Page, "Return of the Boltzmann Brains" (15 November 2006), http://arXiv:hep-th/0611158, accessed 19 May 2008.

32. Michael Ruse, "Evolutionary Theory and Christian Ethics," in *The Darwinian Paradigm* (London: Routledge, 1989), 262, 268–69.

33. Paul Kurtz, *Forbidden Fruit: The Ethics of Humanism* (Buffalo: Prometheus, 1988), 65.

34. William Rowe has dismissed as "absurd" the suggestion that objective moral values and duties would not exist in the absence of God, and Keith Yandell concurs with Richard Swinburne that moral truths, being necessarily true, cannot depend on God for the explanation of their truth. (See William Lane Craig and Antony Flew, *Does God Exist?*, ed. Stan Wallace [Aldershot, UK: Ashgate, 2003].) But when we realize that for both Swinburne and Yandell, the proposition *God exists* is not true in every possible world, whereas *Objective moral values exist* is, then it is obvious why they cannot countenance moral values' being grounded in God.

The mainstream Christian tradition has held that God's existence is broadly logically necessary, so that God can be the explanatory basis of necessary truths. Such truths, being explained not by God's will but by God's nature, could not have been false but are nonetheless not explanatorily ultimate. One could thus agree with Yandell that "there is no such thing as explaining that a necessary truth is true *rather than false*" (my emphasis). But it does not follow that there is no such thing as explaining that (or why) a necessary truth is true. Intriguingly, Yandell does allow that a metaphysical *analysis*, rather than *explanation*, can be given, according to which necessary moral principles are true in virtue of the existence of some necessary being. What I call an "explanation" Yandell calls an "analysis" because he has built into his definition of "explanation" that it must eliminate possible falsehood. But whether we call such an account of the basis of morality an explanation or an analysis, it clearly grounds necessary moral truths asymmetrically in some necessary being. Yandell even gives us the two candidates for the ground of necessary moral truths: God or abstract objects. I agree that these are the alternatives before us.

35. Richard Taylor, *Ethics, Faith, and Reason* (Englewood Cliffs, N.J.: Prentice-Hall, 1985), 83.

36. Ibid., 83–84.

37. Michael Ruse, *Darwinism Defended: A Guide to the Evolution Controversies* (London: Addison-Wesley, 1982), 275.

38. Jordan Howard Sobel, *Logic and Theism: Arguments For and Against Beliefs in God* (Cambridge: Cambridge University Press, 2004), 93–94.

39. Dennett, *Breaking the Spell*, 241–42.

40. Alvin Plantinga, *The Nature of Necessity*, Clarendon Library of Logic and Philosophy (Oxford: Clarendon Press, 1974), 132.

41. Dennett, *Breaking the Spell*, 244.

42. Ibid., 242.

43. I myself am actually very much in sympathy with a nominalist construal of *abstracta* of all sorts; but then it is mere assertion that there can be no proofs from "sheer logic" for the reality of any mind-independent objects. The point remains that in the ontological argument such a proof has been offered. So why is it unsound?

44. See J. P. Moreland and William Lane Craig, *Philosophical Foundations for a Christian Worldview* (Downer's Grove, Ill.: InterVarsity, 2003), 496–99.

Chapter 4

1. An earlier version of this paper was read at an American Philosophical Association symposium with Paul Moser on God, Death, and the Meaning of Life. I want to thank Paul for his comments.

2. And, in part, because I came to discern the profound dimensions of Christian faith that stand apart from its doctrine of post-mortem salvation.

3. N. T. Wright makes the case for classical Hellenic religion and ancient Judaism in *The Resurrection of the Son of God* (Minneapolis: Fortress Press, 2003).

A similar case can be made for many tribal religions, in spite of talk of "ancestor spirits" and the like, not to mention Confucianism. It is less clear what to say about Hindu and Buddhist doctrines of reincarnation. See also Alan F. Segal, *Life After Death: A History of the Afterlife in Western Religion* (New York: Doubleday, 2004). Segal takes the evidence to show that nearly every human culture enshrines one—often several—envisionments of an afterlife. But, as noted, many of these promise a kind of existence hardly worth risking one's life for.

4. I should be clear here that I do not pretend that these three responses exhaust the possibilities.

5. Those who are subjectivists about value will judge that my reflections are, in various ways, misdirected. An atheist who is a subjectivist about values will, I suppose, find life meaningful just in case, or to the extent that, the things he or she values are brought into being.

6. In his *Life After Death* (488–89), Segal argues that the problem of justice—especially the punishment of the wicked, for example, the Romans—constituted a primary motivation for the development by the ante-Nicene Fathers of the idea of a disembodied post-mortem existence of the soul in heaven or hell, in the face of the evident failure of the urgently awaited and immanently expected arrival of the eschaton.

7. Bertrand Russell, "A Free Man's Worship," reprinted in Russell, *Mysticism and Logic* (Totowa, N.J.: Barnes and Noble, 1981), 41.

8. Albert Camus, *The Stranger*, trans. Gilbert Stuart (New York: Knopf, 1981), 154.

9. So de Unamuno's saint, the priest Don Emmanuel: "The other [kingdom] is here. Two kingdoms exist in this world. Or rather, in the other world. . . . Ah, I don't really know what I'm saying. . . . Let men think and act as they will, let them console themselves for having been born, let them live as happily as possible in the illusion that all this has a purpose" (*Abel Sanchez and Other Stories* [South Bend: Regnery-Gateway, 1956], 246–47), and "Like Moses, I have seen the face of God—our supreme dream—face to face, and as you already know and as the Scripture says, he who sees God's face, he who sees the eyes of the dream, the eyes with which He looks at us, will die inexorably and forever. And therefore, do not let our people, so long as they live, look into the face of God. Once dead, it will no longer matter, for then they will see nothing . . ." (ibid., 253). One may hear echoes here of Dostoyevsky's Inquisitor. But so to read de Unamuno is, I think, a grave error.

10. James Frazer, *The Golden Bough*, abr. ed. (New York: Macmillan, 1963), 826–27. A recent vigorous articulation of this view is Victor Stenger's *God: The Failed Hypothesis—How Science Shows That God Does Not Exist* (Amherst, N.Y.: Prometheus, 2007).

11. Larry Arnhart develops a version of this view—though one with which I am not entirely in agreement—in his *Darwinian Natural Right: The Biological Ethics of Human Nature* (Albany: State University of New York Press, 1998).

12. Alvin Plantinga, *Warrant and Proper Function* (New York: Oxford University Press, 1993), chap. 11.

13. For a recent, more extended discussion, see Eric Wielenberg, *Value and Virtue in a Godless Universe* (Cambridge: Cambridge University Press, 2005).

14. For a frightening example, see http://www.alternet.org/story/20666/, accessed 19 May 2008.

15. I have too gloomy an estimate of human nature to indulge in the utopian dreams of some humanists, to say nothing of the fantastic hopes of millenarian Christians. But that sober reflection diminishes neither the satisfactions that life can offer nor the dignity of efforts to improve the human condition.

16. In what follows, I will be holding Jews and Christians to account for biblical morality, and ignoring the long, rich history of subsequent theological reflection on these matters. But this seems fair enough, to the extent that a Jew or Christian sees Scripture as being at the heart of his or her faith.

17. So that here insult is added to injury, and irony to malfeasance. For there is no sin against which Jesus railed more than against the sin of hypocrisy. The Pharisees, a prominent target of Jesus' anger, were not as bad as the Gospels portray them to be. Sadly, Christendom, measured by its own standard, surely is.

18. Thus ill repaying the hospitality of Jethro, the priest of Midian, who was his father-in-law. Nor had the Midianites committed any act of aggression against Israel.

19. But compare Matt. 19:19. The usual apologetic—that Jesus is merely insisting that we get our priorities straight and put loyalty to God first—ignores the sense of the texts. The current political rhetoric of the evangelical right lends to these passages an especially ironic flavor. Equally morally baffling is Luke 16.

20. Mark 4:11-12 even suggests that God does not *want* all sinners to have a change of heart and to be forgiven. A decidedly bracing response to these difficulties invokes the divine command theory of moral obligation. The divine command theory faces its own problems. The familiar one is the Euthyphro dilemma. Here, however, the maneuver is precisely to stare down the moral horrors of the Bible by accepting one horn of the dilemma. Whatever God wills is, solely in virtue of being divinely willed, righteous—even genocide, child sacrifice, and the like.

But there is another, less familiar, problem for divine command theories: Why (morally) ought we to obey God's commands? It's no use saying: because God commands us to obey them. For that is just another command, and it begs the question to be told that we have an obligation to obey it because it comes from God. It follows, then, that there is at least *one* source of moral obligation—indeed a fundamental one—that cannot be grounded in a divine command. We make no progress by observing that our obligation to obey God is grounded in God's having created us. So God may have, but that obliges us to obedience only if there is a moral principle that enjoins obedience to one's creator; and what obliges us to that principle?

The divine command theorist has one recourse. Suppose, as appears to be the case (for example, Leviticus 20, 26:14-39), God's commandments take the form: Do C *or else*. Well, *that* gives us reason to obey God. But it also reduces the moral "ought" to a prudential "ought"—a result most theists will hardly welcome.

21. A dramatic expression of this idea is given by Heb. 9:22.

22. Richard Swinburne, *Responsibility and Atonement* (New York: Oxford University Press, 1989), 154.

23. I have serious doubt that this is what Paul himself has in mind in Romans. See, for example, Alan F. Segal, *Paul the Convert* (New Haven, Conn.: Yale University

Press, 1990), and Evan Fales, "The Road to Damascus," *Faith and Philosophy* 22 (2005): 442–59. The doctrine and practice of substitutionary sacrifice has, of course, a long history within Judaism, and the early church would have been entirely at home in it. The connection between Jesus and the Paschal lamb (and hence with the *akedah*) is patent, and there is a hint that the Gospel writers went further and incorporated into the Passion narratives the sacrificial practice of the scapegoat (which carries the sins of the people into the desert; cf. Lev. 16:5f.): some ancient manuscripts give the name of the man released by Pilate as Jesus Barabbas, that is, Jesus the Son of the Father. *These* doctrines *do* make sense to me, but that is another story.

24. Robin Collins, "Understanding Atonement: A New and Orthodox Theory," http://home.messiah.edu/~rcollins/Atone.htm, accessed 19 May 2008; and Marilyn McCord Adams, *Horrendous Evils and the Goodness of God* (Ithaca: Cornell University Press, 1999).

25. I do not mean to suggest that their faith does not strengthen Christians in their efforts to lead good lives. But many things can strengthen such a resolve, and atheists, in my experience, are able to draw upon resources that, judged by their fruits, are at least as effective.

26. There is, to be sure, the antecedent question whether Jesus was indeed raised. But there is, even prior to this, the question whether the Passion narratives should be understood to assert such a thing (and were so understood by the early church). I believe there is reason to think not: see Fales, "Taming the *Tehom*: The Sign of Jonah in Matthew," in Robert Price and Jeffrey Lowder, eds., *Empty Tomb: Jesus Beyond the Grave* (Buffalo: Prometheus, 2005), 307–48.

27. And if the boy forgives, will the celestial harmony be restored? Will Iustitia reascend her throne? Will the angelic host cease their weeping and raise once more their voices in hymns of praise? So Ivan: "It's not worth it, because those tears are unatoned for. They must be atoned for, or there can be no harmony. But how? How are you going to atone for them? Is it possible? By their being avenged? But what do I care for avenging them? What do I care for a hell for oppressors? What good can hell do, since those children have already been tortured? And what becomes of harmony, if there is hell? I want to forgive. I want to embrace. I don't want more suffering. And if the sufferings of the children go to swell the sum of sufferings which was necessary to pay the price for truth, then I protest that the truth is not worth such a price. I don't want the mother to embrace the oppressor who threw her son to the dogs! She dare not forgive him! Let her forgive him for herself, if she will, let her forgive the torturer for the immeasurable suffering of her mother's heart. But the sufferings of her tortured child she has no right to forgive; she dare not forgive the torturer, even if the child were to forgive him! And if that is so, if they dare not forgive, what becomes of harmony? Is there in the whole world a being who would have the right to forgive and could forgive?" *The Brothers Karamazov*, trans. Constance Garnett (New York: Random House, 1950), 290–91.

28. Wiesel, "Job: Our Contemporary," in *Messengers of God: Biblical Portraits and Legends*, trans. Marion Wiesel (New York: Summit, 1976), 235.

29. Elie Wiesel, *The Trial of God (As It Was Held on February 25, 1649, in Shamgorod)* (New York: Random House, 1979); also *Souls on Fire* (New York: Random House, 1972), 107f.

30. Adams, *Horrendous Evils and the Goodness of God*, 104.

31. Adams, in fact, concedes that, in *moral* terms, beatitude does not make up for horrendous evils suffered in this life. Rather, God ensures that through intimacy with the divine, a person will be able to incorporate her suffering into a life that, taken as a whole, is meaningful and precious. I do not understand how this is to be done by God, and neither, perhaps, does Adams herself.

32. John Locke, *An Essay Concerning Human Understanding*, Bk. IV, Ch. XVIII; and J. S. Mill, "Mr. Mansell on the Limits of Religious Thought," reprinted in Nelson Pike, ed., *God and Evil* (Englewood Cliffs, N.J.: Prentice-Hall, 1964), 37–45.

33. Kierkegaard understood the religious to transcend the ethical, and, to his credit, he is honest about it. To his shame, he accepts it.

34. And yet even the atheist cannot forget that Ivan and Alyosha are brothers. And we too wish to claim Alyosha as an imaginary brother of our hearts, whom we love.

35. Thus, dialectically, an atheist may, for the sake of argument, concede to (Jewish and Christian) theists the existence of God and the veridicality of Scripture, and employ the arguments adduced above to draw out the consequences. In effect, this essay then offers a *reductio* of (Judeo-Christian) theism.

36. We find all three expressed, for example, by Camus—for example, in *Letters to a German Friend*, Fourth letter: "For a long time we both thought that this world had no ultimate meaning and that consequently we were cheated. I still think so in a way. But I came to different conclusions from the ones which you talk about. . . . You never believed in the meaning of this world, and you therefore deduced the idea that everything was equivalent and that good and evil could be defined according to one's wishes. You supposed that in the absence of any human or divine code the only values were those of the animal world—in other words, violence and cunning. Hence you concluded that man was negligible and that his soul could be killed. . . . And, to tell the truth, I, believing I thought as you did, saw no valid argument to answer you except a fierce love of justice which, after all, seemed to me as unreasonable as the most sudden passion.

Where lay the difference? Simply that you readily accepted despair and I never yielded to it. Simply that you saw the injustice of our condition to the point of being willing to add to it, whereas it seemed to me that man must exalt justice in order to fight against eternal injustice, create happiness in order to protest against the universe of unhappiness. Because you turned despair into intoxication . . . you were willing to destroy man's works. . . . Meanwhile, refusing to accept despair and that tortured world, I merely wanted men to rediscover their solidarity in order to wage war against their revolting fate." In Camus, *Resistance, Rebellion, and Death*, trans. Justin O'Brien (New York: Knopf, 1961), 27–28.

Chapter 5

1. Perhaps the best-known proponent of this kind of view is Kierkegaard, who verged on the belief that if the claims of religion were even consistent they would be unworthy of faith. I think, however, that this kind of strict fideism is very much a minority position among believers. It may of course be that, measured by scientific canons of evidence, some religious beliefs—particularly beliefs of revealed

religion—would find only weak support if any. And if this is so, then there may be room for a position something like Kierkegaard's. But that is far from claiming that religious beliefs in general enjoy no objective support whatever. The question, on the present understanding of what it means to "get scientific" about them, is simply one of how much support they enjoy, and what kind of support it is.

2. Some might suspect that any "scientific" evaluation of science as a source of knowledge would run a risk of being question-begging. But the evaluation of science as a knowledge source is exactly what the philosophy of science is all about. And in a broad sense to be outlined in the next section, this endeavor may be viewed as scientific.

3. David Hume, *An Enquiry Concerning Human Understanding*, ed. L. A. Selby-Bigge and P. H. Nidditch (New York: Oxford University Press, 1975), 115n1.

4. For an argument to this effect, see Jonathan L. Kvanvig and Hugh J. McCann, "Divine Conservation and the Persistence of the World," in *Divine and Human Action*, ed. T. V. Morris (Ithaca: Cornell University Press, 1988), 13–49.

5. See, for example, Marc A. Musick, et al., "Spirituality in Physical Health and Aging," *Journal of Adult Development* 7 (2000): 73–85.

6. William James, *The Varieties of Religious Experience* (New York: Longman, Green & Co., 1902), 424–27.

Chapter 6

1. I believe the pattern began in the United States around 1870 or so. For a defense of this claim and a detailed treatment of the pattern's development from 1870 to 1930, see Julie Reuben, *The Making of the Modern University* (Chicago: University of Chicago Press, 1996).

2. Thomas Nagel, *The Last Word* (New York: Oxford University Press, 1997).

3. Property P is an emergent property of some particular x at level l_n just in case P is a property of x at l_n, and no amount of knowledge of (or descriptive statements about) entities at subvenient levels below l_n would justify a prediction of (or logically entails a descriptive statement about) P at l_n. In this sense an emergent property (or a statement about it) is surprising and unexpected relative to knowledge of (or statements about) lower levels.

Since the late 1950s they have been characterized ontologically: Property P is an emergent property of some particular x at level l_n just in case P is a property of x at l_n, and there are no determinates P' of the same determinable D as P such that some particular at a level below l_n exemplifies P or P'. In this sense an emergent property is *sui generis*. For a classic comparison of the epistemic and ontological characterizations, see Ernest Nagel, *The Structure of Science* (Indianapolis: Hackett, 1979), 366–80.

4. For a good treatment of this period, see William Lyons, *Matters of the Mind* (New York: Routledge, 2001), 1–78.

5. Note the dates of the articles in parts 2 and 3 of David M. Rosenthal, ed., *Materialism and the Mind-Body Problem* (Englewood Cliffs, N.J.: Prentice-Hall, 1971).

Cf. Steven J. Wagner and Richard Warner, eds., *Naturalism: A Critical Appraisal* (Notre Dame, Ind.: University of Notre Dame Press, 1993).

6. I think it is wrong to call the problem "multiple realization." Instead, I prefer "multiple exemplification." See J. P. Moreland, "The Knowledge Argument Revisited," *International Philosophical Quarterly* 43 (June 2003): 219–28.

7. John Searle, *The Rediscovery of the Mind* (Cambridge: MIT Press, 1992); *The Mystery of Consciousness* (New York: The New York Review of Books, 1997); *Mind: A Brief Introduction* (New York: Oxford University Press, 2004); David Chalmers, *The Conscious Mind* (New York: Oxford University Press, 1996); Colin McGinn, *The Mysterious Flame* (New York: Basic Books, 1999); Jaegwon Kim, *Mind in a Physical World* (Cambridge: MIT Press, 1998); *Physicalism, or Something Near Enough* (Princeton: Princeton University Press, 2005), 8–22, 32–69; *Philosophy of Mind* (Boulder: Westview, 1996; 2d ed., 2006). Kim's journey is especially interesting. His 2006 edition of *Philosophy of Mind* contains a fair and respectful treatment of several arguments for substance dualism, while the 1996 edition hardly considers the view worth taking seriously. Especially revealing is the shift from *Mind in a Physical World*, where Kim leaves the problem of consciousness up in the air while suggesting that type identity theory may be needed for a naturalist treatment of phenomenal consciousness, to *Physicalism, or Something Near Enough*, in which Kim embraces a narrow, nuanced version of epiphenomenalist emergent dualism. Cf. J. P. Moreland, "If You Can't Reduce, You Must Eliminate: Why Kim's Version of Physicalism Isn't Close Enough," *Philosophia Christi* 7 (Spring 2005): 463–73.

8. For a naturalist treatment of secondary qualities, see Frank Jackson, *From Metaphysics to Ethics* (Oxford: Clarendon, 1998), chap. 4. For the role of indexicals in debates about naturalism, see op cit., 18–21; Geoffrey Madell, *The Identity of the Self* (Edinburgh: University of Edinburgh Press, 1981).

9. On aesthetics, see Frank Sibley, "Aesthetic and Nonaesthetic," *The Philosophical Review* 74 (April 1965): 135–59. On ethics, see Panayot Butchvarov, *Skepticism in Ethics* (Bloomington: Indiana University Press, 1989), 1–10; John Rist, *Real Ethics: Rethinking the Foundations of Morality* (Cambridge: Cambridge University Press, 2003); Paul Copan, "The Moral Argument," in *The Rationality of Theism*, ed. Paul Copan and Paul K. Moser (London: Routledge, 2003), 149–74; Jackson, *From Metaphysics to Ethics*, chap. 5; Wilfred Sellars and John Hospers, eds., *Readings in Ethical Theory* (Englewood Cliffs, N.J.: Prentice-Hall, 1970), part 2. While clear parallels exist in twentieth-century Anglo-American philosophical treatments of ethics and aesthetics, the recent history of aesthetics is not as clean-cut relative to my pattern as is ethics. See Paul Guyer, "History of Aesthetics [Addendum]," in *Encyclopedia of Philosophy* (Detroit: Thomas Gale, 2d ed., 2006), 1:63–72.

10. Timothy O'Connor, *Persons & Causes* (New York: Oxford University Press, 2000); Timothy O'Connor and Jonathan D. Jacobs, "Emergent Individuals," *The Philosophical Quarterly* 53 (October 2003): 540–55.

11. For a discussion of the issues mentioned in the paragraph to follow, see J. P. Moreland, *Universals* (Montreal: McGill-Queen's University Press, 2001).

12. Terence Horgan, "Nonreductive Materialism and the Explanatory Autonomy of Psychology," in *Naturalism*, ed. Wagner and Warner, 313–14.

13. J. P. Moreland, "The Argument from Consciousness," in *The Rationality of Theism*, ed. Copan and Moser, 204–20; "Should a Naturalist Be a Supervenient Physicalist?" *Metaphilosophy* 29 (January/April 1998): 35–57; "Naturalism and Libertarian Agency," *Philosophy and Theology* 10 (1997): 351–81; "Naturalism, Nominalism, and Husserlian Moments," *The Modern Schoolman* 79 (January/March 2002): 199–216; "Timothy O'Connor and the Harmony Thesis: A Critique," *Metaphysica* 3, no. 2 (2002): 5–40.

14. Nagel, *The Last Word*, 130.

15. Ibid., 4.

16. Ibid., 76.

17. Ibid., 3–35.

18. Ibid., 138.

19. Ibid., 143.

20. Ibid., 135.

21. Ibid., 128–33.

22. Ibid., 127–30.

23. Ibid., 132–33.

24. Ibid., 13–35.

25. Nicholas Rescher, *The Limits of Science* (Berkeley: University of California Press, 1984), 22.

26. I shall not bother to distinguish among statements, sentences, or propositions, though there are interesting differences in the way each figures into self-refutation. See Joseph M. Boyle Jr., Germain Grisez, and Olaf Tollefsen, *Free Choice: A Self-Referential Argument* (Notre Dame, Ind.: University of Notre Dame Press, 1976), 122–52.

27. See Michael J. Loux, *Substance and Attribute* (Dordrecht, Holland: D. Reidel, 1978), 17–18, 21–22.

28. Cf. Nagel, *The Last Word*, 4. On page 3 Nagel clearly has in mind the question of the objectivity of reason to which he plans to give a rationalist answer. But on page 4 he moves without warning into the two second-order questions and, in context, he seems to equate them.

29. Ibid., 76.

30. See J. L. Mackie, *The Miracle of Theism* (Oxford: Clarendon, 1982), 141.

31. Alvin Plantinga, *Warrant and Proper Function* (New York: Oxford University Press, 1993), 194–237.

32. Ibid., 222–23.

33. Ibid., 234–37.

34. Ibid., 235.

35. A particularly egregious instantiation of this atheist dilemma and the employment of a dismissive strategy to split its horns is Anthony O'Hear, *Beyond Evolution: Human Nature and the Limits of Evolutionary Explanation* (New York: Oxford University Press, 1997). O'Hear explicitly argues that there are numerous

aspects of human beings (the normativity and universality of our faculties, judgments, and search for [and discovery of] knowledge and truth in epistemology, ethics, aesthetics; consciousness, self-consciousness; veridical perception of mind-independent, irreducible, objective secondary qualities; agency and freedom) that lie beyond the limits of scientific naturalist, particularly Darwinian, explanation. O'Hear also acknowledges that his argument can be employed by theists as an argument for God's existence. But in the space of one small paragraph, O'Hear dismisses such theistic employment out of hand on the grounds that (1) it has been refuted by Kant's critique of the arguments for God, and (2) such employments invariably generate a vicious infinite regress of explanation that theists stop by utilizing the incoherent notion of God as a logically necessary being. In a way analogous to Nagel, the failure of this dismissive strategy has the result that by acknowledging the inadequacy of naturalistic evolutionary theory to account for a wide range of admittedly irreducible, uneliminable, non-natural facts, O'Hear has provided materials for strengthening the case for theism (214).

Chapter 7

1. Jacques Maritain, *Man and the State* (Chicago: University of Chicago Press, 1951), 77.

2. These nontheistic alternatives such as Jainism, Taoism, or Buddhism have difficulty grounding human rights and dignity and objective moral values. An *impersonal* ultimate reality, it seems, cannot adequately ground *personal* virtues such as love, kindness, and compassion. Ninian Smart, scholar of Asian philosophy and religion, observes that the "concept of the importance of the historical process is largely foreign to these faiths," adding that "the notion of a personal God is altogether less prominent." Ninian Smart, "Religion as a Discipline," in *Concept and Empathy*, ed. Donald Wiebe (New York: New York University Press, 1986), 161. So, though I respond to naturalism here, my argument would apply to any nonpersonal metaphysic of ultimate reality.

3. Incidentally, I respond to various Humean sorts of objections that attempt to diminish the force of objections to natural theology: see chap. 8 in Paul Copan, *Loving Wisdom: Christian Philosophy of Religion* (St. Louis: Chalice, 2007); Copan, "Hume and the Moral Argument," in *In Defense of Natural Theology: A Post-Humean Assessment*, ed. James F. Sennett and Douglas Groothuis (Downer's Grove, Ill.: InterVarsity, 2005), 200–25; and Paul Copan and Paul K. Moser, "Introduction," in *The Rationality of Theism* (London: Routledge, 2003), 1–10.

4. J. Budziszewski, *What We Can't Not Know* (Dallas: Spence, 2003).

5. Nicholas Rescher, *Moral Absolutes: An Essay on the Nature and Rationale of Morality*, Studies in Moral Philosophy, vol. 2 (New York: Peter Lang, 1989), 43.

6. David O. Brink, "The Autonomy of Ethics," in *The Cambridge Companion to Atheism*, ed. Michael Martin (Cambridge: Cambridge University Press, 2006), 149.

7. Kai Nielsen, *Ethics without God*, rev. ed. (Buffalo: Prometheus, 1990), 10–11.

8. C. S. Lewis, *The Abolition of Man* (San Francisco: HarperSanFrancisco, 2001), 83–101.

9. Robert M. Adams, *Finite and Infinite Goods: A Framework for Ethics* (New York: Oxford University Press, 1999), 20.

10. Robert Audi notes that *dignity* is the ground of *rights*. When those rights are not observed, this violates one's dignity. "Dignity . . . provides a bridge between the axiological and the deontic, between value and obligation." *Moral Knowledge and Ethical Character* (New York: Oxford University Press, 1997), 263, 264.

11. In *Thomas Reid's Inquiry and Essays*, ed. Keith Lehrer and Ronald E. Beanblossom (Indianapolis: Bobbs-Merrill, 1975), 84–85.

12. See Essay 3 in Thomas Reid, "Of the First Principles of Morals," in *Essays on the Active Powers of the Human Mind* (Cambridge, Mass.: MIT Press, 1969), 364–67.

13. Thomas Reid, Essay 7, "Whether Morality Be Demonstrable," in "Essays on the Intellectual Powers of Man," ed. D. Stewart, *The Works of Thomas Reid*, vol. 2 (New York: Bangs and Mason, 1822), 381.

14. Audi, *Moral Knowledge and Ethical Character*, part 3.

15. Daniel Dennett, *Darwin's Dangerous Idea* (New York: Simon and Schuster, 1995), 510.

16. For some explorations on this topic, see Gerard Casey, "Ethics and Human Nature," *American Catholic Philosophical Quarterly* 77, no. 4 (Fall 2003): 521–33. James B. Reichmann, *Evolution, Animal "Rights," and the Environment* (Washington, D.C.: Catholic University of America Press, 2000).

17. See Alvin Plantinga, *Warranted Christian Belief* (New York: Oxford University Press, 2001), 202.

18. Richard Dawkins, *The God Delusion* (Boston: Houghton Mifflin, 2006), 226, 227.

19. Daniel C. Dennett, *Breaking the Spell: Religion as a Natural Phenonemon* (New York: Viking, 2006), 305 (his italics).

20. Ibid.

21. Brink, "The Autonomy of Ethics," 150. Brink gives a list of what he calls "commonsense morality" (cf. properly basic moral intuitions mentioned in the first section): "compliance with norms prohibiting aggression (at least, unprovoked aggression), enjoining cooperation, fidelity, and aid, and condemning individuals who free-ride on the compliance of others" (157). Cf. Audi's list of "basic duties": fidelity (promise-keeping, truth-telling), "non-injury, reparation, justice, gratitude, beneficence, and self-improvement" (*Moral Knowledge and Ethical Character*, 279).

22. William Rowe, "Reflections on the Craig-Flew Debate," in *Does God Exist? The Craig-Flew Debate*, ed. Stan W. Wallace (Burlington, Vt.: Ashgate, 2003), 66.

23. For such reasoning, see Michael Martin, *Atheism, Morality, and Meaning* (Amherst, N.Y.: Prometheus, 2002). This rape example is found in Michael Martin, "Atheism, Christian Theism, and Rape." Available at http://www.infidels.org/library/modern/michael_martin/rape.html, accessed 21 May 2008.

24. Even though, as this tradition argues, human sin has introduced evil and corruption into the world, the goodness of human nature, though damaged and distorted by evil, still remains. On how Christian theism best helps us come to

terms with evil, see Gordon Graham, *Evil and Christian Ethics* (Cambridge: Cambridge University Press, 2001).

25. See Paul Copan, "The Moral Argument," in *The Rationality of Theism*, ed. Copan and Moser, 149–74.

26. Cf. Adams, *Finite and Infinite Goods.*

27. David O. Brink, *Moral Realism and the Foundation of Ethics* (Cambridge: Cambridge University Press, 1989); and Martin, *Atheism, Morality, and Meaning.*

28. Richard N. Boyd, "How to Be a Moral Realist," in *Essays on Moral Realism*, ed. Geoffrey Sayre-McCord (Ithaca: Cornell University Press, 1988).

29. Brink, "The Autonomy of Ethics," 153.

30. Brink, *Moral Realism*, 120, 156–67.

31. Ned Block, "Consciousness," in *A Companion to the Philosophy of Mind*, ed. Samuel Guttenplan (Oxford: Blackwell, 1994), 211 (his italics).

32. Jaegwon Kim, *Philosophy of Mind* (Boulder: Westview, 1996), 8.

33. Colin McGinn, *The Problem of Consciousness* (Oxford: Blackwell, 1990), 10–11.

34. Paul Davies, "The Birth of the Cosmos," in *God, Cosmos, Nature and Creativity*, ed. Jill Gready (Edinburgh: Scottish Academic Press, 1995), 8–9.

35. Richard Swinburne, *The Coherence of Theism* (Oxford: Oxford University Press, 1977), 204; Keith Yandell, "Theism, Atheism, and Cosmology," in *Does God Exist?* ed. Stan Wallace, 96; Louis P. Pojman, *Philosophy of Religion* (Mountain View, Calif.: Mayfield, 2001), 167; Stephen C. Layman, *The Shape of the Good: Christian Reflections and the Foundation of Ethics* (Notre Dame, Ind.: University of Notre Dame Press, 1994), 44–52. Layman does acknowledge, however, that human value is difficult to account for given naturalism.

36. As Saul Kripke argued, there is a *metaphysical* necessity that, in this case, is discovered a posteriori. On this and the moral argument, see C. Stephen Evans, "Moral Arguments," in *Companion to Philosophy of Religion*, ed. Philip Quinn and Charles Taliaferro (Oxford: Blackwell, 1997), 346–47.

37. "*Addition is possible* is necessarily true because *Numbers exist* is necessarily true and numbers have certain essential properties," notes William Lane Craig. He also points out that theistic thinkers like Swinburne and Yandell *also* hold the problematic belief that "God exists" is not true in every possible world. Thus, their failure to make the intrinsic connection between God and objective moral values is not surprising. See Craig's final comments in *Does God Exist?*, ed. Stan W. Wallace, 168–73; and his "Theistic Critiques of Atheism," in *The Cambridge Companion to Atheism*, ed. Michael Martin, 83–84.

38. Ibid.

39. Dennett made this point at The Future of Atheism conference (the Greer-Heard Forum) in New Orleans on 24 February 2007, where he reinforced his rejection of *essentialism*!

40. Louis P. Pojman, "A Critique of Contemporary Egalitarianism: A Christian Perspective," *Faith and Philosophy* 8 (October 1991): 501.

41. Daniel C. Dennett, "Atheism and Evolution," in *The Cambridge Companion to Atheism*, ed. Martin, 144. With remarkable confidence, Dennett latches on to an oscillating model of the universe, which means an infinite number of opportunities to produce life: "It had to happen eventually" (146, 147). Such optimism is misplaced, as it is contradicted by the physical evidence (the Hawking-Penrose Singularity Theorem in 1970 helped lead to the demise of this theory): the universe is not eternal. As Stephen Hawking reminds us: "Almost everyone now believes that the universe, and *time itself*, had a beginning at the Big Bang." Stephen Hawking and Roger Penrose, *The Nature of Space and Time* (Princeton: Princeton University Press, 1996), 20. For an examination of this and other cosmological models, see chaps. 7 and 8 in Paul Copan and William Lane Craig, *Creation Out of Nothing: A Biblical, Philosophical, and Scientific Exploration* (Grand Rapids/Leicester, U.K.: Baker Academic/Apollo, 2004).

42. Del Ratzsch, *Nature, Design, and Science* (Albany: State University of New York Press, 2001), 68.

43. McGinn, *The Problem of Consciousness*, 10–11.

44. See Vance G. Morgan, "The Metaphysics of Naturalism," *American Catholic Philosophical Quarterly* 75, no. 3 (Summer 2001): 409–31.

45. Alvin Plantinga, "Natural Theology," in *Companion to Metaphysics*, ed. Jaegwon Kim and Ernest Sosa (Cambridge: Blackwell, 1995), 347.

46. George I. Mavrodes, "Religion and the Queerness of Morality," in *Rationality, Religious Belief, and Moral Commitment*, ed. Robert Audi and William J. Wainwright (Ithaca, N.Y.: Cornell University Press, 1986), 225, 226.

47. C. Stephen Layman, *The Shape of the Good*, 138–44.

48. See John E. Hare, *The Moral Gap: Kantian Ethics, Human Limits, and God's Assistance* (Oxford: Clarendon Press, 1996); John E. Hare, *God and Morality: A Philosophical History* (Oxford: Blackwell, 2007), 122–183.

49. Martin's *Atheism, Morality, and Meaning* makes much use of this approach. For a response, see Paul Copan, "Morality and Meaning Without God: Another Failed Attempt," *Philosophia Christi* 6, no. 2 (2004): 295–304.

50. See Roderick Firth, "Ethical Absolutism and the Ideal Observer," *Philosophy and Phenomenological Research* 12 (1952): 317–45. Firth, a Quaker, considered the Ideal Observer theory to be harmonious with belief in God *as* the Ideal Observer: "an ideal observer will be a partial description of God, if God is conceived to be an infallible moral judge" (333). (Firth's religious affiliation was pointed out to me by Firth's former student at Brown University, Charles Taliaferro [24 May 1999].)

51. Dennett, *Darwin's Dangerous Idea*, 507. Dennett writes: "It might seem then that 'rule worship' of a certain kind is a good thing, at least for agents designed like us. It is good not because there is a certain rule, or set of rules, which is probably the best, or which always yields the right answer, but because having rules works—somewhat—and not having rules doesn't work at all" (507).

52. Michael Ruse, "Evolutionary Ethics: A Phoenix Arisen," in *Issues in Evolutionary Ethics*, ed. Paul Thompson (Albany: State University of New York Press, 1995), 236.

53. Ibid., 235.

54. Michael Ruse and E. O. Wilson, "The Evolution of Ethics," in *Religion and the Natural Sciences*, ed. J. E. Huchingson (Orlando: Harcourt Brace, 1993), 310–11. For discussion on this, see Matthew H. Nitecki and Doris V. Nitecki, *Evolutionary Ethics* (Albany: State University of New York Press, 1993), 8.

55. In the *Origin of Species*, Darwin himself speaks of "laws impressed on matter by the Creator" and of life "having been originally breathed by the Creator into a few forms or into one." *Origin of Species* (New York: Thomas Y. Crowell, n.d. [corr. ed.]), 459, 460.

56. Ruse and Wilson, "Evolution of Ethics," 311. This example can also be found in Ruse's "Evolutionary Ethics: A Phoenix Arisen," 241–42, where he humorously refers to the termites' "rather strange foodstuffs"!

57. Michael Ruse, *The Darwinian Paradigm* (London: Routledge, 1989), 262, 268.

58. Larry Arnhart advocates some counterintuitive notions given his naturalistic view of human morality, which he takes to be rooted entirely in our animal nature. If, as Arnhart argues, the good is desirable and the desirable is that which humans generally desire, we are left with difficult moral pills to swallow: besides this point of implicitly encouraging males to act according to their promiscuous inclinations, Arnhart's moral perspective (a) denies a universal "altruistic selflessness" as normative, but instead advocates a more restrictive love of one's own kinship group as an extension of self-love (which seems to encourage tribalism); and (b) he agrees with Aristotle that power, wealth, and prestige are "naturally" desired by humans (but it is a non sequitur to say these are therefore good). See Larry Arnhart, *Darwinian Natural Right: The Biological Ethics of Human Nature* (Albany: State University of New York Press, 1998). For a response to Arnhart, see Hare, *God and Morality*, 65–72.

59. Randy Thornhill and Craig T. Palmer, *A Natural History of Rape: Biological Bases of Sexual Coercion* (Cambridge, Mass.: MIT Press, 2000).

60. Francis Crick, *The Astonishing Hypothesis* (New York: Scribner's, 1994), 3.

61. On this problem, see Victor Reppert, *C. S. Lewis's Dangerous Idea: In Defense of the Argument from Reason* (Downers Grove, Ill.: InterVarsity, 2003).

62. Charles Darwin, "Letter to William Graham Down" (3 July 1881), in *The Life and Letters of Charles Darwin Including an Autobiographical Chapter*, vol. 1, ed. F. Darwin (London: Murray, 1887), 1:315–16.

63. Charles Darwin, *Descent of Man*, 2d ed (London: Murray, 1874), 486. David Hume's position anticipates Darwinism: reason is "the slave of the passions, and can never pretend to any other office than to serve and obey them." Morality itself is "more properly felt than judg'd of." For Hume, one can never locate vice "till you turn your reflexion into your own breast, and find a sentiment of disapprobation, which arises in you, towards this action." *A Treatise of Human Nature*, ed. L. A. Selby-Bigge (Oxford: Clarendon, 1740; repr. 1888), 2.3.3, 415; 3.1.2, 470, 468–69.

64. Mavrodes, "Religion and the Queerness of Morality," 219.

65. Elliott Sober, *Philosophy of Biology* (Boulder, Colo.: Westview, 1993), 202–08.

66. Plantinga, *Warranted Christian Belief*, 219n29.

67. Richard Rorty, "Untruth and Consequences," *The New Republic* (31 July 1995): 32–36.

68. Kai Nielsen, "Naturalistic Explanations of Theistic Belief," in *A Companion to Philosophy of Religion*, ed. Quinn and Taliaferro, 402.

69. Martin, *Atheism, Morality, and Meaning*, 45.

70. Richard Boyd, "How to Be a Moral Realist," 106. See also Russ Shafer-Landau, *Moral Realism: A Defence* (New York: Oxford University Press, 2005).

71. Thomas Nagel, *The View from Nowhere* (New York: Oxford University Press, 1986), 111, 113.

72. Richard Dawkins, *A Devil's Chaplain* (Boston: Houghton Mifflin, 2003), 34. Ironically, Dawkins waxes quite "unscientific" in his book *The God Delusion*, in which he rails against "religious morality."

73. Marc D. Hauser, *Moral Minds* (New York: HarperCollins, 2006).

74. Derk Pereboom, *Living Without Free Will* (Cambridge: Cambridge University Press, 2001), xiii–xiv.

75. Summarized from Thomas L. Carson, *Value and the Good Life* (Notre Dame, Ind.: University of Notre Dame Press, 2000), 194.

76. Ibid., 198. Carson adds that nothing is *explained* by assuming that moral properties are constituted by natural facts: "The best explanations of human behavior available to us at the present time do not make use of claims to the effect that moral facts are constituted by natural facts . . . and it is a mystery how those properties cause or explain observable phenomena" (198–99). Simply to *posit* that moral properties have been instantiated by nature—that they have emerged from (or "supervened upon") natural ones—is a far cry from *explaining* how this is so.

77. Bertrand Russell, *Human Society in Ethics and Politics* (London: Allen & Unwin, 1954), 124.

78. Edward O. Wilson, *Consilience* (New York: Random House, 1998), 268, 269.

79. Jonathan Glover, *Humanity: A Moral History of the Twentieth Century* (London: Cape, 1999), 41, 42.

80. John Searle, *Minds, Brains, and Science* (Cambridge, Mass.: Harvard University Press, 1986 repr.), 87, 88, 92.

81. Simon Blackburn, *Being Good: A Short Introduction to Ethics* (New York: Oxford University Press, 2001), 133, 134.

82. J. L. Mackie, *The Miracle of Theism* (Oxford: Clarendon, 1982), 115.

83. J. L. Mackie, *Ethics: Inventing Right and Wrong* (London: Penguin, 1977). Mackie argued that even if ethics were subjective—or even false—a person could still remain firmly committed to them (16)! But surely this commitment may be irrelevant or even harmful (consider Stalin or Pol Pot, who were committed—wrongly—to their perverse moral vision).

84. Michael Shermer, *The Science of Good and Evil: Why People Cheat, Gossip, Care, Share, and Follow the Golden Rule* (New York: Holt, 2004), 56–57.

85. C. S. Lewis, *Miracles* (New York: Macmillan, 1960), 37.

86. Ibid., 38, 37.

87. Elliott Sober and David Sloan Wilson, *Unto Others* (Cambridge, Mass.: Harvard University Press, 1998), 301–2.

88. Taken from Bill Watterson, *The Authoritative Calvin and Hobbes: A Calvin and Hobbes Treasury* (New York: Universal Press Syndicate, 1990), 105.

89. Robin Le Poidevin, *Arguing for Atheism* (London: Routledge, 1996), 86.

90. Steven Pinker, "The Moral Instinct," *New York Times* (January 13, 2008). Available at http://www.nytimes.com/2008/01/13/magazine/13Psychology-t.html?_r=1&oref=slogin&pagewanted=print, accessed 1 February 2008.

91. In addition to considerations of diet, clothing, ceremonial purity, and the like, we should keep in mind that Old Testament ethics (Mosaic legislation in particular) commonly assumes a departure from the divine ideals in Genesis 1-2 (the implications of the divine image and lifelong monogamous commitment). The Law of Moses often takes for granted human hard-heartedness (cf. Matthew 19:8) and a divine accommodation to, and the regulation or restriction of, negative ancient Near East social structures (for example, polygamy, slavery, patriarchalism, primogeniture, and the like) *without* approving of them. That said, Mosaic legislation often presents a vast improvement over other ancient Near East cultures, including the elevated status of women and slaves, the accountability of all persons under the law (including kings and nobles), and far less severe punishments. For a detailed discussion, see Paul Copan, "Is Yahweh a Moral Monster? The New Atheists and Old Testament Ethics," *Philosophia Christi* n.s. 10, no. 1 (2008): 7–37.

92. See Linda Zagzebski, *Divine Motivation Theory* (Cambridge: Cambridge University Press, 2004).

93. One egregious example is David Brink's "The Autonomy of Ethics."

94. Robert M. Adams, "Divine Commands and Obligation," *Faith and Philosophy* 4 (1988): 272.

95. Adams, *Finite and Infinite Goods*, 255.

96. John Hare, *The Moral Gap*.

97. H. O. Mounce, "Morality and Religion," in *Philosophy of Religion*, ed. Brian Davies (Washington, D.C.: Georgetown University Press, 1998), 278.

98. On the Euthyphro question, see William P. Alston, "Some Suggestions for Divine Command Theorists," in *Christian Theism and the Problems of Philosophy*, ed. Michael D. Beaty (Notre Dame, Ind.: University of Notre Dame Press, 1990); Thomas V. Morris, "Duty and Divine Goodness" and "The Necessity of God's Goodness," in *Anselmian Explorations* (Notre Dame, Ind.: University of Notre Dame Press, 1987); Paul Copan, "The Moral Argument," in *The Rationality of Theism*; and William J. Wainwright, *Religion and Morality* (Burlington, Vt.: Ashgate, 2005).

99. John M. Rist, *Real Ethics: Rethinking the Foundations of Morality* (Cambridge: Cambridge University Press, 2001), 1.

100. Jacques Maritain, *Moral Philosophy* (New York: Scribner's, 1964), 439.

Chapter 8

1. Part of my analysis of evangelical atheism also appears in chapter 1 of my book, *The Evolution of Terrestrial and Extraterrestrial Life* (Goshen, Ind.: Pandora, 2008).

2. We should distinguish between *negative atheists*, who support their atheism by showing that standard arguments for the existence of God are unsound, and *positive atheists*, who try to show that there are good grounds for disbelieving in God. "Positive atheists reject the theistic God and with it belief in an afterlife, in a cosmic destiny, in a supernatural origin of the universe, in an immortal soul, in the revealed nature of the Bible and Qur'an, and in a religious foundation of morality. Positive atheism . . . also rejects the theistic and pantheistic aspects of Hinduism as well as the lesser gods of Theravada Buddhism and Jainism." Michael Martin, "Atheism," in *The New Encyclopedia of Unbelief,* ed. Tom Flynn (Amherst, N.Y.: Prometheus, 2007), 88–89.

3. Sam Harris, *Letter to a Christian Nation* (New York: Knopf, 2006), 55–56.

4. Michael Shermer, *How We Believe: The Search for God in an Age of Science* (New York: Freeman, 2000), 10; Shermer's italics.

5. Richard Dawkins, *The God Delusion* (Boston: Houghton Mifflin, 2006), 31, Dawkins's italics.

6. Ibid., 109.

7. Victor J. Stenger, *God: The Failed Hypothesis* (Amherst, N.Y.: Prometheus, 2007),15.

8. Ibid., 11, 233. See: 17; 40–43; 228–30.

9. Dawkins, *The God Delusion*, 31; Dawkins's italics.

10. Ibid., 156.

11. Quotation taken from *Communion and Stewardship: Human Persons Created in the Image of God,* http://www.vatican.va/roman_curia/congregations/cfaith/cti_documents/rc_con_cfaith_doc, accessed 21 May 2008.

12. Michel Onfray, *Atheist Manifesto: The Case Against Christianity, Judaism, and Islam,* trans. Jeremy Leggatt (New York: Arcade, 2005), 15.

13. In advancing his scientific explanation for religion, Dennett relies on the concept of *meme*—a culturally transmitted idea—adapted from the work of Richard Dawkins. See: Daniel C. Dennett, *Breaking the Spell: Religion as a Natural Phenomenon* (New York: Viking, 2006). Not all students of evolutionary matters will grant that such things as memes in culture, which parallel genes in biology, exist. "Many evolutionary biologists dismiss memes and memetics as little more than pseudoscientific wordplay. For one thing, the analogy between genes and memes is notoriously weak. Genes mutate rarely; memes mutate rapidly. Genes are digital (they're made of DNA, which is made of four distinct chemicals); memes aren't. Nor has memetics produced any persuasive explanations of previously unexplained phenomena. . . . The existence of a God meme is no better established than the existence of God." H. Allen Orr, "The God Project: What the Science of Religion Can't Prove," *The New Yorker* (3 April 2006), 82–83.

14. Daniel C. Dennett, "Why Getting It Right Matters: How Science Prevails," in *Science and Religion: Are They Compatible?* ed. Paul Kurtz (Amherst, N.Y.: Prometheus, 2003), 158. "I would place Professor Dennett in the broad tradition of naturalist explanation of religion which includes Ludwig Feuerbach, Karl Marx, and Sigmund Freud. Whatever the benefits of religions, Dennett and these writers believe that they arise entirely inside human minds. No spiritual realities exist outside us.

Natural explanations may be given of the origins of belief in God. Now I hesitate to mention this, but this is clearly a rather circular argument, which presupposes its conclusions." See Alister McGrath's contribution to this volume, p. 29.

15. Gary Wolf, "The Church of the Non-Believers," *Wired* (November 2006): 182–93.

16. Christopher Hitchens, *God Is Not Great: How Religion Poisons Everything* (New York: Twelve, 2007), 4.

17. Ibid., 46–47.

18. Ibid., 12.

19. Onfray, *Atheist Manifesto*, 67.

20. Ibid., 219.

21. Sam Harris, *The End of Faith: Religion, Terror, and the Future of Reason* (New York: Norton, 2004), 236.

22. Ibid., 131.

23. Harris, *Letter to a Christian Nation*, 85; author's italics.

24. Harris, *End of Faith*, 123.

25. Ibid., 110.

26. Ibid., 129.

27. Ibid., 131.

28. Dawkins, *The God Delusion*, 306.

29. Ibid., 308.

30. Alister McGrath, "Dawkins, God, and the Scientific Enterprise: Reflections on the Appeal to Darwinism in Fundamentalist Atheism," in *Intelligent Design: William A. Dembski and Michael Ruse in Dialogue*, ed. Robert B. Stewart (Minneapolis: Fortress Press, 2007), 103. See: Alister E. McGrath and Joanna Collicutt McGrath, *The Dawkins Delusion: Atheist Fundamentalism and the Denial of the Divine* (Downers Grove, Ill.: InterVarsity, 2007).

31. Tom Pyszcznski, Sheldon Solomon, and Jeff Greenberg, *In the Wake of 9/11: The Psychology of Terror* (Washington, D.C.: American Psychological Association, 2003), 148.

32. Harris, *End of Faith*, 79.

33. Dawkins, *The God Delusion*, 278.

34. Marilynne Robinson, "Hysterical Scientism: The Ecstasy of Richard Dawkins," *Harper's Magazine* (November 2006), 84.

35. Unless otherwise noted all biblical references are from the New Revised Standard Version.

36. St. John Chrysostom, Homily IX.5.162, in *The Homilies of St. John Chrysostom*, A Library of the Fathers of the Holy Catholic Church (Oxford: Parker, 1842).

37. Francis Bacon, *The Advancement of Learning*, cited in Peter M. J. Hess, "God's Two Books: Special Revelation and Natural Science in the Christian West," in *Bridging Science and Religion*, ed. Ted Peters, Gaymon Bennett, and Kang Phee Seng (Minneapolis: Fortress Press, 2003), 123–40.

38. *Belgic Confession*, Article 2, "By What Means God i̶n̶ ... cited by Hess, ibid.

39. See Ted Peters, *God—The World's Future*, rev. ed. (Mi... Press, 2000), 55–67.

40. Referring to the Talmud, Qur'an, and the New Testame... "None of them is a work of revelation. Who would have done the re... *Manifesto*, 77.

41. Martin Luther, "Heidelberg Disputation," in *Luther's Works*, A... ...Vols. 1–30, ed. Jaroslav Pelikan (St. Louis: Concordia, 1955–1967); ed. Helmut T. Lehmann (Minneapolis: Fortress Press, 1955–1986), 3 ...

42. Charles Sanders Peirce, *Collected Papers of Charles Sanders P...* Hartshorne and Paul Weiss, 8 vols. (Cambridge, Mass.: Harvard Univer... 1931–1958), 6:461; or *The Essential Peirce: Selected Philosophical Writings*, ed. Houser, Christian Kloesel, Peirce Edition Project, 2 vols. (Bloomington Univesity Press, 1992–1998), ...

43. Ibid., 6:40; and 2:440, respectively.

44. Wolfhart Pannenberg, *Theology and the Philosophy of Science*, trans ... McDonagh (Louisville, Ky.: Westminster John Knox, 1976), 310. Pannenberg's i... ics. The God hypothesis for Pannenberg does more than merely make us wait ... a future revelation; it provides an expanded horizon for explaining present real... This leads Nancey Murphy to comment that the "best approach" for connecting sci... ence with theology "is to argue that theology is a science (or very science-like), but that it deals with reality at a higher level of complexity than do the other sciences — it takes its place at the top of the hierarchy of sciences. A somewhat similar view is that of Wolfhart Pannenberg who argues that theology is the science that provides the most all-encompassing context for the other sciences." Nancey Murphy, "Evidence of Design in the Fine-Tuning of the Universe," in *Quantum Cosmology and the Laws of Nature*, ed. Robert John Russell, Nancey Murphy, and C. J. Isham (Vatican City State and Berkeley: Vatican Observatory and CTNS, 1993), 424.

45. Robert John Russell, *Cosmology: From Alpha to Omega* (Minneapolis: Fortress Press, 2008), chap. 10.

Index